The Method is the Message

The Method is the Message

Rethinking McLuhan Through Critical Theory

Paul Grosswiler

**BLACK
ROSE
BOOKS**

**Montréal / New York
London**

Black Rose Books No. AA252
Hardcover ISBN: 1-55164-075-9 (bound)
Paperback ISBN: 1-55164-074-0 (pbk.)
Library of Congress Catalog Card Number: 97-79524

Canadian Cataloguing in Publication Data

Grosswiler, Paul
Method is the message : rethinking McLuhan
through critical theory

Includes bibliographical references and index.
Hardcover ISBN: 1-55164-075-9 (bound)
Paperback ISBN: 1-55164-074-0 (pbk.)

1. McLuhan, Marshall, 10911-1980. 2. Marx, Karl, 1818-1883.
3. Mass media and culture. 4. Information theory. I. Title.

P90.G76 1997   302.23'092   C96-900781-7

Cover design: Associés libres, Montréal

**BLACK
ROSE
BOOKS**

C.P. 1258	250 Sonwil Drive	99 Wallis Road
Succ. Place du Parc	Buffalo, New York	London, E9 5LN
Montréal,Québec	14225 USA	England
H2W 2R3 Canada		

To order books in North America: (phone) 1-800-565-9523 (fax) 1-800-221-9985
In Europe: (phone) 081-986-4854 (fax) 081-533-5821

Our Web Site address: http://www.web.net/blackrosebooks

A publication of the Institute of Policy Alternatives of Montréal (IPAM)
Printed in Canada

Table of Contents

Acknowledgements

On its ten-year journey toward becoming a book, this project has gone through its own dialectic: from non-being, to being, to negation, to becoming. It first occurred as an improbable hunch in 1987 that Marshall McLuhan's ideas of media and social change closely matched Marxism's dialectics. The idea formed slowly as a tangential interest to my dissertation on McLuhan's visual and acoustic typologies in media, aesthetics and ideology. It first emerged in writing as an awkwardly long paper in 1989. After one aspect of the project was presented at an International Communication Association session in 1991, it remained dormant until 1995, when the *Canadian Journal of Communication* offered me a chance to overhaul and update an article on McLuhan, Marxism and critical theory. This revision led me to similar books being published in Canada and England that emboldened me to propose the newly expanding project as a book manuscript. A university press editor led me to Black Rose Books, which then encouraged me to add new chapters on cultural studies and postmodernism.

Along the way, many hands and words have helped shape this project and helped it survive occasional lapses into desuetude. That it has persisted is testimony to the strength of the voices that have supported and guided the project through the last ten years. These are the people who have kept this project alive over the years, and whom I wholeheartedly thank:

Pat Peritore, Don Ranly, Keith Sanders and Joye Patterson for shepherding the serendipitous collision of McLuhan and Marxism.

Don Brenner for enthusiastically permitting me to write this project initially and urging me to submit it for publication.

Rowland Lorimer, Nancy Duxbury and Jo-Anne Ray at the *Canadian Journal of Communication*, as well as my reviewers, for the guidance and the opportunity to overhaul a major aspect of the project and for ushering it into print. That article is based largely on chapters 5 and 7.

Judith Stamps, Nick Stevenson and Liss Jeffrey, whom I know only through their writing, for going against the interpretive grain in their analysis of McLuhan.

Jean Wilson for steering me to Black Rose Books.

Dimitrios Roussopoulos and Jean Nataf for creating the title and bringing this project into book form.

Jim Pinson for his insights early on into McLuhan and Marx, although through a contrasting lens.

Tim Cole for his humour during morning runs in the final months of writing.

Naomi Jacobs, Pat Dooley, and Cynthia Mahmood for their inspiring examples as scholarly authors and friends.

Danny Guthrie, Patti Zimmerman, Jonathan Tankel, and Eric Peterson for their textbook orders, bibliographies and libraries.

Joyce Grosswiler for introducing McLuhan's ideas to me in 1965, and for sharing her experience, creativity and artistry in a book publishing collective in Denmark.

Ray and Frieda Grosswiler for wanting a copy of anything I have ever written. My father also taught me patience and persistence. He died a few months before Black Rose Books accepted the manuscript.

Bella and Roxy, for their presence—Bella at the beginning of this work and Roxy at the end. They slept by the computer and only spoke to me or licked my face in my dreams.

Leif Ray Tessier Grosswiler for providing the creative spark that led to the completion of this project. His birth a few days after my father's death and his first year embody being and becoming in the most life-affirming and celebrative sense, a sense that I hope pervades this book.

Marie Tessier for believing in me and in this project for the entire decade since its inception, even when my own belief wavered. Her love is the one undialectic aspect of life—constant and unchanging.

1

Synthesizing McLuhan and Marx

Comparing Methods

One of the many jokes repeated by Marshall McLuhan goes like this: "A caterpillar gazing at the butterfly is supposed to have remarked, 'Waal, you'll never catch me in one of those durn things.'"[1] The joke illustrates part of McLuhan's media and social change theory, the "reversal of the overheated medium."[2]

> The principle that during the stages of their development all things appear under forms opposite to those that they finally present is an ancient doctrine. Interest in the power of things to reverse themselves by evolution is evident in a great diversity of observations, sage and jocular.[3]

The "jocular" observation about the dowdy, furry caterpillar, made with a disgusted frown about the resplendent butterfly, as well as the "ancient doctrine" that it illustrates, resembles a passage from a "sage" observer who represents the "ancient doctrine" of dialectical theory, philosopher Georg Hegel. Only instead of a caterpillar and a butterfly, Hegel described a bud, a blossom, and fruit,

> The bud disappears in the bursting forth of the blossom, and one might say that the former is refuted by the latter; similarly, when the fruit appears, the blossom is shown up in its turn as a false manifestation of the plant, and the fruit now emerges as the truth of it instead.[4]

According to political scholar Chris Sciabarra, Hegel, as well as Karl Marx, focused on the "unity-in-contradiction" between things in existence and things in the process of becoming, this after Hegel rediscovered Aristotle's philosophy of being as process and movement. The concept of *Aufhebung*, in which each step of change both "preserves and abolishes, maintains and annihilates its previous movement,"[5] is at the heart of dialectical method as practiced by Hegel and, with modifications, by Marx.

This book stems from the unexpected observation that the method of McLuhan's theory of media and social change—modeled in part on the principle behind the joke of the caterpillar and the butterfly—resembles both Hegel and Marx's dialectical methodology, which Marx used to analyze social relations and history. Hegel's bud has become McLuhan's caterpillar, and the blossom has become the butterfly. The blossom and butterfly refute the bud and caterpillar, and as the fruit turns up as the truth of the process, the butterfly renders the caterpillar false. The only missing element in Hegel's example is the caterpillar's disbelief and lack of recognition of its future as featured in McLuhan's humor.

The thesis to be presented here is that methodological similarities between McLuhan and early humanist Marxism, along with Western Marxism, form a methodological bond between McLuhan's media studies and Marx's political economy studies that is stronger than the differences between them. Despite decades of labeling McLuhan a "technological determinist," by numerous descendants of Marxism in the neo-Marxist and post-Marxist fields of cultural studies and postmodernism, these critical and social theorists should reappraise and reclaim McLuhan's, as well as Marx's, dialectical methods and their media and social theories.

The gulf between Marx and McLuhan might appear so vast that opposing sides would concede that these two social philosophers had only one thing in common: both rejected being members of the movements they created, although the reasons for the rejection probably were different. "I'm a stodgy conservative," McLuhan said. "If there are going to be McLuhanites, you can be sure that I'm not going to be one of them."[6] Hearing the outrageous ideas of his followers, Marx exclaimed, "but I am not a Marxist."[7]

If there were one unbridgeable gap between McLuhan and Marxism it may best be illustrated by the title of one of McLuhan's most important and popular books, *Understanding Media: The Extensions of Man* (1964). Had Marx undertaken an analysis of media, which he did not, he certainly would have objected to the goal of "understanding" stated by the title. As Marx wrote in the eleventh thesis on Feuerbach, "the philosophers have only interpreted the world, in various ways; the point, however, is to change it."[8] McLuhan's ultimate goal, however, moves beyond understanding to intervening in media development, so that, as he said, "we can, if we choose, think things out before we put them out."[9]

This book allies itself with Marx's explicit and McLuhan's implicit goal in making a distinction between understanding and action as the difference may be applied to communication theory. While a methodological accommodation between McLuhan and Marxism might be possible, the question must be raised about what the reason for such a project would be. The purpose of this book is to reconcile McLuhan and Marxism in order to contribute to the history of critical communication research, including qualitative and Marxist-based research. In faulting McLuhan's communication theory for its lack of proper social scientific method and other normative values of administrative methodology, mainstream positivist research has been able to dismiss McLuhan.[10] An argument can be made that McLuhan offers fertile ground for empirical social science research,[11] however, McLuhan's dialectical theory and qualitative approach make him better suited in alliance with the critical communication theorists.[12] By illustrating the methodological foundation shared by McLuhan and Marxism, McLuhan's media theories may find a home in Marxist-based research and cultural studies.

Building this methodological bridge between McLuhan and Marxism would be a simpler project except for the fact that McLuhan consistently attacked or dismissed Marx, socialism and communism in his own work.[13] McLuhan's biographer, Philip Marchand, wrote that McLuhan developed a contempt for Marxism early in his life as he cautiously approved of fascism's rejection of both socialism and capitalism. Later, McLuhan predicted that his theory focusing on the means of communication would supersede Marx's theory of the means of production. McLuhan also considered his work a satirical look at both capitalism and socialism.[14]

Responding in kind, Marxist scholars for the most part have attacked McLuhan for failing to include essential elements of the social process in his writing, including private property, class struggle, and the fight for liberation.[15] At their least vitriolic, McLuhan's critics have labeled him a Catholic conservative.[16] The criticisms share the assertion that if there is anything McLuhan was not, he was not a revolutionary.

The differences between McLuhan's and Marx's thinking might have been too great to permit a thesis arguing similarities between their methodologies if there were not a few scholars who have more strongly linked McLuhan and Marx.[17] Media scholar Carolyn Marvin, for example, argued that the similarities are only superficial, but sociologist Tom Nairn was prepared to match McLuhan and Marx, or neo-Marxists, quite extensively, to the point of arguing that if criticism of McLuhan separated his significant historical phenomena from his mythology, Marxism could look at a productive force it failed to consider, the media.

British cultural studies, led by Raymond Williams, has responded negatively to McLuhan for thirty years, as has US cultural studies, notably reflected in the work of James Carey.[18] But this critical field has come nearly full circle with one cultural sociologist, John B. Thompson, applying the theories of political economist Harold Innis and McLuhan as one of three foundations in his study of media and social practices.[19] British sociologist Nick Stevenson has strongly called for a historical reappraisal of McLuhan[20] and Canadian cultural studies scholar Jody Berland has incorporated McLuhan's spatial analysis in her research on cultural technologies.[21]

McLuhan and postmodern media and social theories have gone hand in hand in the writings of many media scholars, some of whom have warmly regarded McLuhan and his theories.[22] These include French philosopher Jean Baudrillard, postmodern theorist Charles Jencks, historian Mark Poster, and literary critic John Fekete in recent work. Others have applied his theories at other times under others' names, including critical historian Donald Lowe, art sociologist Janet Wolff, and in other work, Poster.[23] Nevertheless, McLuhan still retains the stigma of a technological determinist among many postmodernist writers and critics, including Douglas Kellner, Steven Best, Stanley Aronowitz, and Henry Giroux.[24]

In searching for methodologies that are multi-perspectival, it is often a form of dialectics that contemporary communication scholars call for. It is to this field-wide call for new methodologies of critical rather than administrative theories, for example, that this book is aimed. The current resurfacing of McLuhan's theories among a diverse group of theorists in cultural studies and postmodernism illustrates McLuhan's continued relevance to critical communication approaches. For Canadian communication historians David Crowley and David Mitchell, Thompson, and communications scholar Joshua Meyrowitz, McLuhan maintains a central position.[25] McLuhan also has been revisited by neo-Marxists like Armand Mattelart, and included in the social semiotics discussions of Klaus Jensen and the ethnographic studies of James Lull.[26] Cultural studies itself, with its methodological openness and defiant spirit, embodies McLuhan. Even as postmodernists label McLuhan a technological determinist and attempt to move beyond him, much of his dialectical analysis seems ever more applicable and relevant in light of their concerns.

Within this pluralist group of scholars, McLuhan offers relevance, both theoretically and methodologically, to critical communication research in cultural studies and postmodernism. The dialectical methodology of McLuhan, allied with other critical theory paradigms and their dialectic methods, offers a bond that would bridge diverse researchers. Stripped of mythology and reinforced in his dialectic and historical methodology, McLuhan offers a theory of media evolution and human intervention that Marxism has missed. McLuhan's methodology forms a bond with Hegelian and Marxist dialectics and its descendants in the critical theory of Walter Benjamin, Theodor Adorno, and Max Horkheimer, as well as in the new generation of cultural studies scholars, postmodernists and more generally, in Canadian media theory.

The primary methodological studies used here to discuss dialectics and compare dialectical theory with McLuhan come from a Marxist art historian, Arnold Hauser, who weighs the positives and negatives of McLuhan, Canadian political theory scholar Judith Stamps, and several other political theory scholars, including Scott Warren, Donald Lowe, and Patrick Peritore, as well as Frankfurt theorist Erich Fromm.[27] The critical media and social universe that is set in motion by McLuhan's dialectical theory will be described and McLuhan's dialectical theory will be compared with the theories of Frankfurt School critical theorists Benjamin, Horkheimer and Adorno.[28] McLuhan's assessment by neo-Marxist and post-Marxist cultural studies and postmodernists also will be explored in order to historically reappraise McLuhan in light of contemporary critical media and social theories.

For example, as recent Canadian scholarship in critical theory and cultural studies has begun to reawaken to the work of McLuhan and re-establish his place among communication theorists, Stamps has connected his communication theories with the Frankfurt School.[29] Other relatively recent Canadian scholarship, by Liss Jeffrey, Paul Heyer, Donald and Joan Theall, and Pamela McCallum, has debated the relationship between McLuhan and critical theory.[30] US scholarship by Carey, as well as my own work, has also taken some note of the similarities between McLuhan's and Benjamin's media theory.[31] Other US research has reassessed McLuhan from critical perspectives.[32] In Europe, postmodernists like Baudrillard have adapted McLuhan's theories, as have British cultural studies scholars Thompson and Stevenson. Much of this recent scholarship runs counter to or tempers decades of negative scholarly assessment of McLuhan, which was more dismissive in the United States than in Canada or Europe, and which represents part of a new reassessment of McLuhan that was not possible during his lifetime.

The central argument to be made is that McLuhan's method, like the early Marx's radical dialectical method, was not a mechanistic, technological determinism. Few critics until recently, have noticed that

McLuhan was mining the interstices of media change for openings that allow human awareness and change, or in another word, praxis. This study attempts to reclaim McLuhan from this misreading by showing that his method was open-ended and process-oriented, not only in his early work, but in the later and posthumous work as well. This effort could be compared to the Western Marxist reclamation of the early Marx's radical dialectics in a departure from the scientific socialism of Eastern Marxists.

The similarities of the dialectical methodologies of McLuhan and early Marxism, as well as in later Western Marxism and the Frankfurt School, form a bond between McLuhan's media studies and Marx's political economy. Although mainstream US communication research, Marxist-based and critical research both largely rejected McLuhan, this book will argue that McLuhan's dialectical theory and qualitative historical approach make him well-suited to an alliance with critical communication and social theorists.

This book will provide a narrative description and comparison of the theoretical underpinnings of both McLuhan's and Marx's methodologies as found in their works and as interpreted by other scholars. Marx's methodology has come to be called dialectical materialism, although that name was contrived by his followers in nineteenth-century Russia.[33] Dialectics, the name this study will use for Marx's approach, has a rich history beginning in pre-Socratic Greek philosophy, sidetracked in Aristotelian philosophy and revitalized in nineteenth century German philosophy by Hegel, Marx's teacher. Dialectics has been the methodology followed by Western Marxists, including existentialists, but abandoned by Eastern Marxists in favor of the Leninist version—some say distortion—of Marxism.[34]

McLuhan did not name his methodology, although he formulated the seeds of what he called the laws of the media, a tetradic or four-part process, later in his life in one journal article and a letter to the editor of a second journal.[35] The laws became the basis for two more co-authored books that were published posthumously.[36] The laws of media, however, did not contradict his earlier approach. The laws were built on a methodology of analyzing media evolution that McLuhan employed in his seminal works, *The Gutenberg Galaxy: The Making of Typographic Man* (1962) and *Understanding Media*. That unnamed methodology will be called the "hybrid media" methodology.

Evolution of McLuhan's Dialectical Theory

McLuhan developed his dialectical theory over several decades. It can best be understood in relation to his concepts of visual and acoustic space, as well as to two other key concepts, "the medium is the message" and the "global village." McLuhan drew knowledge together from disparate fields, creating his web of concepts by first borrowing and then departing from theorists including Innis and social philosopher Lewis Mumford. The kernel of McLuhan's media theory, in turn, was developed by his "disciples," among them humanities scholar Walter Ong, who focused on the shift from orality to literacy.[37] Others were influenced by his thinking, including media theorist Neil Postman in his jeremiad against television, and Meyrowitz in his study of the blurring of social place and distinctions because of electronic media.[38]

McLuhan's thought did not spring fully formed in his most widely read work of the 1960s, *The Gutenberg Galaxy* and *Understanding Media*. As with many of McLuhan's ideas, his dialectic of sensory balance began by borrowing, coming from an area outside mass communication theory and the social sciences. It began with New Criticism literary theory, which approached language as ambiguous and studied poems in their context and for subliminal effects rather than their "content," or dictionary meaning.[39] In the 1930s at Cambridge University, McLuhan studied the "auditory imagination" of poet T.S. Eliot and the emphasis on sound in the poetry of W.B. Yeats and Gerard Manley Hopkins.[40] Out of this literary approach grew the notion that the senses that are dominant in the perceiver alter perception significantly. This suggested a visual mode of perception and an auditory mode, which is not primarily logical, linear or sequential.

At St. Louis University in the late 1930s, McLuhan was introduced to medieval philosopher St. Thomas Aquinas' notion of the human senses working in unison. The notion supported the idea that experience is shaped by the individual's mix of senses.[41] Aquinas discussed the *sensus communis*, or common sense as a device for putting concentions together in an internal sense.[42] This notion has its roots in Aristotle, who postulated that the *sensus communis* translated each sense into the other senses to offer a unified, integral image of perception to the mind.[43]

Debt to Harold Innis

Before McLuhan had melded the *sensus communis* notion with media, a seed of McLuhan's most popular aphorism, the "medium is the message," came to him in part from Innis. In the 1940s, McLuhan encountered Innis' idea that media possess characteristics apart from the messages they transmit.[44] Innis said newspapers increased interest in the immediate, while decreasing temporal continuity, and radio centralized government. Innis divided media into two groups evolving dialectically: time-binding and space-binding, meaning that different media extended social control over time or in space. He was studying the implications of the dominant media for the nature of knowledge and civilization.

Speech was for Innis the ultimate and preferred time-binding medium, although stone and tablets also were time-binding. By contrast, the lighter and more mobile papyrus and paper increased social control over space, fostered empire and lessened the durability of the message. Innis broached the idea that in oral discourse all the senses act together in cooperation and rivalry but he did not develop any notion that media are extensions of the senses.[45]

Early in the 1950s, McLuhan combined the literary ideas of Yeats and Eliot with the political ideas of Innis and proposed that each medium emphasizes sight or sound. This emphasis deeply influences the world views of individuals using the medium.[46] Thus, the medium is the message.

However, McLuhan departed dramatically from Innis in assessing the social effects of electronic media. Carey quotes Oscar Wilde's quip about Niagara Falls—"It would be more impressive if it ran the other way"—to comment on communication theory running from Innis' "great achievement" to McLuhan.[47] Innis did not hypothesize, as McLuhan did, the return to a decentralized, deeply participant, positive communication web through the electronic media. Innis wrote in the early 1950s that the modern communications media, cinema and radio, made communication more difficult. The new media intensified the negative and destructive cultural effects of media monopoly found in the space-binding print media.[48]

As the champion of oral communication, Innis, had he lived longer, would have strongly disagreed with McLuhan's later position that the electronic media share the positive cultural potential of oral communication and reverse the direction taken by print media to retribalize culture. For Innis, electronic media extended the bias of print media toward space.[49] Carey opposed the "modern utopian" view, although not attributed to McLuhan, that the electronic media will by their nature help societies transcend nationalism and create a global village. According to Carey, the opposite is occurring: "We are witnessing the imperial struggle of the early age of print all over again but now with communication systems that transmit messages at the extremes of the laws of physics."[50]

8

McLuhan was aware that he sharply departed from Innis' conclusion regarding electronic media, but he attributes the difference to Innis' "technological blindness."[51] McLuhan argued that Innis failed to apply the time-binding power of the ear as a structural principle to radio, and Innis followed conventional thought by mistakenly including radio within visual culture. McLuhan maintained that electric media have decentralizing psychic and social effects. McLuhan further argued that while the visual power of print media extends monopoly control over space, the auditory power of electronic media abolishes space and time. Electric technology is immediate, ubiquitous and decentralizing, which in political terms leads to the tribe rather than the nation. Electric technology favors the integral and organic rather than the fragmentary and mechanical.

Mumford's "Neotechnics" in the "Global Village"

McLuhan also borrowed the idea that electric culture is organic and capable of creating the village form on a global scale. This he borrowed from Mumford. Within two years after Innis' death in 1952, McLuhan began to employ a concept that he had first encountered in St. Louis in the 1930s in Mumford's *Technics and Civilization,* that a civilization based on electricity was organic and directly opposed to the preceding mechanistic civilization based on steam.[52] Mumford argued that electrical technology, or neotechnics, had the intrinsic potential to decentralize society and destroy the concentrated power of the State and industry amassed by mechanical technology, or paleotechnics.[53] Carey summarized Mumford's argument as including the idea that only the outmoded social form of capitalism prevented neotechnic culture from realizing its potential for peace and order.

Mumford foreshadowed McLuhan's idea that print media upset the balance of the human sensorium and that electronic technology restores the organic and the aesthetic. Carey, however, found that McLuhan probed similar ideas through literary sources without the complexity and moralism of Mumford.[54] By the 1960s, Mumford had rejected the dualism of paleotechnic and neotechnic and replaced it with the observation, much like Innis', that electronic technology had created a society devoted to the mechanical values of power, domination, production, wealth and publicity—not human values. In this alignment with Innis' position, Mumford attacked McLuhan's defense of electronic technology and its agencies, which Mumford believed were leading to totalitarianism.

To be fair to McLuhan's evolution, he morally inveighed against mass culture in *The Mechanical Bride: Folklore of Industrial Man* (1951) before assuming the neutrality of his major works of the 1960s, a neutrality that was often interpreted as an uncritical acceptance of the new electronic media.[55] In the 1970s, he developed the concept of "discarnate man," the electronic media audience member who could travel to many places through the media, but whose identity had ceased to be physical and had become a phantom image. This disembodied state troubled McLuhan because it destroyed private identity and seemed to be creating TV children who were unfocused, lazy and illiterate.[56]

"Visual" and "Acoustic" Space

The dialectic of "visual" and "acoustic" sensory space in terms of media, which is central to the dialectical theory that was fully expressed in *The Gutenberg Galaxy* and *Understanding Media* in the 1960s, also evolved in the early 1950s at the University of Toronto's Centre for Culture and Technology, which McLuhan directed.[57] Visual space is an empty container that separates objects. Associated with print culture, visual space is linear, sequential and logical. Created by the enclosure of space as a static quantity in architecture, visual space encompasses history from the introduction of the phonetic alphabet until the invention of the telegraph. Acoustic space has no boundaries, centre or sense of direction. Associated with oral and electronic culture, acoustic space is multisensory, simultaneous, immediate, resonant, natural and analogical. Acoustic space encompasses history before the introduction of the alphabet and since the invention of the telegraph. In McLuhan's terminology, acoustic space also is audio-tactile, and he endlessly categorized all objects and attitudes according to their sensory bias, visual or acoustic/audio-tactile.

In 1960, McLuhan struck on the idea that as the senses interact; the dominant sense translates the others into its own mode of perceiving. Any extension of a sense in a medium alters the overall pattern of the sensorium.[58] This idea emerged in full form in *The Gutenberg Galaxy*. Literary scholar Donald Theall describes this work as centering on a series of contrasts governed by visual and acoustic dualism. On the visual side is the written, linear, individual-civilized, phonetic alphabet and print. On the acoustic side is the oral, auditory, tactile, mosaic or non-linear, tribal-participatory, ideogrammatic and script. In McLuhan's dialectic, the invention of the alphabet changed the oral universe of tribal societies into linear form, creating a specialization that did not exist in oral culture's audio-tactile universe.[59] The introduction of movable type alienated the individual from the manuscript culture of the Middle Ages, fragmenting sensory life with an intense visual bias. The discovery of electricity—beginning with the telegraph in 1844 and intensifying with radio in the 1920s and television in the 1950s—reversed the visual bias of the intervening four hundred years and returned the individual to an acoustic, or audio-tactile environment, Theall writes.

Attempting to bridge the sensorium and the medium, McLuhan linked print and speech as extensions of the body that amplify or inhibit different senses.[60] Speech amplifies the auditory sense, and print amplifies the visual sense. McLuhan adapted Aquinas's *sensus communis* so that common sense, or a ratio of the senses, shapes thought processes by transforming and translating information from the individual senses.

Theall criticizes McLuhan for his "rather naive psychology" and pointed to problems in McLuhan's treatment of individual sensory mechanisms and sensory interplay. He suggests that "visual," "acoustic," and "tactile" in McLuhan's works have idiosyncratic meanings that on the surface appear wrong.[61] The terms are completely beyond normal definitions. The visual is not restricted to physical vision. Vision could be visual, but it also could be tactile. McLuhan usually used visual with geometric vision, but tactile with light and colour vision. For McLuhan, the medium of colour television is a tactile rather than a visual medium. This definition was based on the light-transmitting properties of television. He also implied that the interplay of the senses involved in colour vision make it "tactile," although Theall points out that geometric vision possibly involves more interplay according to most theories of vision. McLuhan was playing with popular, as well as many specialized senses of the term visual. "Visual" is tied to geometric vision, perspective and print-orientation as well as alienation and individualism.

Conversely, some written literature can be acoustic, as in Eliot's "auditory imagination." McLuhan also thought that two-dimensional painting is "visual" or "acoustic" based on its style.[62] The illusion of linear perspective, achieved after the discovery of the vanishing point and development of geometry, led to visual painting. The abandonment of linear perspective after Paul Cézanne and the multiple perspectives of cubism are acoustic because the image has to be perceived as a whole rather than from a fixed point of view.

"Tactility" as Synaesthesia

The dialectic of sensory balance remained a key part of McLuhan's arguments in *Understanding Media,* notably in the extension of his ideas to the modern media of film, the newspaper, radio and television, and the fine arts.[63] "Tactility" is an interplay of the senses, or synaesthesia, that became possible through electronic media in contrast to the fragmented visual sensory system created by print media.[64] McLuhan also adopted the theory that media are extensions of the human body. Because each medium is an extension of the nervous system or sensory system, each medium affects the ratio between the senses.[65]

McLuhan attempted to build a dialectical theory of sense-perception and sense-extension that stayed with his work until the end, although the theory became overshadowed by his interest in right versus left hemispheres of the brain, which in essence posed an acoustic versus visual space dialectic.[66] Also, his later interest in figure-ground relationships and the tetradic "laws" of media still were based on a dialectic of sensory balance. Visual space, for example, examines figure abstracted from ground. Acoustic space focuses on ground, or environment, as a unified sense experience containing the figure.[67]

The persistence of the sensory dialectic became clear in McLuhan's two posthumous works. He traced the cause of visual or geometric space to the phonetic alphabet, which intensified vision and suppressed ground by isolating and detaching figures. The alphabet also split the conscious and unconscious. This split contrasts with the pre-alphabet, "old acoustic 'common sense' of space," which was spherical, multisensory and multidimensional. Visual space is a human-made artifact opposed to the natural, environmental form of acoustic space. Visual space, created by the eyes when their operation is abstracted from the other senses by the phonetic alphabet, is continuous, connected, homogeneous and static.[68]

Chapter Outlines

Chapter 2 will explore McLuhan's ideas about Marx and Marxism, focusing in the second section on McLuhan's only full analysis of Marx, found in *Take Today: The Executive as Dropout* (1972). McLuhan was unwavering in his negative reading of Marx, socialism, communism and dialectics; however, McLuhan based his rejection on the argument that communism has been achieved as a social effect of technology. McLuhan's more extensive analysis of Marx offers a more tempered view than his earlier condemnation of Marxism.

A case has been made by other scholars, based on parallels between McLuhan and Marx, that challenges McLuhan's consistent dismissal of Marxism and essentially describes McLuhan as a Marxist. By contrast, Marxist scholars have almost unanimously returned the attack against McLuhan. Chapter 3 will review those comparisons and criticisms along with critiques of McLuhan's social theory, providing a larger context for measuring McLuhan against Marxist theory.

The word "dialectics" has appeared in the attempt to measure the common ground between McLuhan and Marx. The arguments of McLuhan and his critics have touched on dialectics, but never centered on the methodology itself. Chapter 4 will draw together the references to dialectics found in the works of McLuhan and his critics. The chapter will then define dialectics as a methodology stretching from pre-Socratic philosophers through Marx and beyond to critical theory.

Chapter 5 will focus on McLuhan's two methods of media analysis: his early hybrid media concept and his later tetradic laws of media. As these two approaches are being described, the chapter will discuss the confluences of McLuhan's method and Marxist dialectics.

Chapter 6 will provide a broad outline of the media environments that McLuhan's methodology generates. The chapter will describe this historical, socio-political-economic galaxy, as well as the media galaxies of the arts and the mass media.

Although contemporaries, the neo-Marxist Frankfurt School theorists and McLuhan never made published references to each other. Yet, as dialectical theorists, McLuhan, Horkheimer, Adorno, and Benjamin share central ideas about the media in their seminal works. Chapter 7 will present points of convergence between McLuhan and the Frankfurt School.

Chapter 8 will chart the crescendo of negative responses that later reverse themselves into a positive reassessment among cultural studies scholars, the direct descendants of the Frankfurt School critical theorists. As a rapidly evolving and theoretically diverse approach to communication issues, cultural studies has come nearly full circle in its response to McLuhan with a more positive reception.

Cultural studies has haltingly but hopefully reawakened to McLuhan's theories in several major new works that have begun to historically re-evaluate and reclaim his dialectical approach for contemporary media and social theory after decades of negative criticism. In the writings of many media and social theorists, postmodernism and McLuhan's social theories have increasingly gone hand in hand. Chapter 9 will chronicle how, despite the warm regard for McLuhan by postmodernists, his theories appear at times under the names of others and he still bears the negative label of a technological determinist.

Chapter 10 will discuss issues raised by critical communication theory, as well as McLuhan's reception among contemporary cultural studies and postmodern scholars who work under the umbrella of critical media and social theories. This chapter will demonstrate how McLuhan's theories fit within today's critical communication theory tradition and offer a fruitful research base for critical media research.

NOTES

1. Marshall McLuhan, *Understanding Media: The Extensions of Man* (New York: Mentor, 1964), 46.
2. Ibid., 51.
3. Ibid., 46.
4. Georg Hegel, *Phenomenology of Spirit*, trans. by A. V. Miller (Oxford: Oxford University Press, 1977), 2, quoted in Chris Sciabarra, *Marx, Hayak, and Utopia* (Albany, NY: SUNY Press, 1995), 80.
5. Ibid.
6. Marshall McLuhan, *Letters of Marshall McLuhan,* eds. Matie Molinaro, Corinne McLuhan, and William Toye (Toronto: Oxford University Press, 1987), 179.
7. Chris Sciabarra, *Ayn Rand: The Russian Radical* (University Park, PA: Pennsylvania State University Press, 1995), 6; N. Patrick Peritore, "Radical Dialectics" (University of Missouri, Columbia: Department of Political Science, 1985, unpublished paper), 18.
8. Karl Marx, "Theses on Feuerbach," *The Marx-Engels Reader,* ed. Robert C. Tucker, 2nd ed. (New York: Norton, 1978), 145.
9. McLuhan, *Understanding Media,* 57.
10. James M. Curtis, "McLuhan: The Aesthete as Historian," *Journal of Communication* 31 (summer 1981): 149; Bruce E. Gronbeck, "McLuhan as Rhetorical Theorist," *Journal of Communication* 31 (summer 1981): 118-119; Paul Levinson, "McLuhan and Rationality," *Journal of Communication* 31 (summer 1981), 185; David R. Olson, "McLuhan: Preface to Literacy," *Journal of Communication* 31 (summer 1981): 136-137.
11. Levinson, "Rationality," 187.
12. Judith Stamps, "The Bias of Theory: A Critique of Pamela McCallum's 'Walter Benjamin and Marshall McLuhan: Theories of History,'" *Signature: A Journal of Theory and Canadian Literature* 1, no. 3 (1990): 44-62; Judith Stamps, *Unthinking Modernity: Innis, McLuhan and the Frankfurt School* (Montréal: McGill-Queen's University Press, 1995).
13. Marshall McLuhan, *The Mechanical Bride: Folklore of Industrial Man* (New York: Vanguard Press, 1951), 34, 40; McLuhan, *Understanding Media,* 49, 51, 58, 160, 198, 265; Marshall McLuhan, with Quentin Fiore and Jerome Angel, *War and Peace in the Global Village,* (New York: Bantam Books, 1968), 4-5, 136; Marshall McLuhan, with Harley Parker, *Counterblast* (New York: Harcourt, Brace and World, 1969), 56, 96, 128, 139; Marshall McLuhan, with Barrington Nevitt, *Take Today: The Executive as Dropout,* (New York: Harcourt, Brace Jovanovich, 1972), 61-78; McLuhan, *Letters,*

157, 373, 402-403, 405; Marshall McLuhan, with Bruce Powers, *The Global Village: Transformations in World Life and Media in the Twenty-first Century* (New York: Oxford University Press, 1989), 96.

14. Philip Marchand, *Marshall McLuhan: The Medium and the Messenger* (New York: Ticknor and Fields, 1989), 27, 144, 186.

15. Hans M. Enzensberger, *The Consciousness Industry* (New York: Seabury Press, 1974), 118-119; Sidney Finkelstein, *Sense and Nonsense of McLuhan* (New York: International Publishers, 1968), 110-112; Armand Mattelart, *Mass Media, Ideologies and the Revolutionary Movement* (Atlantic Heights, NJ: Sussex, 1980), 8, 10, 20-21; John Fekete, "McLuhanacy: Counterrevolution in Cultural Theory," *Telos* 15 (spring 1973): 75-123.

16. Daniel J. Czitrom, *Media and the American Mind: From Morse to McLuhan* (Chapel Hill, N.: University of North Carolina Press, 1982), 165; Donald F. Theall, *Understanding McLuhan: The Medium is the Rear View Mirror* (Montréal: McGill-Queen's University Press, 1971), 60.

17. Carolyn Marvin, "Innis, McLuhan and Marx," *Visible Language* 23 (summer 1986): 355-359; Patrick Brantlinger, *Bread and Circuses: Theories of Mass Culture as Social Decay* (Ithaca, NY: Cornell University Press, 1983), 265-271; Tom Nairn, "McLuhanism: The Myth of Our Time," in *McLuhan; Pro and Con*, ed. Raymond Rosenthal (Baltimore, MD: Penguin, 1968), 140-152. Stamps, *Unthinking Modernity*; Nick Stevenson, *Understanding Media Cultures: Social Theory and Mass Communication* (London: Sage, 1995), 114-143; John B. Thompson, *Ideology and Modern Culture* (Stanford, CA: Stanford University Press, 1990), 225-226.

18. Raymond Williams, "Paradoxically, If the Book Works It to Some Extent Annihilates Itself," in *McLuhan Hot and Cool*, ed. Gerald E. Stearn (New York: Dial Press, 1967), 188-191; Raymond Williams, *Television: Technology and Cultural Form* (Hanover, NH and London: Wesleyan University Press, 1992), 120-122; James Carey, "Harold Adams Innis and Marshall McLuhan," in *McLuhan: Pro and Con*, ed. Raymond Rosenthal (Baltimore, MD: Penguin, 1968), 270-308; James Carey, "McLuhan and Mumford: The Roots of Modern Media Analysis," *Journal of Communication* 31 (summer 1981): 162-178; James Carey, "Walter Benjamin, Marshall McLuhan, and the Emergence of Visual Society," *Prospects: An Annual of American Cultural Studies* 12 (1987): 29-38; James Carey, "Space, Time, and Communication: A Tribute to Harold Innis," in *Communication as Culture: Essays on Media and Society* (Boston: Unwin Hyman, 1989), 142-172; James Carey, with John J. Quirk, "The Mythos of the Electronic Revolution," in *Communication as Culture. Essays on Media and Society* (Boston: Unwin Hyman, 1989), 113-141.

19. Thompson, *Ideology,* 225-226.

20. Stevenson, *Media Cultures,* 114-143.

21. Jody Berland, "Angels Dancing: Cultural Technologies and the Production of Space," in *Cultural Studies*, ed. Lawrence Grossberg, Cary Nelson, and Paula Treichler (New York: Routledge, 1992), 38-51.

22. Jean Baudrillard, "Requiem for the Media," in *For a Critique of the Political Economy of the Sign* (St. Louis: Telos Press, 1981), 164-184; Jean Baudrillard, *Simulations* (New York: Semiotext(e), 1983); Charles Jencks, *What is Post-Modernism?* (New York: St. Martin's Press, 1986), 47, 55; Mark Poster, *The Mode of Information: Post-Structuralism and Social Context* (Chicago: University of Chicago Press, 1990), 2, 15, 45, 76; John Fekete, *Moral Panic: Biopolitics Rising* (Montréal-Toronto: Robert Davies Publishing, 1994), 16, 33, 38, 39, 336, 337, 355.

23. Donald M. Lowe, *History of Bourgeois Perception* (Chicago: University of Chicago Press, 1982); Mark Poster, *Foucault, Marxism and History: Mode of Production vs. Mode of Information* (Cambridge, MA: Polity Press, 1984); Mark Poster, "The Mode of Information and Postmodernity," in *Communication Theory Today*, ed. David Crowley and David Mitchell (Stanford, CA: Stanford University Press, 1994), 173-192; Janet Wolff, *The Social Production of Art*, 2nd ed. (New York: New York University Press, 1993), 35-40.

24. Douglas Kellner, "Resurrecting McLuhan? Jean Baudrillard and the Academy of Postmodernism," in *Communication: For or Against Democracy*, eds. Marc Raboy and Peter A. Bruck (Montréal: Black Rose Books, 1989), 131-146; Douglas Kellner, *Jean Baudrillard: From Marxism to Postmodernism and Beyond* (Stanford, CA: Stanford University Press, 1989), 60-76; Steven Best and Douglas Kellner, *Postmodern Theory: Critical Interrogations* (New York: Guilford Press, 1991), 267-268; Stanley Aronowitz and Henry A. Giroux, *Postmodern Education: Politics, Culture, and Social Criticism* (Minneapolis: University of Minnesota Press, 1991), 192-193.

25. David Crowley and David Mitchell, eds., *Communication Theory Today* (Stanford, CA: Stanford University Press, 1994); John B. Thompson, "Social Theory and the Media," in *Communication Theory Today*, 27-49; Joshua Meyrowitz, "Medium Theory," in *Communication Theory Today*, 50-77.

26. Armand Mattelart, *Mapping World Communication: War, Progress, Culture*, trans. Susan Emanuel and James A. Cohen (Minneapolis: University of Minnesota Press, 1994), 125-128; Klaus Bruhn Jensen, *The Social Semiotics of Mass Communication* (London: Sage, 1995), 4-5, 11, 98-99; James Lull, *Inside Family Viewing: Ethnographic Research on Television Audiences* (London: Routledge, 1990), 23, 149, 171.

27. Arnold Hauser, *The Sociology of Art*, trans. Kenneth J. Northcott (Chicago: University of Chicago Press, 1982), 611-617; Scott Warren, *The Emergence of Dialectical Theory: Philosophy and Political Inquiry* (Chicago: University of Chicago Press, 1984); Erich Fromm, *Marx's Concept of Man* (New York: Ungar, 1961); Lowe, *Bourgeois Perception*; Peritore, "Radical Dialectics"; Stamps, *Unthinking Modernity*.

28. Walter Benjamin, "The Work of Art in the Age of Mechanical Reproduction," in *Illuminations*, ed. Hannah Arendt, trans. Harry Zohn (New York: Schocken Books, 1969), 217-251; Max Horkheimer and Theodor Adorno, *Dialectic of Enlightenment*, trans. John Cumming (New York: Continuum, 1987).

29. Stamps, "Bias of Theory"; Stamps, *Unthinking Modernity*.

30. Liss Jeffrey, "The Heat and the Light: Towards a Reassessment of the Contribution of H. Marshall McLuhan," *Canadian Journal of Communication* 14 (winter 1989): 1-29; Paul Heyer, "Probing a Legacy: McLuhan's Communications/ History Twenty-Five Years After," *Canadian Journal of Communication* 14 (winter 1989): 30-45; Donald Theall and Joan Theall, "Marshall McLuhan and James Joyce: Beyond Media," *Canadian Journal of Communication* 14 (winter 1989): 46-63; Pamela McCallum, "Walter Benjamin and Marshall McLuhan: Theories of History," *Signature: A Journal of Theory and Canadian Literature* 1, no. 1 (1989): 71-89.

31. Carey, "Benjamin and McLuhan"; Paul Grosswiler, "A Dialectical Synthesis of Marshall McLuhan and Critical Theory," (paper presented at the annual meeting of the International Communication Association, Chicago, Ill., May 1991); Paul Grosswiler, "The Dialectical Methods of Marshall McLuhan, Marxism, and Critical Theory," *Canadian Journal of Communication* 21, no. 1 (1996): 95-124.

32. Marjorie Ferguson, "Marshall McLuhan Revisited: 1960s Zeitgeist Victim or Pioneer Postmodernist?" *Media, Culture and Society* 13, no. 1 (1991), 71-90; Michael Bross,

"McLuhan's Theory of Sensory Functions: A Critique and Analysis," *Journal of Communication Inquiry*, 16, no. 1 (1992): 91-107; Barry Brummett and Margaret Carlisle Duncan, "Toward a Discursive Ontology of the Media," *Critical Studies in Mass Communication* 9, no. 3 (1992): 229-249; Paul Grosswiler, "The Shifting Sensorium: A Q-Methodology and Critical Theory Exploration of Marshall McLuhan's Visual and Acoustic Typologies in Media, Aesthetics and Ideology" (Ph.D. diss., School of Journalism, University of Missouri, Columbia, MO., 1990).

33. Robert C. Tucker, ed., *The Marx-Engels Reader*, 2nd. ed. (New York: W. W. Norton, 1978), xx.

34. Hauser, *Sociology of Art*, 331-426; Warren, *Dialectical Theory*, 64-68; Fromm, *Marx's Concept*, 40-60; Rius, *Marx for Beginners* (New York: Pantheon, 1976), 70-77.

35. Marshall McLuhan, "McLuhan's Laws of the Media," *Technology and Culture* 16, no. 1 (January 1975): 74-78; Marshall McLuhan, "Laws of the Media," *Et Cetera* 34, no. 2 (June 1977): 173-179.

36. Marshall McLuhan, with Eric McLuhan, *Laws of Media: The New Science* (Toronto: University of Toronto Press, 1988); and McLuhan and Powers, *Global Village*.

37. Walter Ong, *Orality and Literacy: The Technologizing of the Word* (New York: Methuen, 1982).

38. Neil Postman, *Amusing Ourselves to Death: Public Discourse in the Age of Show Business* (New York: Penguin, 1985); Joshua Meyrowitz, *No Sense of Place: The Impact of Media on Social Behavior* (New York: Oxford University Press, 1985).

39. Marchand, *Medium and Messenger*, 34.

40. Ibid., 37, and Marshall McLuhan, *Culture is Our Business* (New York: McGraw-Hill, 1967), 164, citing T.S. Eliot from *The Use of Poetry and the Use of Criticism* (London: Faber and Faber, 1933), 118: "What I call the auditory imagination is the feeling for syllable and rhythm, penetrating far below the conscious levels of thought and feeling, invigorating every word, sinking to the most primitive and forgotten, returning to the origin and bringing something back, seeking the beginning and the end."

41. Ibid., 48.

42. McLuhan, *Letters*, 281.

43. Ibid., 277.

44. Marchand, *Medium and Messenger*, 112.

45. Ibid., 113.

46. Ibid., 119.

47. Carey, "Space, Time," 142.

48. Ibid., 165-169

49. Ibid., 160.

50. Ibid., 170.

51. Marshall McLuhan, introduction to *The Bias of Communication*, by Harold A. Innis (Toronto: University of Toronto Press, 1964), xii-xiv.

52. Marchand, *Medium and Messenger*, 123, citing Lewis Mumford, *Technics and Civilization* (New York: Harcourt, Brace and World, 1934).

53. Carey, "McLuhan and Mumford," 171.

54. Ibid., 174-177.

55. McLuhan, *Mechanical Bride*, v. "To keep everybody in the helpless state engendered by prolonged mental rutting is the effect of many ads and entertainment alike. Since so many minds are engaged in bringing about this condition of public helplessness, and since these programs of commercial education are so much more expensive and influential than the relatively puny offerings sponsored by schools and colleges,

it seemed fitting to devise a method for reversing the process. Why not use the new commercial education as a means to enlighten its intended prey?"

56. Marchand, *Medium and Messenger*, 238.

57. Ibid., 123-124.

58. Ibid., 140.

59. Theall, *Rear View Mirror*, 81.

60. Ibid., 84-85.

61. Ibid., 85-89.

62. McLuhan, *Understanding Media*, 28.

63. Theall, *Rear View Mirror*, 137.

64. Ibid., 148.

65. Ibid., 124.

66. McLuhan and Powers, *Global Village*, 54-55.

67. Ibid., 25-26.

68. McLuhan and McLuhan, *Laws of Media*, 17-18, 22.

McLuhan's Understanding of Marx

Dismissing Marx and His Method

McLuhan was unwavering in his negative reading of Marx, socialism, communism and dialectical methodology, but McLuhan based his rejection on the argument that communism has been achieved as an effect of technology.[1] Unfortunately, McLuhan's attacks were offered in summary form, often containing no more than a sentence. Only one extended discussion of Marx was attempted in McLuhan's published work, but it was in *Take Today: The Executive as Dropout*, a lesser known work written after the zenith of McLuhan's public attention had passed and the criticisms against him had levelled off.[2] This chapter will summarize McLuhan's understanding of Marx chronologically, focusing on his fuller analysis of Marx in *Take Today* in the second section .

Biographer Philip Marchand documents McLuhan's early and abiding contempt for Marxism. In the 1930s, McLuhan cautiously supported fascism's analysis of world problems in urging a return to "heroic enterprises," and in rejecting socialism and capitalism.[3] Going against the grain of progressive politics at the University of Wisconsin in Madison, McLuhan was the only possible Republican graduate student in the late 1930s.[4] Later, he predicted his theory of change based on the means of communication would supersede Marx's theory based on the means of production.[5] He also considered his work a satirical probe of capitalism and socialism.[6]

In *The Mechanical Bride: Folklore of Industrial Man* (1951), McLuhan commented sparingly on Marxism, berating Marxists for trying to solve the conflict between modern technology's pursuit of ease and profits and religion's call for moral duty through the suppression of religion.[7] A few pages later, he put forth the notion that Marx argued technology would win socialism's battles without political assistance—an argument McLuhan used to explain the acceptance of women in the labour force and the economic logic of feminism.[8]

Despite earlier condemnations McLuhan introduced an idea, expanded in later works, that communism has already been realized, although the association with communism was largely negative, and connoted "replaceable parts," "uniform products," and lack of individualism.

> Thus, it may very well be that the effect of mass production and consumption is really to bring about a practical rather than theoretic communism. When men and women have been transformed into replaceable parts by competitive success drives, and have become accustomed to the consumption of uniform products, it is hard to see where any individualism remains.[9]

McLuhan did not return to this theme until *Understanding Media: The Extensions of Man,* in 1964, where he comments more frequently on Marx. In this text he gave technologically-driven communism a more positive spin.[10] *The Gutenberg Galaxy: The Making of Typographic Man* briefly mentioned that Marx, Vladimir Lenin and communism are irrelevant when compared to the nature of oral society in shaping attitudes that favour public media over private media in the Soviet Union.[11] The work's other reference to Marxism was in a quote from historian Carleton Hayes, where he argued that anti-nationalist philosophies such as Marxism and Christianity have been put into the service of nationalism since the 1800s.[12]

In *Understanding Media*, McLuhan reported that Europeans could exclaim that Americans had realized communism—i.e., that rich and poor consumed the same goods and lived the same lives—and, as a result, he could find no correlation between income and social class:

> When Europeans used to visit America before the Second War they would say, "But you have communism here!" What they meant was that we not only had standardized goods, but everybody had them. Our millionaires not only ate cornflakes and hot dogs, but really thought of themselves as middle-class people. What else? How could a millionaire be anything but "middle-class" in America unless he had the creative imagination of an artist to make a unique life for himself? Is it strange that Europeans should associate uniformity on environment and commodities with communism? … The highest income cannot liberate a North American from his "middle-class" life. The lowest gives everybody a considerable piece of the same middle-class existence. That is, we really have homogenized our schools and factories and cities and entertainment to a

great extent, just because we are literate and accept the logic of uniformity and homogeneity that is inherent in Gutenberg technology. This logic, which has never been accepted in Europe, has suddenly been questioned in America, since the tactile mesh of the TV mosaic has begun to permeate the American sensorium.[13]

According to McLuhan, Marx and his followers did not understand the "dynamics of the new media of communication" because they were still using the machine as their unit of analysis at the moment when electronic technology, including the telegraph, began to reverse the mechanical form. McLuhan concluded that it was poor timing.[14] He then called Marx an "impressionable recipient" of theories elevating human labour to an aesthetic level as the machine was substituted for that work.[15] While appearing to attempt to play down Marx's importance, McLuhan, without explanation, noted that Marx strikes fear in contemporary society, comparing him to Machiavelli.[16]

McLuhan also offered his thesis that "linguistic media shape social production, as much as do the means of production" as a deep subversion of Marx's dialectic. After all, McLuhan contended, the knowledge that material production affects daily life is a commonplace.[17] In the section "Hybrid Energy," McLuhan appeared to be replacing the mode of information, or the medium, for the mode of production, dismissing Marx in the process. It is my contention that in building this understanding, what McLuhan does is retain the essence of dialectical methodology as he makes the medium the moving social force. He attributed the power to retribalize to radio, reversing individualism into fascist or Marxist collectivism.[18]

The theme of an immanent communism is augmented in *War and Peace in the Global Village* (1968), which McLuhan wrote that the service environment created by the press, highways, postal service, steam and railroad in the nineteenth century was available to workers far in excess of what services could be obtained by private, individual resources.

By Karl Marx's time, a "communism" resulting from such services so far surpassed the older private wealth and services contained within the new communal environment that it was quite natural for Marx to use it as a rear-view mirror for his Utopian hopes. The paradox of poverty amidst plenty had begun. Even the pauper lived, and lives, in an environment of multi-billion dollar communal services.[19]

However, Marx went on to state that the mechanical, communal service environment gave way to the electric information environment, which superseded the territorial goals of business and politics. As a result he felt that "by now Communism is something that lies more than a century behind us, and we are deep into the new age of tribal involvement."[20]

Another attack on Marx in this work charged that he failed to understand that new technologies create new environments, which in turn act on the human sensorium. Marx was thus able to describe changes to which he could assign no causes.[21] That Marx did not understand causality is found in *Counterblast* (1969).

> Russia stands pat on the status quo ante 1850 that produced Marx. There culture ends. The Russian revolution reached the stage of book culture. Marx never studied or understood causality. He paid no attention to the railway or the steamboat. Russia strives to have a 19th century of consumer values but remains a tribal or corporate and non-visual culture.[22]

Counterblast reiterated the idea that Marx's *Communist Manifesto* is a "rear view mirror of a *fait accompli*," and Marxists are devoted to a "revolution that took place in our service environments over a century ago."[23] Marx—in an evaluation that is more likely to inspire pity rather than fear of him—was misled: "It was the absence of the power to probe or to observe the environment of his time that misled Marx in his *Communist Manifesto* (1848). What became the nightmare of the Communist threat from then until now was a misunderstanding of events that had already occurred."[24]

Marx was a "victim" blind to the new environment, and the class struggle was "a spectre of the old feudalism" that distorted the new middle classes. As an intellectual enthralled by Gutenberg technology and mass production, Marx "would have revolted from our global upsurge of tribal man."[25] Meanwhile, the information environment creates a tribal communism.[26]

These critiques of Marx are consistent with views expressed in his letters and in his posthumous work. One letter referred to an unpublished manuscript arguing that Marx, along with Machiavelli and Hobbes, offered "emotional strategies" rather than conceptual systems.[27] In another letter, he wrote that England had achieved communism by 1830 "in terms of (industrial) services available to the ordinary man." Communism, which "happened long before Karl Marx," is "when travel and information and education services are available to the ordinary person."[28]

> Today, with the multi-billion dollar service environments available to everybody, almost for free, (these include the massive educational and information world of advertising) it means that we have plunged very deep into tribal Communism on a scale unknown in human history. I asked the group [at the Bilderberg Conference on international themes at Elsinore, Denmark]: "What are we fighting Communism for? We are the most Communist people in world history."[29]

In a letter to the editor that responded to an article attacking McLuhan, psychologist R.D. Laing, and anthropologists Claude Levi-Strauss and Conrad Lorenz, McLuhan reproached the "Marxist hang-up" that human labour does not alter the total environment:

> Marxists have chosen to ignore the "invisible" or total information environment created by industrial hardware. Marx ignored the "flip" or reversal that occurred in his own time. That is, when public services, available to the ordinary worker, exceeded all power of private wealth to provide these same services for the wealthiest persons in the world.[30]

This theme was reiterated in a letter to author Jonathan Miller in which McLuhan wrote that all classical economists, including Marx, ignored the new service environments as they studied labour, markets, products, rents and prices.[31] Even after death, McLuhan's stand against Marxism remained firm. The assertion from *Counterblast* that Marx did not study or understand causality was recapitulated verbatim in the posthumous work, *The Global Village: Transformations in World Life and Media in the Twenty-first Century* (1989).[32]

McLuhan's Extended Comment on Marx

These thematic forays against Marx are consistent throughout McLuhan's writings, changing from a position of relative neutrality and moving toward hostility. However, they are all glancing blows against Marx rather than sustained offensives. McLuhan's single sustained treatment of Marx as part of economic history is found in *Take Today: The Executive as Dropout*.[33] In this treatment, however, rather than launch an offensive, McLuhan was much more sympathetic, drawing parallels between Marx and Charles Darwin, Alexis de Tocqueville and Charles Dickens. In other references to the latter three, McLuhan credits them with insights and advances that were ahead of their times.

McLuhan first linked Marx's finding of the "chink in the 'iron law of wages'" with Darwin's focus on the "missing link" of nature. Thus, both thinkers stand on the cusp of change from the print era to the electronic era. Also, because of his "ignorance of his predecessors" in English thought, Marx enjoyed status as an immigrant observer in England—having an anti-environment: his "medieval" Prussian culture. Marx shared this anti-environmental advantage, which McLuhan reserved for the role of the artist, with de Tocqueville. Finally, like Dickens, Marx was shocked by his experience of the new industrial society.[34]

McLuhan credited Marx with finding the flaws in liberal capitalist economist David Ricardo's insistence on matching labour and product. Marx, McLuhan approvingly noted, observed that the work process made a profit as he traced the origins of value, price and profit in the market process in extensive historical studies of exchanges in a market that had perfected the equation of translating products of all labour into monetary terms.[35] In McLuhan's terminology, matching is a practice of the visual culture of the print era; making is a practice of the pre-print oral era and the post-print electronic era. McLuhan quoted from Marx's *Capital* to illustrate: "In other words, Marx saw money as the magical transformer of all things whatever to money prices. As a member of the literati, he sought the matching principle, or the common denominator of 'socially necessary labour,' as the underlying drama of the nineteenth century."[36]

At this point in his argument, McLuhan faulted Marx for his focus on the dehumanizing aspects of the industrial age, thereby mistaking the new service environments as "mere crumbs for the poor from the tables of the rich," when in fact, they were available to rich and poor alike.[37] But rather than the nearly indictable offense this mistake seemed to be in other McLuhan writings, in this discussion McLuhan equates Marx's error with Aristotle's failure to consider the service environments of the phonetic alphabet and currency. Marx, in turn, ignored the environment created by steam's alteration of the work process, an oversight of innovations he shares with economists from his time to the present.[38]

McLuhan quoted Marx's *A Contribution to the Critique of Political Economy* as evidence that Marx was unaware of the "dynamic interface among environments as such..." The message of steam as a new "medium," McLuhan argued, is that it speeds up the "social surround" not the products it produces. But Marx, like all economists then and since, was not able to see this new environment.[39]

McLuhan further translated Marx into figure and ground terms, writing that the figure for Marx was the commodity of hourly labour and the ground was the social process of production for market.

> The market had newly "alienated" or separated the "labour power" from the man in the mechanical age. Under preindustrial conditions, labour power had, as it were, remained embodied in the whole man. This man was not an independent worker but dependent on a man-master relationship. The market broke this personal bondage and freed "labour power" to sink or swim on the competitive market waves, along with its possessor
>
> In his historical analysis, Marx clearly separated the labour process from the forms it may assume "under particular social conditions." For him, the labour process had now broken away from the agrarian household with its tribal bonds of kinship and personal subordination. Thus for Marx, the labour process comes to include all commodity exchange. It does not include consumer satisfactions since these are to be assumed as a necessary condition or motive for exchange.[40]

McLuhan supported his analysis with another lengthy quote from *Capital* on how the labour process changes with human nature. He then asserted that Marx developed his concepts in "the rear-view historical mirror" rather than join "the existential struggle of the Kierkegaards and the Rimbauds." As the latter probed "where it's at," Marx was one stage behind, along with other unnamed Western intellectuals of modern times who insisted on "translating all processes into matching categories and classifications." McLuhan wrote that Marx's vision of a socialist age in which "man assumes control of the production process" and becomes "master of his own history" to "get with the historical process" was both "whimsical and hopeful."[41]

What Marx ignored, according to McLuhan, was the new service environments spinning off from the products of the work process. Further, McLuhan argued that Marx, hemmed in by his classifications, failed to consider the total system that he claimed to study. The *coup de grace* against Marxists is this: "In the electric-information environment the old categories of 'class' and 'economics' and 'history' are meaningless.

For fifty years the West has provided the same multibillion-dollar services for rich and poor."[42]

Of the "class struggle," McLuhan wrote that this time-honoured conflict between owners and workers is abstracted from the service environments created by new media in the attempt to be scientific. Although this Marxist goal was "noble and feasible," Marxist analysis did not follow when science "went through the vanishing point into acoustic or resonant space" with Albert Einstein's relativity theory.[43] As products of "Western literati" and their sensory assumptions, Marx's followers were surprised by the electric phase of the new hidden environments that retrieved many forms of primitivism and brought revolution outside highly literate and industrialized societies. Marx "used a utopian rear-view mirror to advocate the takeover of all technologies for an overall social programming 'to make history.' He was not prepared for the takeover of nature and history alike by the instant information environment."[44]

McLuhan repeated the refrain that communism had been realized in the West before Marx was born, but he grouped Marx with other utopian or anti-utopian thinkers such as George Orwell who focused on the period before their own.[45] And, according to McLuhan, if Marx did not break through the limitations of his time, it was not for want of trying through the use of dialectics.

> Lineal classification as a basis for science and historical evolution had been pushed to its limit and now performed the flip or reversal that is incidental to ultimate development. Marx went all the way to the boundaries of scientific classification seeking an outlet into a "field theory" via Hegelian dialectic. He was certain that "everything is interconnected." He was unprepared for interplay, the resonant interval where the new action is. The old action had been in the cosmic connections of "the great chain of being," whose common denominator was "matter-in-motion." He was also unprepared for the sudden nowness of the past in the speed-up of the electric age. The new electric speed-up had created the interval that was classified by the old scientists as the missing link.[46]

Electronic media and culture, McLuhan wrote, "bypassed the Hegelian process of interconnectedness, restoring the structure of acoustic space to Western experience... Acoustic space is, like a pun, a resonant sphere whose centre is everywhere and whose boundaries are nowhere."[47]

It would appear that McLuhan thought Marx tried to make the transition although unsuccessfully. He continued:

> To the visual man, the effort to define and to visualize this space is unnerving. Even contemporary scientists persist in making visual models to explain and confuse their publics concerning nonvisual processes. Marx eventually repudiated the Marxist expositors of his perception of social process, but he remained meshed in his own paradigm trap.[48]

In McLuhan's summary analysis, Marx was commended for noting that products tended to be translated into a store of money, taking on the aspect of capital, and that capitalists built on this tendency although it worked against consumer needs. But despite this insight, McLuhan wrote, Marx and other economists were not aware of the electric media speed-up and its effect on creating wealth.[49]

This extended discussion of Marx is offered to show that McLuhan's analysis of Marxism was not completely one-dimensional or a caricature, which are among charges to be aired in the next chapter. Unfortunately, this discussion of Marx occurred in a work that followed the height of McLuhan's popularity in the 1960s and is not one of McLuhan's seminal works. While McLuhan consistently dismissed or attacked Marx, he attempted an analysis that allowed Marx a serious hearing. In fact, McLuhan's criticisms of Marx are extremely similar to those made within the past decade by postmodernist historian Mark Poster.[50] McLuhan's critique of dialectics foreshadows the critiques of postmodernist Jean Baudrillard and neo-Marxist Armand Mattelart. McLuhan's demand for a field theory also foreshadows the view of British cultural studies scholar Raymond Williams.[51]

NOTES

1. Marshall McLuhan, Understanding Media (New York: Menor, 1964), 198-199.
2. Marshall McLuhan, with Barrington Nevitt, *Take Today: The Executive as Dropout* (New York: Harcourt, Brace, Jovanovich, 1972), 61-78.
3. Philip Marchand, *Marshall McLuhan: The Medium and Messenger* (New York: Ticknor and Fields, 1989), 27.
4. Ibid., 42.
5. Ibid., 144.

6. Ibid., 186.
7. Marshall McLuhan, *The Mechanical Bride: Folklore of Industrial Man* (New York: Vanguard, 1951), 34.
8. Ibid., 40.
9. Ibid., 55.
10. McLuhan, *Understanding Media*, 198.
11. Marshall McLuhan, *The Gutenberg Galaxy: The Making of Typographic Man* (Toronto: University of Toronto Press, 1962), 31.
12. Ibid., 265-266, citing Carleton Hayes, *Historical Evolution in Modern Nationalism* (New York: Smith Publishing, 1931), 289.
13. McLuhan, *Understanding Media*, 198-199.
14. Ibid., 49.
15. Ibid., 51.
16. Ibid., 160.
17. Ibid., 58.
18. Ibid., 265.
19. Marshall McLuhan, with Quentin Fiore and Jerome Angel, *War and Peace in the Global Village* (New York: Bantam, 1968), 4-5.
20. Ibid.
21. Ibid., 136.
22. Marshall McLuhan, with Harley Parker, *Counterblast* (New York: Harcourt, Brace and World, 1969), 56.
23. Ibid., 96, 128.
24. Ibid., 139.
25. Ibid., 140.
26. Ibid., 97.
27. Marshall McLuhan, *Letters of Marshall McLuhan*, ed. Matie Molinaro, Corinne McLuhan, and William Toye (Toronto: Oxford University Press, 1987), 157.
28. Ibid., 373.
29. Ibid.
30. Ibid., 402, citing Michael Wood, "The Four Gospels," *New Society* (December 18, 1969).
31. Ibid., 405.
32. Marshall McLuhan, with Bruce Powers, *The Global Village: Transformations in World Life and Media in the Twenty-first Century* (New York: Oxford University Press, 1989), 96.
33. McLuhan, with Nevitt, *Take Today*, 61-78.
34. Ibid., 61.
35. Ibid.
36. Ibid., 62.
37. Ibid.
38. Ibid., 63.
39. Ibid.
40. Ibid., 65-66.
41. Ibid., 66-67.
42. Ibid., 68.
43. Ibid., 69.
44. Ibid., 70-71.
45. Ibid., 75.

46. Ibid.
47. Ibid., 76
48. Ibid.
49. Ibid., 78.
50. Mark Poster, *Foucault, Marxism and History: Mode of Production vs. Mode of Information* (Cambridge, MA: Polity Press, 1984), 57; and Mark Poster, "The Mode of Information and Postmodernity," in *Communication Theory Today*, eds. David Crowley and David Mitchell (Stanford, CA: Stanford University Press, 1994), 173-175.
51. Jean Baudrillard, "Requiem for the Media," in *For a Critique of the Political Economy of the Sign* (St. Louis, Telos Press, 1981), 164-169; Armand Mattelart and Michele Mattelart, *Rethinking Media Theory*, trans. James A. Cohen and Marina Urquidi (Minneapolis: University of Minnesota Press, 1992), 115; Raymond Williams, "Paradoxically, If the Book Works It to Some Extent Annihilates Itself," in *McLuhan: Hot and Cool*, ed. Gerald E. Stearns (New York: Dial Press, 1967), 190.

Marxism's Understanding of McLuhan

Assessing McLuhan's Social Theory

Despite McLuhan's many anti-Marx protests, several scholars have made a case, based on parallels between McLuhan and Marx, that contradicts McLuhan's consistent dismissal of Marxism. They call McLuhan a Marxist, to some extent. Marxist scholars, in contrast, almost unanimously return the attack against McLuhan. Before turning to those comparisons and criticisms, however, two negative critiques (by historian Daniel Czitrom and literary scholar Donald Theall) and one positive evaluation (by political theorist Judith Stamps) of McLuhan's social theory will be reviewed to provide a larger context for measuring McLuhan against Marxist theory.

Claiming McLuhan is essentially without a social theory, Czitrom notes that McLuhan borrowed from his mentor, political economist Harold Innis, the tools—dialectical theory—to add a theory of social change to his aesthetic doctrine.[1] Innis, according to Czitrom, "employed a dialectical method to explain the rise and fall of civilizations. Whereas Hegel focused on Nation States and Marx on modes of production, Innis substituted communications media to identify the great epochs."[2]

The strength of McLuhan's promise is embodied in the French notion of "McLuhanisme"—the "commitment to serious examination of culture." Czitrom argued, however, that implicit in McLuhan's study of culture via the literary theory of New Criticism was a conservative, apolitical social theory. New Criticism studied how literature produces psychological states in an emphasis of form over content in which authorial biography and history were not important. McLuhan's literary criticism was both neo-Catholic and anti-modern.[3]

Czitrom also argues that McLuhan's concept of "technological naturalism," by which technology modifies humans, offered "a trick of vision, not a true social theory" that substitutes myth for history. McLuhan's "glorification" of television became "an apology for corporate interests that controlled the medium" as he abandoned the "critical theory" stance of Innis. Czitrom classifies McLuhan as part of a broader trend toward synchronic analysis of language, communication, myth and cultural forms in areas such as structural anthropology, linguistics and semiotics. All have an affinity with New Criticism, although Czitrom concedes that McLuhan helped legitimate new areas of cultural study.[4]

Theall calls McLuhan "an aesthet[e] in a world of social and political upheaval" who is apolitical but is conservative when he is intentionally political. Theall explains that an aesthete like McLuhan was thrust in the role of social commentator because the 1960s social movements began with a revolution in lifestyles. He characterized the sixties as an aesthetic revolution with social and political implications.[5] Although Theall and Czitrom both describe McLuhan as a Catholic committed to conservative political positions, McLuhan's sharpest critics suggest that his philosophy is totalitarian, as seen in his commitment to the views of Ezra Pound and Wyndham Lewis, who both praised totalitarian regimes. McLuhan also shared Lewis's view of the State as work of art. Despite McLuhan's claims to being apolitical, Theall suggests that such views introduce the possibility of a totalitarian philosophy.[6]

Theall offers *The Mechanical Bride: Folklore of Industrial Man* as evidence of McLuhan's lack of a basic sociological theory. The book made no mention of Max Weber or Emile Durkheim and showed "no serious awareness of Marx."[7] Concentrating on the role of the uncommitted observer allowed McLuhan to avoid discussions of religion and politics, in accord with the New Criticism. Theall suggests that while endorsing the status quo, McLuhan endorsed the new Catholic liturgical values of the 1940s and 1950s in his electronic-era concepts of participation, community and retribalization. McLuhan was seen as someone who promised to link the aesthetic insights of surrealism and symbolism to an analysis of the perceived world and the nature of culture. He also promised to integrate the popular arts, which others in art italicized were of value, with the fine arts. He promised to provide for the arts some of the credibility of the human sciences.[8]

Theall argues that McLuhan's vision needed a strong social theory rather than the textual emphasis of New Criticism. McLuhan, however, showed no interest in the theoretical ways in which Marx or others might have aided him in achieving his synthesis. McLuhan showed no awareness of Marxism's relevance to his brand of determinism, and in fact, said many times that Marx never studied causality. Theall adds that with a shallow understanding of sociology and structural anthropology, McLuhan failed to present his findings in terms of any social theory of why media come to be and how they interact politically.[9] In the end, McLuhan was unable to overcome the weaknesses imposed by his limited theoretical tools in order to fulfill his promise.

Offering a more positive reading, Stamps would agree that the influence of New Criticism, as well as McLuhan's key notion of sensory perception, fed into his understanding of Innis. However, she argues that these two influential theories helped him formulate his brand of critical theory through exposure to Innis. Sensory perception theory formed the basis for his negative dialectics; the New Criticism provided McLuhan with a call for a new rhetoric that would end the dominance of logic, or dialectics, and in which neither logic or rhetoric would dominate.[10]

McLuhan came to Innis' texts after *The Mechanical Bride* and incorporated his ideas into *The Gutenberg Galaxy: The Making of Typographic Man*, his next book. Stamps also believes that Marxists would have benefited from a similar encounter with Innis. In *The Gutenberg Galaxy* McLuhan pursued the material bases of media messages and addressed historians.[12] Stamps echoes the critics of McLuhan's works from *Understanding Media: The Extensions of Man* onward who vilify McLuhan for drifting toward technological determinism, pseudo-science, ahistoricism and dogmatism. Despite this, her alliance of McLuhan with the critical political economy of Innis and the Frankfurt School through the continuing critique of modernity and use of negative dialectics under a different name, keeps him within the critical theory camp.[13]

Parallels Between McLuhan and Marx

In finding similarities between Marx and McLuhan, commentaries range from passing references to more extended analyses. In a limited comparison, media scholar Neil Postman suggests that the "McLuhanesque" idea that media form will determine the nature of content reflects Marx's observation in *The German Ideology* that storytelling and song, which were required for epic poetry, disappeared when the printing press was introduced. Postman writes that although Marx did not fully explore this, he understood the press was a form for discourse that determines different content and audiences.[14]

In a more extended and positive comparison between Marx and McLuhan, literary scholar Patrick Brantlinger equates Marx's focus on economic modes of production as primary causal factors in history, including the base structure's influence on the cultural superstructure, with McLuhan's stress on the mass media the main causal factor in history. The parallel finally breaks down in McLuhan's assertion that political action is futile because social change occurs beyond human control, whereas Marxism insists on the need for political action, or praxis, to effect change.[15] Brantlinger further adds that another parallel between Marx and McLuhan is their sense of history as "progressive and catastrophic." For McLuhan, each new medium radically changes social life. McLuhan also parallels Marx's alienation of labour in arguing that visual culture's separation of the producer and consumer leads to social decay.[16]

Sociologist Tom Nairn attempted an alignment of McLuhan and Marxism by questioning why the media of human communications have only recently become an intellectual subject. He notes that communication was not a problem, or an area of interest, for Hegel or Marx.[17] He answers this question by citing general social development since the last part of the nineteenth century, before which time communication media "fitted society like a glove." The alienation, or reification, formerly attributed to material conditions, today might be attributed to "various forms of estrangement of language from reality."[18]

Nairn adds to this the new electric media techniques, which have offered a solution to many communication problems. By forcing communication to fill the new vehicles for communication, the new information environment creates a crisis.[19] Nairn accepts the Marxist model of society, containing the economic base structure and the cultural superstructure. However, he notes that the model needed to be adapted to contemporary society because modern media no longer fit society as did traditional media. He writes, "Conscious culture does not echo or transform such a change, as it did the cotton mill, or the railway, for instance; it is the change."[20] Consciousness under the old model was a product of the base structure, but mass media change the scale of society, making consciousness a part of the structure, as well as becoming part of the economy. Nairn further notes that media void the gap between structure and superstructure in the classical Marxist model.

McLuhan echoed Marx's epochs of world history, of primitive societies without alienation, historical societies that exert control over nature by forfeiting that unity, and the society of the future with its unity regained at a higher level and its complete control over the environment. Capitalism, Nairn argues, has made the material realization of this future society possible and created the communications media to help regain Marx's unity. He suggests that capitalism is restrained from doing this by its social forms.

Nairn contends that although this should be the message of McLuhan's slogan, "the medium is the message," McLuhan's thesis is

wrapped in myth. For example, the "global village" was created historically by European imperialism rather than mythically by television.[21]
And, rather than a village, imperialism has created "a cruel class society
tearing humanity in two," made and sustained by "private property and
the gun." The social forms of capitalism prevent the emergence of a
global village, in which McLuhan insists society already lives.

> That we now could live in a "global village," that our actual
> experience prefigures this more and more in its form, thanks
> to new media, is another and different point. The potential of
> electric media is, in fact, in contradiction with a great deal of
> the actual social world. And the actual, historical and social
> grasp of the meaning of such media depends more than any-
> thing else on seeing the contradiction.[22]

According to Nairn, McLuhan's myth lay in ignoring these contradictions and, by believing the new media have ended history, he denied
any chance of the historical understanding of social processes.
McLuhan's mythology abstracts consciousness from history by making
one aspect of that process, the medium, a single cause of the rest.

Nairn suggests that further research in McLuhan's work ought to
separate the historical significance of the media discussed from the
mythological form used; "to put it crudely: after Hegel, Marx put history on its feet, right way up; McLuhan has turned it upside down
again: criticism of McLuhan must inevitably try and put it on its feet
once more."[23]

In constructing a historical theory of communication, McLuhan
offered social theory a myth to debunk—a task which Nairn called a
measure of McLuhan's achievement. McLuhan realized the importance
of media more acutely than others. Criticism of his thinking could be a
major impetus in rethinking basic ideas about society.[24]

In contrast to Brantlinger's and Nairn's fruitful comparisons of Marx
and McLuhan, other scholars argue the Marx/McLuhan parallels are
superficial. Still others argue that McLuhan's similarities to Marx wither
into a caricature of technological totalitarianism. Media scholar Carolyn
Marvin finds only superficial similarities between Innis and McLuhan
and Marx, pointing to conceptual problems in Innis' categories of spatial and temporal bias and in his analysis of the interaction of media
with social organizations. For similarities, Innis and Marx both set in
motion a historical logic of material causes that expose progress as an
illusion; consciousness turns on itself, leading to destruction, death and

injustice. Also, Innis' vision of unalienated communication resembles Marx's unalienated labour. Marvin collapsed McLuhan into Innis for her discussion, explaining that McLuhan applied to perception what Innis attempted to do for social institutions.[25]

In a more thorough analysis that rejects any real shared ideas between Marx and McLuhan, author Sidney Finkelstein argues that although McLuhan's vision of an economic transformation of society through electronic media may appear similar to socialism, "McLuhan seems like Marx seen through a distorting mirror." The false parallels include the reappearance in future society of qualities of early tribal society.[26] Marx, however, keyed in on the rise of private property and antagonistic social class relations as the impelling forces for progressive change away from early society through feudalism and capitalism, and back toward an improved version of common property through the dialectical negation of monopoly capitalism.[27] McLuhan retained the idea of progress through leaps and disasters, but stripped his approach of factors such as private property or the formation of social classes. He focused instead on the phonetic alphabet, printed books and electric technology, all acting outside of human criticism or intervention.[28] In their place, McLuhan put a growing force, "a move toward totalitarian control of the world's natural resources, labour and markets by the great interlocking industrial corporations," which ultimately is a vision of "human history with the humans who created it left out."[29]

Marxists Cast Out McLuhan

Marxist social theorists uniformly cast McLuhan in similar terms as Finkelstein, emphatically disavowing any parallels between Marx and McLuhan. Only social art historian Arnold Hauser identifies any redeeming qualities in McLuhan. Recent Canadian scholarship has also argued for parallels between McLuhan and Marxism, while still arguing that McLuhan was not a Marxist.

Hans Enzensberger, one of the few Marxist thinkers who ascribe a positive role to the mass media in socialist change, charges that McLuhan lacks analytic categories for analyzing social processes and is "incapable of any theoretical construction." Calling McLuhan's work an attempt to "stand Marx on his head"—in all likelihood an effort to play on Marx's claim of having stood Hegel on his head, or rather, turned him on his feet—Enzensberger finds that McLuhan suppresses all problems of the economic base through idealist tendencies and by belittling the notion of class struggle. Enzensberger calls McLuhan's "gospel" of the new primitive's return to prehistoric tribal existence on a higher level a "vague humanism."[30] He sounds only one positive note on McLuhan, interpreting the aphorism that "the medium is the message" as a sign that the bourgeoisie have all the means to communicate, but, being ideologically sterile, have nothing more to say.[31]

Neo-Marxist writer Armand Mattelart more systematically dismembers the "fetish" that the mass media are autonomous agencies that transcend the societies in which they occur, and thus allow them to appear to be a natural force. Rather than being understood as instruments of the ruling class' struggle to dominate oppressed classes, McLuhan's media are independent actors in the technological drama and a primary influence on society. In this drama, the ruling class is able to denounce the media's influence.[32] The communication revolution, under the rule of capitalist relations, obscures the true nature of class confrontation and seeks to be a substitute for Lenin's "revolutionary moment." McLuhan incorrectly perceived technology as an apolitical actor neutral to class interests.[33]

Mattelart argues the opposite, that the media, as agents of the ruling class, give material form to the notion of change within the capitalist system, which is in fact, the negation of change. The media's task is to reproduce this ideology in order to prevent any change in the capitalist mode of production. The media become imperialism's instrument for putting into orbit McLuhan's "global village," which Mattelart says is created by the ruling class to neutralize the dominated classes with the illusion of integration into the world. McLuhan's theory is imperialism's way of fostering false consciousness through the new media while declaring that the media bring "liberation," "participation," and even a concept of "communism." Rather than a true democratization of mass media however, the in-depth participation engendered by the new media heralded by McLuhan represent the status quo because they do not challenge passive participation or the receiver's consumer status.[34] Mattelart's comments about African experience with Western mass media strongly denounced "McLuhanesque myths," including the "global village," which belies the dominant position of the West as a transmitter that, in effect, has used media to colonize and dominate an Africa far removed from a global communication network.[35]

In a lengthy critique of "McLuhanacy," Marxist literary critic John Fekete writes that McLuhan's neocapitalist account of the effects of dominant mass media environments removes the essential elements of social history: praxis, class struggle and the fight for liberation. McLuhan develops "a powerful bourgeois ideological form of manipulative-hegemonic neocapitalist structural modifications."[36] His theory of media as sensory extensions affecting sensory balance reifies, or objectifies, human activity so that the objectifications—the media—are forever alienated and fetishized with power over human beings. Concrete forms of neocapitalist alienation become general forms of humanity, freezing social development as historical facts become essences.[37] "McLuhanacy is the ideological otherness of counter-revolutionary neocapitalist reification of the production and reproduction of everyday existence. This is the main source of its appeal, power, and barbarity," Fekete argues.[38]

Fekete also asserts that McLuhan abstracts from and preserves existing class-determined forms and social uses of communication because his theory ignores the political, economic and military dimensions of power, as well as ownership and class interests of the mass media. McLuhan also moves away from the media's socio-historical determinations, treating media not "in terms of social relations among human beings, but as relations between human beings and things, as well as among things themselves." McLuhan's "technocratic" ideology excludes questions of human need, interest, value and goals.[39]

According to Fekete, McLuhan's historical periods, based on cultural changes and corresponding media-influenced sensory changes, equate roughly with Marxist historical periods. The first era is primitive, an audile tribal culture with the oral technology of speech. The second is pre-capitalist, a visual culture with writing and the phonetic alphabet. The third is capitalist, which is an extreme visual culture with the mechanical technology of print. And fourth is monopoly capitalist, an audio-tactile culture with the electronic technology of television. Fekete continues on to state that the main issue with McLuhan is the rise and fall of visuality, although within this context his periods are vague and contradictory.[40] He charges that at its heart, McLuhan's cultural ideology is a religious myth of the fall of detribalization and the salvation of retribalization, with technology as the main feature of all the cultural formations. In this process, social theory is reduced to ecology and history disappears into a technology-driven search for equilibrium.[41]

Next Fekete argues that a concept of sensory extension and balance is the "epicentre" of McLuhan's whole theory, providing a direct relationship between the individual and the technological environment. He calls the concept "an ideological construction whose standpoint is that of corporate social integration, harmony, equilibrium" and that precludes conscious revolutionary change by paralleling the psychic and social order through the model of biological homeostasis.[42] In the social order, the human organism extends and imbalances itself through media, which alter the organism's sense-ratios, creating discomfort and numbness following a cycle of irritation and counter-irritation seeking balance—until released by electronic media. The theory of history, in sum, is the history of disease.[43] Unable to resist the impact of media on the senses, human beings are left with only "technocratic manipulative options," reprogramming the human nervous system to adjust. Fekete asserts that McLuhan "accepts the fact of reification, the rule of technology, and suppresses the consciousness of alienation by insisting that technology is really ourselves and by denying that the objectified praxis has really been alienated from us."[44]

Fekete argues that McLuhan's theory cannot be interpreted as mechanical materialism, focusing on technology, or a subjective idealism, focusing on the sensorium. He contends that because McLuhan identifies subject and object as one—in other words, human beings and the media that dominate them similarly—McLuhan dissolves the dialectical dualism of subject-object into a monism of one-dimensional reification in which the alienated subject is surrounded by an alienated existence. This, Fekete wrote, presents a process described by Frankfurt School theorist Herbert Marcuse.[45] McLuhan becomes, in Fekete's words, "the apologist of counter-revolution" and "the major bourgeois ideologue of one-dimensional society."[46]

Marxist Art Historian: Another View

In sharp contrast to these criticisms, Hauser's scholarly exploration of all forms of art—the visual arts, literature, film, theater and music, as well as the mass media, popular art and music—finds a small but at times positive niche for McLuhan's interpretation of mass culture.[47] Faulting McLuhan's doctrines for being examples of "the exaggeration and simplification with which the media of mass culture present phenomena," Hauser hails McLuhan as the first to give "proper emphasis" to the effects of electronic media as compared to the effects of print media and film.[48] Still, Hauser challenges McLuhan on nearly every point. For example, to McLuhan's preference for the spoken over the written word, Hauser counters:

> The impression made by the spoken word may, because of its immediacy, be stronger than in a written communication; the liveliness of the impression does not, however, guarantee a deeper interpretation with more nuances of the communica-

tion in question. A written text at least offers more reliable clues for proper interpretation than the fleeting sound of the spoken word.[49]

Hauser continued to rebut McLuhan's visual versus acoustic dualism point by point, concluding that television signals the "victory and not the defeat of visuality," despite the addition of the acoustic process in television.[50] These central shortcomings aside, McLuhan's theory has "special significance" for Hauser because the theory introduced the idea of "technical reproducibility" into the "realm of culture." Hauser applauds McLuhan for popularizing an idea similarly held by Frankfurt School critical theorist Walter Benjamin, that film and photography introduced the age of technical reproducibility of works of art. Hauser is probably correct in suggesting that McLuhan had not heard of or read Benjamin, who held that mechanical reproduction through film released "concrete visual sensuality from the dominance of abstraction and poetic expression from that of literature."[51] Hauser disagrees with McLuhan's identification of the book, rather than film, as the first mechanically reproduced medium. Hauser argues that despite similar technical processes, a gulf separates reproduction of a printed text, which is not identical with the literary work, and reproduction of graphic art, which is the same work.

Hauser chides McLuhan for his "double romanticization of the historical process," of mourning a lost golden age and forecasting a utopian future. Hauser is more receptive to the idea of electronic media as extensions of the nervous system and concedes that "McLuhan is at least right insofar as we can no more escape from them (media) than we can from our own nerves." And Hauser recasts the aphorism "the medium is the message" in probably its least aphoristic form, when he writes, "...everything we have to say is the product of the way in which we can express it."[52]

In overcoming his "coquettish formulation," scholars should not deny McLuhan's having brought to critical consciousness the fact that the medium is part of the message being communicated. In Hauser's Marxist theory, medium and message are definable only in a dialectical relationship.[53] As a dialectical relationship, however, medium and message are still separate parts, as are form and content. Hauser contends that by negating the content of media and art's verbal, musical and visual structures, McLuhan embraced a concept of the end of art, which, like many of McLuhan's other notions, has a long history. For McLuhan's aesthetics, the consequence is that he did not—in fact, could not—talk about "what makes an artifact into a work of art or a dabbler into an artist."[54]

A Recent Canadian Perspective

Stamps draws together the "critical social scientific" approaches of McLuhan and Innis with those of Benjamin and Adorno. Stamps compares the Canadians with representatives of "German neo-Marxism" to argue that all four shared critical theories of modernity; itself a radical critique of Western political economy and rationality.[55] Although noting that the Frankfurt School was grounded in Marxism, Stamps is not dissuaded by McLuhan's dismissal of Marxism and of dialectics, nor from connecting the four theorists' shared interests in economics, politics, culture and communication.

As for dialectical methods used by these four theorists, Stamps argues that Innis and McLuhan were linked to a long tradition of dialectics in their critical historical analyses of Western views of objectivity and subjectivity. Innis and McLuhan developed their own version of the Frankfurt School's "negative dialectics," although they called it by a different name. She also argues that since the nineteenth century dialectical theorists have critiqued the dichotomy of objectivity and power, as well as Western rationalist ways of perceiving and classifying the world. Stamps offered "negative dialectics," as practiced by the Frankfurt School and the two Canadians, as a way of penetrating these issues.[56]

Stamps' comparison of the Frankfurt School's neo-Marxist dialectics with the thinking of McLuhan and Innis, in addition to Hauser's critique of McLuhan for denying the dialectical relationship of medium and message, and Fekete's charge that McLuhan collapsed the dualism of subject, the human, and object, the media, raise the need to explore the methodology of dialectics, its roots in Greek philosophy, Hegelian and Marxist philosophy, and its relationship to McLuhan's communication theory. The next two chapters will address these issues.

NOTES

1. Daniel Czitrom, *Media and the American Mind: From Morse to McLuhan* (Chapel Hill, NC: University of North Carolina Press, 1982), 172.
2. Ibid., 161.
3. Ibid., 165.
4. Ibid., 180-182.
5. Donald Theall, *Understanding McLuhan: The Medium is the Rear View Mirror* (Montréal: McGill-Queen's University Press, 1971), xiv.
6. Ibid., 60.

7. Ibid., 57.
8. Ibid., 202-204.
9. Ibid., 204-205.
10. Judith Stamps, *Unthinking Modernity: Innis, McLuhan and The Frankfurt School* (Montréal: McGill-Queen's University Press, 1995), 103, 108-109.
11. Ibid., 97.
12. Ibid., 123.
13. Ibid., 124-142.
14. Neil Postman, *Amusing Ourselves to Death: Public Discourse in the Age of Show Business* (New York: Penguin, 1985), 42-43.
15. Patrick Brantlinger, *Bread and Circuses: Theories of Mass Culture as Social Decay* (Ithaca: NY: Cornell University Press, 1983), 266-267.
16. Ibid., 270-271.
17. Tom Nairn, "McLuhanism: The Myth of Our Time," in *McLuhan: Pro and Con*, ed. Raymond Rosenthal (Baltimore, MD: Penguin, 1968), 141-143.
18. Ibid., 143.
19. Ibid., 144-145.
20. Ibid., 146.
21. Ibid., 150.
22. Ibid.
23. Ibid., 151.
24. Ibid., 152.
25. Carolyn Marvin, "Innis, McLuhan and Marx," *Visible Language* 23 (summer 1986): 355, 359.
26. Sidney Finkelstein, *Sense and Nonsense of McLuhan* (New York: International Publishers, 1968), 106.
27. Ibid., 106-109.
28. Ibid., 110.
29. Ibid., 115, 121.
30. Hans Enzensberger, *The Consciousness Industry* (New York: Seabury Press, 1974), 118.
31. Ibid., 119.
32. Armand Mattelart, *Mass Media, Ideologies, and the Revolutionary Movement* (Atlantic Highlands, NJ: Sussex, 1980), 8.
33. Ibid., 10.
34. Ibid., 20-21.
35. Ibid., 229.
36. John Fekete, "McLuhanacy: Counterrevolution in Cultural Theory," *Telos* 15 (spring 1973): 75.
37. Ibid., 76.
38. Ibid., 77.
39. Ibid., 78.
40. Ibid.
41. Ibid., 79.
42. Ibid., 100
43. Ibid., 101.
44. Ibid., 105.
45. Ibid., 106.
46. Ibid., 121.

47. Arnold Hauser, "An Interpretation of Mass Culture," in *The Sociology of Art*, trans. Kenneth J. Northcott (Chicago: University of Chicago Press, 1982), 611-617.
48. Ibid., 611.
49. Ibid., 612.
50. Ibid., 613.
51. Ibid., 614, citing Walter Benjamin, "The Work of Art in the Age of Mechanical Reproduction," in *Illuminations*, ed. Hannah Arendt, trans. Harry Zohn (New York: Schocken Books, 1969), 217-251.
52. Ibid., 615.
53. Ibid., 616.
54. Ibid., 658.
55. Stamps, *Unthinking Modernity*, xi, 4.
56. Ibid., 4-5.

Understanding Dialectics

References to McLuhan and Dialectics

The word "dialectics" has appeared in references attempting to measure the common ground between McLuhan and Marx. The arguments of McLuhan and his critics touched on dialectics, but never centered on the methodology itself. The term also has appeared, as it appears in the references, without explanation or definition. This chapter will draw together the references to dialectics found in McLuhan and his critics. It will then attempt to define dialectics as a methodology stretching from the pre-Socratic philosophers through Marx and beyond to critical theory and McLuhan.

According to McLuhan, if Marx did not break through the limitations of his time it was not for want of trying. He noted that Marx used Hegelian dialectics to seek a "field theory" based on his belief that "everything is interconnected."[1] McLuhan, however, argued that dialectics was ineffective because electronic media and culture "bypassed the Hegelian process of interconnectedness." A "visual man," Marx failed to make the transition and remained caught in a "paradigm trap."[2]

Although McLuhan viewed his thesis—that media shape production as much as the means of production—as a subversion of Marx's dialectics,[3] McLuhan maintained a self-professed debt to political economist Harold Innis, whose method was derived from Hegelian and Marxist dialectics.[4] Historian Daniel Czitrom asserts that McLuhan abandoned Innis' "critical context" and his "moral and political concern with American media imperialism."[5] He also argued that, as a humanist, McLuhan favoured rhetoric and grammar over dialectics in the post-Socratic intellectual debate over which method was superior.[6]

McLuhan himself, as Czitrom observes, envisioned dialectics as being on the wrong side of the dispute in the trivium between its foes, rhetoric and grammar. For McLuhan, dialectics, or logic and philosophy, has a "left-hemisphere" focus on abstraction and absolutes, and promoted correct thought forms regardless of audience.[7] Rhetoric and grammar are right-brain activities, which to McLuhan makes them valuable because rhetoric is the science of transforming audiences with speech, and grammar the ground search for structure and roots.

From the beginning the trivium was beset by rivalry between the brain hemispheres ... with grammar and rhetoric usually holding control of the trivium against the rival claims of the dialecticians. Cicero ... and Quintilian established the basic pattern for civilized education in the West ... as the alignment of encyclopedic wisdom and eloquence. That is, the conjunction of grammar ... and rhetoric provided a balance of the hemispheres.[8]

McLuhan clearly felt he was in a war, fighting on the side of the conservative, traditional grammarian and rhetorician "Ancients" against the dialectician "Moderns" with their "marvelous new systems and methods for organizing knowledge."

The proverbial rivalry between the two camps and their intellectual wars continue apace today, albeit largely unknown to the combatants. With *Laws of Media* we launch a fresh campaign in the war, against the futility of deploying the science of the Moderns of recent decades and centuries to deal with matters of media, as distinct from messages.[9]

McLuhan argued that the earliest expression of "visual" space, or linear thinking associated with the phonetic alphabet and typography, seemed to be based in the ancient Greek science of dialectics, which transformed religion into philosophy. The alphabet gave rise to the dialectic of pre-Socratic philosophers.[10] He maintained that in the print era, a new battle was waged between the Ancients and Moderns, which dialectics won, and which resulted in the casting of rhetoric and grammar in left-hemisphere forms. However, the tables are turning once more with the return to "acoustic" space in this century with electronic media. McLuhan describes his role in that table-turning as providing his tetradic form, which improves on Hegel's triadic syllogism.[11]

In contrast to McLuhan's stated non-dialectical stance and Czitrom's ruling on his position, literary scholar Donald Theall argues that McLuhan's literary tradition emphasized concepts of "'tension,' 'resolution of conflict,' and ... 'reconciliation of opposites.'" As wit and paradox are used often by McLuhan and the New Criticism, McLuhan favoured dialectics.[12] For Theall,

The history of the return of this movement to Hegelianism is well known, since its dialectic nature is rather apparent... A view of the world as a conflict rising out of dialectic interplay is congenial to McLuhan's whole sensibility. His strategy, and he attributes the source of it to H. A. Innis ... is a strategy of interface.[13]

Perhaps McLuhan, in a further analogy to Marx, may be understood in relation to Innis as Engels is in relation to Marx. Literary scholar Patrick Brantlinger observes:

Innis' theories undergo both an expansion and a loss of scholarly rectitude in McLuhan. Perhaps it would be fair to say that McLuhan plays Engels to Innis' Marx. Just as Engels' popularizations rendered Marx's theories more deterministic than they in fact are, so McLuhan transforms Innis' soft technological determinism into something much harder.[14]

And as part of a dialectical process themselves, involving Hegel, Marx, Engels, Innis and McLuhan, perhaps, as sociologist Tom Nairn suggests, "(A)fter Hegel, Marx put history on its feet... McLuhan has turned it upside down again; criticism of McLuhan must inevitably try to put it on its feet once more."[15]

Marxist art historian Arnold Hauser could be counted among those dialectical theorists who would keep part of McLuhan's thought because it brought out the fact that the medium is part of the message being communicated. In Hauser's Marxist theory, medium and message are definable only in a dialectical relationship.[16] In a dialectical relationship, however, medium and message are still separate parts. McLuhan's undialectic mistake, according to Hauser, is negating the content of media.[17]

Canadian political theory scholar Judith Stamps clearly identifies the early McLuhan as a dialectical theorist whose own "negative theory of dialectics" was based on his perception theory and the terms he coined to define it, such as "audio-tactile" and its idea of "dynamic simultaneity."[18] McLuhan's dialectics explored tensions between the elements in a single image and tensions between static and historical viewpoints, leaving the latter in tension and inviting "a negative reading of the spaces between them."[19]

What Is Dialectics?

Having indicated the presence of an inheritance passed, even if inverted in the process, from Hegel to Marx to Innis to McLuhan, despite McLuhan's denials, the problem remains: What is dialectics, theoretically and operationally? Unfortunately, McLuhan's critics pass quickly over this methodological point. Czitrom titles his epilogue "Dialectical Tensions in the American Media, Past and Future," but goes no further than a descriptive definition of dialectics which, when applied to media, consists of "contradictory elements embedded in the history of all modern means of communications."[20]

> For each medium is a matrix of institutional development, popular responses, and cultural content that ought to be understood as a product of dialectical tensions, of opposing forces and tendencies clashing and evolving over time, with things continually giving rise to their opposite. Broadly speaking, these contradictions have been expressed in terms of the tension between progressive and utopian possibilities offered by new communications technologies and their disposition as instruments of domination and exploitation.[21]

Theall's discussion of McLuhan is rife with references to dialectics, but nowhere is the term defined, except in connoting the idea of opposites, tension and duality. He writes that for McLuhan, "man lives in a dialectic between fragmentation and integration."[22] He adds that McLuhan developed the technique of "hateful contraries" in relation to his theory of environments and anti-environments.[23] Theall explains that the latter idea is that anti-environments are needed to make the hidden environment visible. The dialectical process of dialogue—dialectical because it involves two rather than one—helps produce the anti-environment.[24] Theall also talks about the "dialectical interplay between the specialist and generalist" as the major problem of information pollution.[25] Theall argues that war, for McLuhan, "is a conflict without conflict, for the realities of the strife are lost in the system of the dialectic," so that McLuhan is left upholding "the power of technology as a mystical way to salvation."[26] And Theall suggests that author Wyndham Lewis's dialectical theory of art was central to McLuhan's own theory of art as anti-environments.[27]

Accepting McLuhan as a dialectical theorist, Stamps similarly offers an open definition of dialectics, a "post-Hobbes idea about how parts of the world interact" that is based on Socratic dialogue's conversation-based method.

As in any conversation, its main elements are opposing principles or ideas that meet and fuse in a way that results in something truly new... In dialectical processes understood more
abstractly, the parties can be cultures, social classes, economic
systems, or, as in the work of Innis and McLuhan, communications media.[28]

Arguing that Marx had reached an impasse with his dialectic of historical materialism, Stamps suggests that Frankfurt School theorists
Theodor Adorno and Walter Benjamin, as well as Innis and McLuhan,
used negative dialectics to work both with and against historical materialism.[29] Negative dialectics contrasts with dialectics, according to
Stamps, by substituting open-ended interaction of different perspectives for the end product or finality of dialectics as practiced by
Hobbes.[30] It will be argued, however, that early Marxist dialectics was
indeed an open-ended interaction.

The method of negative dialectics approaches history as an "open-
ended series of qualitative changes that emerged at the margins of
dominant institutions." The method provided a way of writing texts
"juxtaposing multiple perspectives" that would allow authors to see
their object of study as a totality without privileging or excluding the
perspectives. Stamps identifies these perspectives as psychoanalytic,
economic, sociological, and technological.[31] Adorno and Benjamin's
totalities were called "constellations," while McLuhan's were "galaxies"
or "mosaics."[32]

Stamps further defines dialectical causation as explaining how
social change occurs by assuming "internal tensions" and "contradictory forces" that pull in the opposite direction. Stamps writes that "this
tension calls for a dialogue and some sort of synthesis, which then
becomes a new social development."[33] Although the Frankfurt theorists
and the Canadian theorists approached the dialectic between material
history and consciousness differently, they all—including McLuhan—
agreed that the analysis must focus on the concrete realities within
which, according to Marx, people make their history.[34]

Marx's Dialectics

Political scholar Chris Sciabarra notes that there are many different
interpretations of Marx. For example, there is the Aristotelian Marx
and the Hegelian Marx, as well as the Leninist Marx, whose theories
have been combined with sciences such as psychology and sociology,

among others. Some scholars stress the younger, "humanist" Marx, while others stress the economic determinism in Marx's later work.[35]

Marxist scholar Robert Tucker writes that for Marx, historical materialism was dialectical because human history revealed a revolutionary pattern of development through opposition and conflict.[36] Marx wrote that he took Hegel's dialectical method and turned it, not Hegel, on its head:

> My dialectic method is not only different from the Hegelian, but is its direct opposite. To Hegel, the life-process of the human brain, i.e., the process of thinking, which, under the name of "the Idea," he even transforms into an independent subject, is the demiurge of the real world, and the real world is only the external, phenomenal form of "the Idea." With me, on the contrary, the ideal is nothing else than the material world reflected by the human mind, and translated into forms of thought...
>
> The mystification which dialectic suffers in Hegel's hands by no means prevents him from being the first to present its general form of working in a comprehensive and conscious manner. With him it is standing on its head. It must be turned right side up again, if you would discover the rational kernel within the mystical shell.
>
> In its mystified form, dialectic ... seemed to transfigure and to glorify the existing state of things. In its rational form it is a scandal and an abomination to bourgeoisdom ... because it includes in its comprehension an affirmative recognition of the existing state of things, at the same time also, the recognition of the negation of that state, of its eventual breaking up; because it regards every historically developed social form as in fluid movement, and therefore takes into account its transient nature not less than its momentary existence; because it lets nothing impose upon it, and is in its essence critical and revolutionary.[37]

Tucker suggests that the dialectic taken from Hegel and then inverted was idealism because Hegel represented history as the self-realization of spirit, or God. For Hegel, the process of spirit becoming itself occurs in the process of knowing and is conducted mostly in the human realm by philosophers.

> This process involves the repeated overcoming of spirit's "alienation" from itself, which takes place when spirit as the

knowing mind confronts a world that appears, albeit falsely, as objective, i.e., as other than spirit. Knowing is recognition, whereby spirit destroys the illusory otherness of the objective world and recognizes it as actually subjective... The process terminates at the stage of "absolute knowledge," when spirit is finally and fully "at home with itself in its otherness," having recognized the whole of creation as spirit.[38]

Tucker writes that Marx first reversed the subject and predicate of Hegel's dialectical process of knowing, following German philosopher Ludwig Feuerbach. Feuerbach, instead of seeing man as self-alienated God, saw God as self-alienated man.[39] Tucker explained that to overcome this alienation, man must take his alienated being, God, back into himself. This reversal brought to Marx a practical use for Hegel: it helped him discover social reality and history, the real social process being man's alienation from himself in the material world, and to apply it to political economy as well as religion.[40] Marx also inverted Hegel's political philosophy so that the State was an outgrowth of economic life rather than the opposite, as Hegel had it.[41] Marx came to explore economics as an area of self-alienation by people who were seen as producers filling their world with created objects. People overlay nature with a human-made "nature." Marx's system had as its cornerstone, a picture of history where, over centuries, people were producing a world in material productive activities. So far in history, though, people had not achieved the state of free and conscious producers; all labour produced involuntarily was "alienated labour." Modern technological development made it materially possible for people to escape from alienated labour by seizing and socializing the technology. This state, which Marx called "positive humanism," in which people produce in freedom, roughly equates with Hegel's state of "absolute knowledge."[42]

Tucker believes that this "original Marxism," contained in writings unknown until the late 1950s, was the unchanging basis for the mature Marxist system. He takes this position despite the fact that the later system favoured an impersonal social theory that emphasized class struggle as the force of history rather than alienation and "positive humanism."[43] Early Marxism is critical, morally aware, existential, as opposed to the orthodox communist Marxism of the former Soviet Union.[44] Yet Tucker argues that the themes appearing in Marx's early work did not disappear in later writings.

Tucker writes that Marx's dialectic in *Capital* stems from an earlier passage in *The Holy Family* dealing with private property and the proletariat as opposites forming a contradictory totality. This totality is moving toward dissolution because private property creates more workers who become conscious of their alienation and thus abolish the totality. The dialectic in *Capital* is based on the capital-labour relationship, or the bourgeois-proletarian relationship. Marx morally opposed wage labour because it is by its nature dehumanizing; it is "alienated labour."[45]

Rius, author of *Marx for Beginners*, wrote that Marx and Engels returned to dialectics as a basis for their theory of social development and as an alternative to visual, mechanistic notions of nature and humanity.[46] From the Greek "dialogue," the core of dialectics is to argue or contend. He added that the Greek philosophers applied dialectics, or the Socratic method, as a system of argument that exposes the contradictions in their opponent's reasoning in order to arrive at the truth. Catholicism's opposition to dialectics suppressed the method until Kant and Hegel revived it.[47] Hegel, Rius wrote, argued human development evolved through a struggle between contraries. The triumph of one contrary in the struggle produces change.[48]

Philosopher Hans Gadamer explores the extent to which ancient Greek dialectic tradition influenced Hegel. He wrote that the connection is obvious in Hegel's development of the concepts of "being," "nothing" and "becoming" as a "homogeneous process in the continuing determination of thought."[49] Sciabarra suggests that dialectics also has been given different meanings in history, including the Aristotelian sense of it as logical discussion and argument.[50] For Hegel, opposing views were conceived of as partial views whose differences could be risen above by constructing them as parts of a greater totality. Others viewed this dialectic as the triadic "thesis," "antithesis," and "synthesis." Dialectical materialism applied this process to economics and used it to analyze history.[51]

In Sciabarra's view, the "dialectical impulse" is best understood as "a technique to overcome formal dualism and monistic reductionism."[52] On the one hand, dualism defines two antagonist and separate spheres, such as good and evil, or body and mind. On the other, Monists try to reduce one part of a pair into a form of the other. Dialectics does neither of these, but "anchors the thinker in both camps," refusing to "recognize these camps as mutually exclusive or exhaustive," and striving to "uncover the common roots of apparent opposites."[53]

Totality is essential to dialectics because, first, it discredits dualism, and, second, it "preserves the analytical integrity of the whole." It refuses to allow reification or removing a part from the whole and conceiving of it as a totality in itself. Further, dialectics looks at the totality synchronically, as a system, and diachronically, in time, or historically. The synchronic analysis allows the system to be analyzed by looking at the relationship between all of its issues and parts. The diachronic analysis looks at the past, present and future of a system, looking at "the dynamic tensions with a system, the internal conflicts or 'contradictions' that require resolution." Finally, for Sciabarra, the dialectical theorist seeks to alter the system rather than to understand it, making dialectics "both critical and revolutionary."[54]

Dialectics as a Method

Political theory scholar Patrick Peritore calls dialectical logic "mankind's oldest mode of thought. A logic of cyclic change, development through internal transmutation, contradiction, the self-negation of the extreme."[55] Rather than a philosophy or a theory of history or a science, however, Peritore suggested dialectics is a method that "negates by determining the larger context, and thus by limiting truth claims— all negation is determination. It totalizes by amassing claims and their contradictories into ever more comprehensive structures... It tests its conceptualizations through actual social praxis."[56] In dialectics, Peritore continues:

> Truth lies in the whole, but the whole is false...Dialectical theory, by becoming true, makes itself false, replaces itself with itself. It is method, not philosophy. Negation and self-negation...A dialectical theory gives itself depth by projecting backward in history the main structures—contradictions which it discovers in the present—in order to find their origins, their necessary and sufficient conditions. This historical projection allows us to project in the opposite direction, into the future... A theory of the future provides the ends, the goals, the telos of our action.[57]

Dialectics works with historical processes and their artifacts, including philosophy, ideology, literature, music and art, which are made dialectical through their contradictions.[58]

Peritore writes that Platonic dialectics grew out of an early limited skepticism, or cross-questioning of definitions designed to destroy the definitions themselves. Next dialectics passed through a middle period of a "dialectics of discovery," in which the cross-questioning ascends to fixed truth. Finally, they became a true dialectics, a "synthesis and division" method using dialectical negation.[59] The first two stages shared the idea that in "common sense" terms, negation means "nothing."[60] Peritore argued that dialectical negation, or "determinate negation," rejects placing an unchanging being against an empty "nothing," in favour of things coming into existence through differentiation and relation.[61]

> Synthesis is the unification of scattered forms under a single generic form... Division finds the natural contradictions and chooses the positive side of each contradiction until it reaches the basic definition of the thing... The whole is active in the part. The process of division is reversible, and a synthesis can be made from part to whole... Now (Plato) sees reality as a complex whole of unchanging and changeable elements, a whole in process of becoming.[62]

According to Peritore, Aristotle took Plato's legacy toward empiricism and the other Greek thinkers reverted to skepticism. Dialectical determinate negation went another route, culminating in Hegel's idealism, which has been described by Tucker. Peritore wrote that Hegel unified Plato's dialectics of discovery—ascending to essences—with his synthesis of division—descending to the parts—in his dialectics of the spirit.[63]

Peritore went on to say that Hegel created a dialectics of the becoming of the Absolute, which comes only at the end of the process, at the centre of which is contradiction. As an example, Peritore offers "being" as the most basic conceptual determination of an object. Yet its being has no meaning unless defined by what the object is not. At its margin, then, is nothingness, the object's determinate negation. "Being" exists only in relation to "nothing," which both negates and determines being without destroying, it because "nothing" needs "being" in order to exist. Because they determine each other, "being" and "nothing" are united by a continuous process, or the higher concept of "becoming." Peritore writes that "being" and "nothing" are mediated, or are negated, determined, cancelled and preserved in a higher synthesis. The "being" of the synthesis is then negated and preserved in a higher synthesis, as Hegel's dialectics creates, annuls, and transcends contradictions on its way to the Absolute.[64]

Marxist art historian Arnold Hauser describes the starting point of Hegelian dialectics as "simply the axiom that A was simultaneously non-A and that everything had a double, even conflicting, meaning."[65]

Hauser argued that dialectics ignores and goes beyond formal Aristotelian logic's principle of noncontradiction.

> If we maintain that A is simultaneously non-A, we are not saying that A and non-A are one and the same—merely that we include the concept of non-A when we speak or think of A. A without non-A as a limit is simply unthinkable. If there were no economy but free competition, no ethic but charity, no artistic style but classicism, neither capitalism nor Christianity nor the Renaissance would have a concrete, tangible meaning. All of these concepts achieve a real meaning only in contrast to what they are not. Hegel, however, in saying that everything was at once itself and its opposite, went further. In the sentence A = non-A, "non-A" does not merely form a limit; it is inherent in A and anticipated by it. What A is can and must, under certain circumstances, become non-A. This is the first and decisive step in dialectic.[66]

Contradiction leads the process forward, as harmony is achieved provisionally, disturbed and restored again. Hauser writes that the majority of conflicting theses are reunited and preserved in the new form rather than destroyed.[67] Contradiction and its negation, which is fulfilling itself with positive content, is the main principle of dialectics. Hauser contends that dialectic contradictions are not formed merely by antitheses, polarities and ambivalences. Contradictions are found in the constitutive function of one moment in the birth of another.

> Hatred is not created by love, sadism by masochism, hubris by humiliation, even though one may be deepened and sharpened by the other. If on the other hand the individual only becomes what he is through society, by wage labour, by exploitation, by alienation caused by the mechanization of work ... both factors achieve an additional, creative, indispensable element through their relationship. Not only is it the case that there would be no poverty, no militant coalition of the workers, and no socialism without the accumulation of wealth, but it is also true that capitalism acquires its full meaning and fulfills its historical role only as a result of these circumstances.[68]

Hauser argues that cultural development expresses the dialectical process in the loss of equilibrium between historical forms, the negation of positive moments, and the transformation of the status quo into movement. The stage of negativity, in which contradictions, outmoded productive forces and new productive forces are all opposed, seeks through "the negation of negation" a new balance of the opposites. "As soon as new productive forces—material or intellectual—disturb the equilibrium of production and consumption, service and reward, striving for recognition and the possibility of success, the process of disturbance and undermining of the system begins."[69]

According to Sciabarra, Marx's dialectical method involved an "unusual" concept of contradiction, leading non-Marxist critics as well as Marxists to claim that Marx violated the principles of Aristotelian logic, including the law of identity, which states that something cannot be both A and non-A. But Sciabarra adds a temporal caveat to the law of identity, arguing that under this law something cannot be A and non-A at the same time. Dialectical contradiction, which Hauser, Peritore and Tucker all argue holds to a different truth than A cannot equal non-A, does not transgress this law because dialectics studies A's development over time. A does equal non-A, but only in a relational aspect.[70] Sciabarra argues that Aristotle's philosophy included "identity and change, being and becoming," the latter of which in each pair presumes the former. Marx took this emphasis and applied it to history, making Marx, as well as Hegel, Aristotle's successors. Also, like Aristotle, Marx did not separate individual parts from the whole, or an instance from its context.[71]

> In his opposition to reification and his comprehension of systemic relations, Marx inherits a dialectical method that is as much an Aristotelian legacy as it is a Hegelian one. Marx absorbs the Hegelian concept of "contradiction," while never discarding Aristotelian logic, or the Aristotelian ontology upon which this dialectic is built. For Marx, the dialectical concept of "contradiction" is relational, not logical. It views each element of duality as inseparable from the other, since each is a precondition of the other's existence…
>
> For Marx, within capitalism, there is a conjunction of polarities that propels the social whole toward some kind of resolution. What distinguishes Marx's understanding of contradiction is not merely the coexistence of opposites, but their unstable movement over time. Marx focuses on both the hostility of opposing spheres, as well as their mutual support.[72]

Peritore noted that Marx can be read in a scientistic, positivist way, as Eastern Marxism reads him, or in a Hegelian, humanistic, and sociological way, as Western Marxism has. Peritore proposes to read Marx another way: through the process of developing the method of dialectics. After developing the "positive humanism" described by Tucker, Marx moves away from espousing any theory of man, or human nature.

> "Human nature" and "society" are not fixed philosophical abstractions but mutable historical relations in process of constant change. Social relations in contradiction, in process of becoming can only be understood in concrete dialectical fashion... To Marx, the relationship between means and relations of production, analytic terms not frozen realities, is subject to "infinite variation and gradations in appearance, which can be ascertained only by analysis of the empirically given circumstances."[73]

Peritore argued that Marx rejects mechanistic and causal "laws of motion" of society, evolutionary modes, the liberal notion of progress and of universal self-interest, the idea that history occurs in stages and the development of modes of production, which have been attributed to him.[74] He maintains that "Marxist dialectics is the radical application of totalizing determinate negation to concrete and contradictory relations of socio-historical process, in order to bring about practical transformations in the interest of the producing classes."[75]

Peritore rejects "dialectical materialism" developed by Engels, Lenin, and later Stalin in orthodox Communist Marxism, by describing it as a distortion of Marxism "transmuted into an ideology of domination within a distorted technocratic state."[76] Similarly, Peritore rejects Western Marxism qua Marxism, although its "liberating quality" "has led to some important socialist experiments the Prague Spring of 1968, Allende's Chile 1970-73, and Solidarity in Poland 1980-1981."[77] In Western Marxism, including existential Marxism and Adorno's negative dialectics, dialectics is used to construct a philosophy or anti-philosophy. Peritore believes "the critical, heuristic, and practical function of dialectics is thereby lost, and indeed, dialectics must forfeit its characteristic totalizing determinate negation in order to be circumscribed within a deductive system... That is, philosophical dialectics are not dialectics."[78]

In Peritore's analysis, Marxism is "radical dialectics," and "pre-philosophical political praxis ... of liberation" that "can only serve the interest of an oppressed class with no stake in the system of reification and domination."[79] The essential element for dialectics is contradiction, which can be mediated and totalized through determinate negation. Peritore explained that

> If contradictions are given, there lies the dialectic. Contradictions are not antinomies, binaries, dichotomies, paradoxes, or any other such repellents to thought, productive of only blockage, and the frustration of mystical acceptance. Contradictions are self-produced oppositions, in which a cultural given shows itself to be process instead of thing by traducing the boundary of its own self-definition and becoming its otherness.[80]

In contrast to Aristotelian logic, which holds it is impossible to unite a thing with its opposite, dialectics, as Hauser argued, shows that "being" is defined only in relation to what it is not. In mediation, "being" and "nothing" transcend the negative self-determination of the original being. One totalization is followed by the next in a process that does not expect or desire totality as an end, because that would be the "death of dialectics and the triumph of reification."[81]

> A unitary string of mediations totalizes a field of self-generated relations. Read backwards, these totalizations are history; the necessary and sufficient conditions for the current moment. Read forward, these totalizations are means-ends relationships; ethical tasks to be accomplished in praxis.[82]

Dialectics only superficially resembles the syllogism, above which according to Hauser is "an empty methodological formula." Dialectics consists of

> two contrastive phases and attitudes: on one hand in the negation and surrender of a dominating view or institution, the rejection of demands which are just coming into being as a result of newly arising forces or legal titles; on the other in the settlement of the antagonism which arises by means of a more complex unity, a new synthesis which embraces the antitheses. The contradiction in the points of view is the origin; their reconciliation is the culmination of the dialectical process.[83]

This reconciliation does not destroy either opposing force, but preserves positive elements and throws away untenable ones.[84] Hauser wrote that dialectics moves between negation and preservation, or *Aufhebung*. Without the latter, dialectics would be no more than negation. *Aufhebung* represents the positive final yield of the process, as the concept is transposed to a higher level, or is overtaken by a more developed form.[85]

> Through this remarkable change ... dialectic achieves its actual significance, its suitability to define and solve problems which could not be handled any other way... Only by dialectic can we explain how an artistic style...can surrender its role as a principle of taste and yet remain a constitutive factor in further development... [N]o really creative style disappears without a trace and cannot be revived in corresponding circumstances. The act of Aufhebung constitutes not only the most strange but also the most fruitful part of the dialectical processes.[86]

In joining the debate over whether Marx's dialectic is deterministic or not, Sciabarra attempts to deflect this criticism, in part, by focusing on the aspect of "interaction" of economic factors with other factors in Marx's dialectical method.[87] Taking the case of Marx's distinction between the economic base and the social superstructure of society, Sciabarra argued that the base is social as well as technological, and it is grounded in individuals at work within society under real conditions. People are part of the material world as well as part of nature and they are conscious of their existence and of their self-consciousness. By acting on the world, people transform it and achieve their potential as both social and conscious entities.[88] According to Sciabarra, Marx thought that "human existence is both natural and social, and it is characterized by free, conscious activity that is the essence of labor. Labor as such transforms both the external world and the laborer himself."[89] Sciabarra contended that Marx was opposed to solely deterministic models of history.[90] It was only in an effort to popularize his theory that Marx emphasized economic development and oversimplified "an otherwise rich dialectical construction."[91]

The Method is the Message

Applying Dialectics in History and Politics

It would appear that Marxism, a fluid process-oriented methodology that opens all of Marx's successors and Marxism itself to a radical critique using Marxist dialectics as a method, has at its basis the spirit of the pre-Socratic philosopher Heraclitus's dictum that you cannot step into the same river twice. Peritore's analysis of dialectics is supported by the writings of historian Donald Lowe and political scientist Scott Warren. The "humanist" Marxist interpretation of critical theorist Erich Fromm provides a commentary of what dialectics can yield. And the work of Mark Poster extends neo-Marxism into a postmodern critique.

Lowe proposed the history of perception as the intermediary link between the content of thought—studied by phenomenology—and the structure of society—studied by Marxism— which unfolds dialectically in historical periods characterized by discontinuity and revolution. Lowe agreed that the concept of determination that occurs through the use of a totalizing and dialectical approach is more complex than the cause and effect concept of linear positivism.[92]

Lowe's historical study of bourgeois perception recovers McLuhan's idea of sensory dialectics and transforms it into a much more complex form. He then incorporated it into Marxist discourse and social theory. Using a Marxist-phenomenological framework, Lowe proposed that perception is the link between the content of thought and the structure of society. Perception, as Lowe framed it, is a reflexive process involving the perceiver, the act of perceiving and the content of the perceived.[93] Perception is defined by three factors: the media, which frame perception; the hierarchy of sensing—whether hearing or seeing dominates—which determines the subject as a physical perceiver; and the epistemic presuppositions, which order the content of the perceived. These factors comprise the field of perception within which knowledge is possible. Two of these factors, the media and the hierarchy of sensing, are categories used by McLuhan.

Sounding like McLuhan but attributing his ideas to Walter Ong, Lowe asserted that "the medium may not be the message, but it determines the message." For the first and second factors, Lowe uses Ong's theory of communication, which identifies four types of media culture: oral, chirographic, typographic and electronic. The four types of media are: speech for oral culture; written language for chirographic culture; the printed book for typographic culture; and all electronic media from the telegraph on for electronic culture. Each type frames knowledge qualitatively differently, and each forms a new layer over the previous one with its residue influencing the future.[94]

According to Lowe, the hierarchy of senses is influenced by the media in each period. Oral and chirographic cultures emphasize hearing and touching.[95] Typographic cultures emphasize sight and formal visual space. Electronic media extend and extrapolate light and sound to alter everyday reality. This creates a new reality that emphasizes seeing and hearing, and is multiperspectival and environmental.

Lowe's description of the epistemic order is adapted from the discourse theory of postmodernist Michel Foucault and proposes that unconscious rules that change as a whole from period to period shape discourse.[96] There is no universal discourse or continuous knowledge. Each culture's epistemic order differs. Oral-chirographic culture was ordered by epistemic rules of "anagogy," based on an absolute God, faith, analogy and metaphor. The switch to typography brought an epistemic order of similitude in which man was the measure in the universe. Later in the typographic era, similitude was replaced by representation-in-space, as science discovered empirical space. Bourgeois society from the late 1700s to 1905 was based on development-in-time, adapting the former epistemic system to include new experiences of time. In the twentieth century, electronic culture has undermined the belief in reason. Space and time are functions rather than the absolute framework. Lowe suggested that the new electronic order is founded on a synchronic system that has destroyed the framework of objective space and time as well as the ideal of individualism.

Lowe qualified this theory, asserting that perceptual fields interpenetrate with the dominant field exerting hegemony over the others. In effect the field of perception is determined by society as a totality, and thus the media, the hierarchy of sensing and the epistemic order are also determined by the society as a whole. The concept that dialectical determinism takes place within some total perceptual field is much more complex than the linear positivist cause and effect associated with bourgeois scientific method, a methodology that Lowe, and McLuhan, call linear thinking.[97]

Lowe uses two social theories: Marxist dialectics and Maurice Merleau-Ponty's phenomenology. Both are anti-positivist but take different approaches. Phenomenology uses intentionality to focus on the lived connections in the intersubjective, real, pre-theoretical life-world in which human beings undertake everyday living. In contrast, Marxism uses dialectics to analyze society as a whole, seeking to unify theory and praxis within an ongoing totality. Marxist knowledge understands the world as a totality that is actively tested and revised through intervention in the world, or praxis. Dialectics also analyzes the world as a multi-level structure. The superstructure—which includes for, example, the media—and its forms of social consciousness are autonomous, yet they are conditioned by the base economic structure. The contradictions of the development of these levels in time are ultimately discontinuous and eventually lead to revolution.[98] The underside of consciousness, alienation, can only be overcome by the unity of consciousness and praxis as dialectics reveals the multi-level structure of social totality in transformation.[99]

Marxist dialectics analyzes the structure of totality in transformation, while phenomenology focuses on the subjectivization of that dialectical structure.[100] Lowe suggests that by explaining the past as a totality of multi-level structures, Marxism offers the most comprehensive historical explanation. However, people in the past experienced their world through their own fields of perception, which phenomenology is able to approach. Marxism also responds to periodization, studying each period as a structure consisting of internal changes as well as periodic changes. Internal changes do not transform the structure, but changes between periods involve transformation. Foucault's discourse theory—which emphasizes historical dislocation—helps explain the discontinuity from one period to another.[101]

Warren noted that for Marx the point of philosophy is to change the world "on the basis of a thorough and non-dogmatically open understanding of the world."[102] This openness of Western Marxism is in stark contrast to the positivism of orthodox Eastern Marxism. Borrowing from Hegel, Marxism conceives of reality as a "concrete totality of open-ended, changing relations." Further, all reality is social because of the social essence of human existence. Marx views everything as a series of relations, with each object possessing the whole within it. Each factor exists in relation to all others and contains the whole of other factors as internal relations.[103]

Warren echoes Lowe's point that Marx does not deal with relations in causal terms of linear determination, which conceive of reality as "externally related, closed and self-contained." Unlike a thing, the basic unit of reality is a concrete, open-ended relation that bridges abstract dualities such as cause and effect, and individual and society. Warren argues that a dialectical work must be "an interlocking whole, not an artificially segmented presentation of what is unified and connected in reality." Philosophy that pursues truth as if it is static and eternal leads to the reification of concepts: "The dialectic is like a swift sparrow; we can shoot it down or put it in a cage, but we can truly understand it only while it is in flight."[104]

Warren describes Marx's notion of history as a synthetic activity involving people and nature in reciprocally determined relationships that are "open-ended in possibility." The person is the "focal subject-object of history." As subject, he or she participates in creating the world. As object, he or she is created by the world. Alienation is an important factor for Warren as well as Lowe. The union of theory and praxis focuses on changing existence, transforming alienation into wholeness and the "realization of creative and artistic talents."[105]

For Western Marxism, Warren argues that dialectics precludes positivist and determinist versions of Marxism because the dialectic requires open-ended relations. Economic forces and social crises create possibilities rather than determine necessities.[106] Because Marxist dialectics views reality as a concrete totality of relations, reality cannot be understood in terms of abstract absolute laws. The internally related totality cannot be reduced to absolute objectivity. The dialectic demands that any examination of an aspect of reality include its "historical character and its relation to the totality of reality."[107]

Warren writes that subjective thought is produced in a shared interaction with reality, or "the dialectic of subject and object."[108] This emphasis on subjective human action argues against a guaranteed end of history. Freedom is only possible if people take history into their own hands in the dialectic of subject and object. Only those who are "intellectually and emotionally emancipated from the existing system" can make revolution. Economic forces alone will determine nothing.[109] In other words, people must free themselves from the reified control of social forces to "begin the transition to the conscious control of their destiny."[110] Freedom does not take place mechanically, although economic forces shape history and progress will not be made unless economic forces also change.[111] Warren's reading of Marxist dialectics shows that the methodology defends no traditions as it examines the relation between the present and the historical totality.[112]

Warren notes that in Marx's dialectical phenomenology, the individual is a "totality of historical, social and natural relations."[113] For Marx, people are nothing other than relations, not "abstract beings squatting outside the world." People are the human world and each one comprises the whole as well as an individual.[114] Neither are people defined by a fixed nature, but rather they are open possibilities. Their full nature is a synthesis that is unfinished, always changing, thereby making people open and historical.[115]

Warren also warns that reification and canonization threaten Marxism. Marx's dialectics includes the discovery that the process of reality cannot be understood by a theory that does not change itself. He argues that "classic" Marxist politics as the "scientific application of correct theory to the already determined processes of human affairs is inadequate."[116] Dialectics "guarantees nothing and expects everything." The revolutionary faces new problems daily. In order to discover what needs to be done, he/she cannot wait on an objective, inevitable course of events.[117]

Unlike Peritore, Warren believes that Western Marxism and critical theory are responses to political and historical transformations in the twentieth century that threaten to reify Marxist dialectics. Orthodox Marxism was inadequate to respond to the fact that in the Soviet Union an anti-democratic political system emerged. Capitalism was entering a post-liberal State with an increase of monopoly structures and growing government intervention in the economy. The assumption of an inevitably progressing revolutionary working class became unworkable, and Marxists had to face the decline of the revolutionary working class.[118] Perhaps most importantly though, was the rise of a technological society that demanded that Marxism be expanded to include "the critique of technical civilization."[119]

Critical Theory on Marx's Dialectics

Erich Fromm is among those who have responded to the above historical conditions, and who have incorporated the newly discovered early "positive humanism" of Marx. Fromm demonstrates that Marx's primary concern is to liberate individuals living in capitalist society in order to overcome alienation and restore the capacity to relate fully to themselves, each other and nature.[120] He added that Marx's central critique of capitalism is not the "injustice in the distribution of wealth," but the "perversion of labour" into alienated labour.[121]

Fromm adheres to Marx's understanding of labour as the expression of individuality, a process in which individuals and nature participate dialectically. By opposing themselves to nature, individuals act on the world and change it, thereby changing and becoming themselves. Fromm wrote that Marx originally called this function "self-activity" rather than labour, later differentiating between free and alienated labour.[122] According to Marx, alienation increases in history as human development increases. Socialism's self-realization is the end of alienation.[123] Alienation develops as private property and the division of labour develop. Under capitalism, work loses the character of self-expression as labour and products "assume an existence separate from the worker." The labour becomes alienated because work is no longer part of the worker's nature. Workers are exhausted and miserable rather than energetic and fulfilled. They feel secure only in leisure time, while at work they feel estranged. In production their relationship to work is felt as alienation. The product becomes an "alien object that dominates" them.[124]

According to Fromm, Marx was concerned with the liberation of workers from work that destroys individuality, making them into things and making the self a "slave of things."[125] The capitalist fetishization of commodities "transforms the relations of individuals into qualities of things themselves."[126] The world of things becomes the ruler of people along with social and political systems.[127] The alienated person who believes he or she has become the master of nature has instead become the powerless slave of things and social forces.[128]

Fromm writes that the alienation of labour is connected with alienation from the self, others and nature, and leads to the "perversion of all values" because the economy becomes the supreme aim of life rather than the development of moral values. Each sphere of life becomes alienated from the others, because in the alienated world of capitalism, needs are not defined as essential.[129] Capitalism creates new needs in workers as if it were exerting an alien power over them. With the crush of objects, the world of alien being also increases and people need money to possess this "hostile being," as the need for money becomes the only real need created by capitalism.[130]

Fromm argues that history has corrected Marx's belief that the working class was the most alienated and that liberation would start with the working class. Marx did not envision the degree to which almost all people would be alienated, especially the growing number of people who manipulate symbols and people instead of machines. He adds that the skilled worker only sells his or her labour, but "symbol manipulators" are hired for "attractive personality packages" that are easy to control. In consumption, Fromm sees no difference between workers and bureaucrats: all crave new things and are passive consumers who are alienated by things that satisfy "synthetic needs" rather than true needs.[131]

Real needs are based in nature and are needed for the individual to realize his or her essence as a human being.[132] The task of the social critic is to make people aware of false needs, which are as urgent and real as true needs but from a subjective viewpoint.[133] That will happen only when production serves people and capital ceases to create and exploit false needs. Fromm argues that unalienated people do not dom-inate nature, but become one with it and are "alive and responsive toward objects, so that objects come to life." The essential elements of socialism include cooperative rather than competitive production and individual participation in planning. In unalienated society, people would no longer be "crippled by alienated modes of production and consumption." People would begin to make living their "main business rather than producing the means for living."[134]

Marx's Dialectics in Postmodernism

Striking a theme explored by McLuhan, post-Marxist and postmod-ern historian Poster emphasizes the important role of media and tech-nology in poststructuralist social theory.[135] The discontinuity of struc-tural change in advanced industrial society is one concept from Foucault's discourse theory that prompted Poster to argue for changing the Marxist analysis of the mode of production to an analysis of the mode of information: the key process in capitalist domination and alienation. Poster argues that the experiences of the twentieth century brought about by advances in media technology necessitate the study of the mode of information.

Poster suggests that labour can no longer be the first principle of Marxist theory. A new principle must account for the increase of infor-mation in social space, and he suggested Foucault's category of dis-course. Poster defends the need for this change by noting that the model of people working on objects cannot be assumed as the manu-facturing system declines and the United States becomes the first ser-vice economy. Labour now means people acting on each other, or on information, or inversely, information acting on people. Most new technologies create and move information. Soon, movement will involve information, not people or goods. People will be immobile as electronic information moves in social space.[136]

Prisons are analogous to information systems in advanced capital-ism. Poster explains that in Foucault's writing, the prison system intro-duced in the nineteenth century—the panopticon—was a way that authorities sought to control the minds of prisoners by making them conscious of being under constant surveillance. In the previous and discontinuous discourse system prisons were places where bodies were punished, not minds, through torture and physical penalties.[137]

Poster argued that the panopticon prison is parallel to computer monitoring of individuals because both cause individuals to conform.

Using media, the prisoner, the patient, the worker and the student are all normalized, giving capitalism a technology of power that can be used in many locations. The computer and media normalize individuals at home, at play, in all daily activities.[138] The media use normalizing criteria in determining their audiences because the media generate little feedback and must organize messages so most viewers will accept them. The receiver must be general, without individuality, not a person but a norm. The receiver must become the norm in order to understand the messages. Although the individual can resist for a while, each receiver gradually accepts the norms displayed on the computer screen and regards them as real. This transformation of the individual into the norm is a continuous surveillance in advanced industrial society. The media extend the reach of normalizing surveillance, creating new modes of domination through alienation and reification of individuals.[139]

Poster argued that Marxism must include the ways media serve, and to some degree, control the ruling class via daily dominatation of communication. He also notes that goods are sold through meanings generated by advertising, while political processes are also shaped by mass media.[140]

Poster suggested that in the age of information, media have replaced face-to-face interaction. Superficially, television contains many features of oral communication. Visual-verbal messages from a stranger are sent to the receiver's home, simulating a friend's visit. In this way media diminish traditional forms. Social reality changes as social interactions combine face-to-face and electronic communication. Poster suggests the computer is extending the alienation Marx saw in the machine. The computer stores dead knowledge rather than dead labour. The computer replaces mental labour rather than physical labour. Also, the computer is opposed to workers like an alien essence dominating the work process.[141]

Dialectics as a methodology described by Tucker, Peritore, Hauser, Stamps, and Sciabarra is demonstrably more rigorous than the sketchy and partial definitions implied by Theall and Czitrom. The open-ended, process-oriented spirit of dialectics as applied to political and social forms by Lowe, Warren, Fromm, and Poster clearly differs from the mechanical causality associated with Eastern Marxism and orthodox communism, as well as points the way from Marxism to postmodernism. How much McLuhan applied this rigorous, open-ended, radical methodology in his writings remains to be argued. The next chapter will identify points of convergence between dialectics, McLuhan's "hybrid media" and his laws of the media, as well as with the critical theory he is accused of abandoning.

NOTES

1. Marshall McLuhan, with Barrington Nevitt, *Take Today: The Executive as Dropout* (New York: Harcourt, Brace, Jovanovich, 1972), 75.
2. Ibid., 76.
3. Marshall McLuhan, *Understanding Media: The Extensions of Man* (New York: Mentor, 1964), 58.
4. Daniel Czitrom, *Media and the American Mind: From Morse to McLuhan* (Chapel Hill, NC: University of North Carolina Press, 1982), 161.
5. Ibid., 181.
6. Ibid., 168.
7. Marshall McLuhan, with Bruce Powers, *The Global Village: Transformations in World Life and Media in the Twenty-first Century* (New York: Oxford University Press, 1989), 33; Marshall McLuhan, with Eric McLuhan, *Laws of Media: The New Science* (Toronto: University of Toronto Press, 1988), 124.
8. McLuhan and Powers, *Global Village*, 33; McLuhan and McLuhan, *Laws of Media*, 124-125.
9. McLuhan and McLuhan, *Laws of Media*, 10.
10. Ibid., 19.
11. Ibid., 125-126.
12. Donald Theall, *Understanding McLuhan: The Medium is the Rear View Mirror* (Montréal: McGill-Queen's University Press, 1971), 39.
13. Ibid.
14. Patrick Brantlinger, *Bread and Circuses: Theories of Mass Culture as Social Decay* (Ithaca, NY: Cornell University Press, 1983), 268.
15. Tom Nairn, "McLuhanism: The Myth of Our Time," in *McLuhan: Pro and Con*, ed. Raymond Rosenthal (Baltimore, MD: Penguin, 1968), 151.
16. Arnold Hauser, *The Sociology of Art*, trans. Kenneth J. Northcott (Chicago: University of Chicago Press, 1982), 616.
17. Ibid., 658.
18. Judith Stamps, *Unthinking Modernity: Innis, McLuhan and the Frankfurt School* (McGill-Queen's University Press, 1995), 103.
19. Ibid., 109.
20. Czitrom, *American Mind*, 184.
21. Ibid.
22. Theall, *Rear View Mirror*, 150.
23. Ibid., 155.
24. Ibid., 159.
25. Ibid., 162.
26. Ibid., 165.
27. Ibid., 167.
28. Stamps, *Unthinking Modernity*, 11-12.
29. Ibid., 18.
30. Ibid., 19.
31. Ibid., 20.

32. Ibid., 21.
33. Ibid., 28.
34. Ibid., 33.
35. Chris Sciabarra, *Ayn Rand: The Russian Radical* (University Park, PA: Pennsylvania State University Press, 1995), 5-6.
36. Robert Tucker, ed., *The Marx-Engels Reader*, 2nd. ed. (New York: Norton, 1978), xx.
37. Karl Marx, *Capital*, in *Marx-Engels*, 301-302.
38. Tucker, *Marx-Engels*, xxi.
39. Ibid., xxii.
40. Ibid., xxiii.
41. Ibid., xxiv.
42. Ibid., xxv.
43. Ibid., xxvi.
44. Ibid., xxvii.
45. Ibid., xxx-xxxi.
46. Rius, *Marx for Beginners* (New York: Pantheon, 1976), 70. This book, it should be noted, is written in the form of a comic book. By comparison, it is no further from book form than the forms of several of McLuhan's books, including *The Medium is the Massage, War and Peace in the Global Village*, and *Counterblast.*
47. Ibid., 71.
48. Ibid., 76.
49. Hans Gadamer *Hegel's Dialectic: Five Hermeneutical Studies*, trans. P. Christopher Smith (New Haven, CN: Yale University Press, 1976), 13.
50. Sciabarra, *Ayn Rand*, 15.
51. Ibid., 16.
52. Ibid.
53. Ibid.
54. Ibid., 17-18.
55. N. Patrick Peritore, "Radical Dialectics," unpublished paper (Department of Political Science, University of Missouri, Columbia, MO., 1985), 1.
56. Ibid., 2-3.
57. Ibid., 3.
58. Ibid., 4.
59. Ibid., 5.
60. Ibid., 10.
61. Ibid., 11.
62. Ibid., 11-12.
63. Ibid., 15.
64. Ibid., 15-16.
65. Arnold Hauser, *The Sociology of Art*, trans. Kenneth J. Northcott (Chicago: University of Chicago Press, 1982), 337.
66. Ibid., 338.
67. Ibid., 339.
68. Ibid., 340.
69. Ibid., 333.
70. Chris Sciabarra, *Marx, Hayak, and Utopia* (Albany, NY: State University of New York Press, 1995), 79.
71. Ibid., 80-81.
72. Ibid., 81-82.

73. Peritore, "Radical Dialectics," 20.
74. Ibid., 21.
75. Ibid., 23.
76. Ibid., 38.
77. Ibid., 39.
78. Ibid.
79. Ibid., 53.
80. Ibid., 53-54..
81. Ibid., 54-55.
82. Ibid., 54.
83. Hauser, *Sociology of Art*, 345.
84. Ibid., 355.
85. Ibid., 360.
86. Ibid., 361.
87. Sciabarra, *Marx, Hayak, and Utopia*, 70-71.
88. Ibid., 72-73.
89. Ibid., 74.
90. Ibid., 75.
91. Ibid.
92. Donald Lowe, *History of Bourgeois Perception* (Chicago: University of Chicago Press, 1982), 16.
93. Ibid., 1-2.
94. Ibid., 2-5.
95. Ibid., 7-9.
96. Ibid., 9-12.
97. Ibid., 14-16.
98. Ibid., 172.
99. Ibid., 173-174.
100. Ibid., 173.
101. Ibid., 175-176.
102. Scott Warren, *The Emergence of Dialectical Theory: Philosophy and Political Inquiry* (Chicago: University of Chicago Press, 1984), 64.
103. Ibid., 65-68..
104. Ibid., 68.
105. Ibid., 69.
106. Ibid., 72-73.
107. Ibid., 76.
108. Ibid., 77.
109. Ibid., 78.
110. Ibid., 79.
111. Ibid., 81-82.
112. Ibid., 76.
113. Ibid., 108.
114. Ibid. 108.
115. Ibid., 138.
116. Ibid., 125.
117. Ibid., 126.
118. Ibid., 145.
119. Ibid., 146.

120. Erich Fromm, *Marx's Concept of Man* (New York: Ungar, 1961), 4-5.
121. Ibid., 42.
122. Ibid., 40-41.
123. Ibid., 43.
124. Ibid., 47-48.
125. Ibid., 48-49.
126. Ibid., 50.
127. Ibid., 52.
128. Ibid., 50-53.
129. Ibid., 54.
130. Ibid., 55.
131. Ibid.., 56-57.
132. Ibid., 62.
133. Ibid., 63.
134. Ibid., 60.
135. Mark Poster, *Foucault, Marxism and History: Mode of Production vs. Mode of Information* (Cambridge, MA: Polity Press, 1984), 44-69.
136. Ibid., 53.
137. Ibid., 97-101.
138. Ibid., 103.
139. Ibid., 115.
140. Ibid., 117-118.
141. Ibid., 165-166.

Understanding McLuhan's Method

Media as "Hybrid Energy"

This chapter will focus on McLuhan's two methods of media analysis, his early "hybrid media" concept and his later tetradic laws of media. As these two approaches are being described, the chapter will discuss confluences between McLuhan's method and Marxist dialectics, as well as the limitations of such a comparison.

Driving McLuhan's early methodology was an open-ended, process-oriented, relation-based, mosaic methodology of hybrid media, based on extension of being, alienation and numbness, transformation, break boundary and reversal, as well as understanding and autonomy—all of which are central elements of Marxist dialectics. The process is based on totalities and constantly interacting media forms. Although McLuhan did not describe the process step by step, he did describe its broad outlines in his early work.

> *The Gutenberg Galaxy* develops a mosaic or field approach to its problems. Such a mosaic image of numerous data and quotations in evidence offers the only practical means of revealing causal operations in history.
>
> The alternative procedure would be to offer a series of views of fixed relationships in pictorial space. Thus the galaxy or constellation of events upon which the present study concentrates is itself a mosaic of perpetually interacting forms that have undergone kaleidoscopic transformation—particularly in our own time.[1]

Extension as Marxist Alienation

Much as Hegel and Marx began with "being" and "nothing," or self-alienation, McLuhan also based his hybrid media analysis on a form of alienation. In his method, media are extensions of bodily senses, parts and consciousness itself, which have been extended into the environment.

> During the mechanical ages we had extended our bodies in space. Today, after more than a century of electronic technology, we have

extended our central nervous system itself in a global embrace, abolishing both space and time as far as our planet is concerned. Rapidly, we approach the final phase of the extensions of man—the technological simulation of consciousness, when the creative process of knowing will be collectively and corporately extended to the whole of human society, much as we have already extended our senses and our nerves by the various media... Any extension, whether of skin, hand, or foot, affects the whole psychic and social complex.[2]

In this excerpt, what was a perpetual process in *The Gutenberg Galaxy* has been ushered into its "final phase," which might find its companion in Hegel's "absolute knowledge" and Marx's socialism. The idea of finality, however, is contradicted in other writings.

Nevertheless, the unit of analysis, the extension, is not viewed in isolation, but in relation to "the whole psychic and social process." McLuhan made it clear that relation is the key as he discusses the "mosaic" process of insight. He declared that media only have meaning in relation to other media. "In fact, (the "mosaic") is the technique of insight...necessary for media study, since no medium has its meaning or existence alone, but only in constant interplay with other media."[3]

The whole process, or totality, is what McLuhan called a "galaxy," which he equated with an "environment" that, again, is process-oriented and interactive.

There might have been some advantage in substituting the word "galaxy" for the word "environment." Any technology tends to create a new human environment...Technological environments are not merely passive containers but are active processes that reshape people and other technologies alike.[4]

The alienated being or extension that McLuhan called media range far beyond the means of mass communication such as books, newspapers, magazines, radio, television, film and recordings, although these are included. A medium is "any extension of ourselves...or any new technology."[5] Automation, machine technology, electric light, speech, writing, print, the telegraph, abstract painting, the railway—all are examples of media. Some of them are also examples of content, or messages, because McLuhan argued that the content of any medium is another medium. As he radically broadened the definition of media, he also compared the media to economic commodities, which are the basis of Marx's analysis in *Capital*: "If the formative power in the media are the media themselves, that raises a host of large matters that can only be mentioned here... Namely, that technological media are staples or natural resources, exactly as are coal and cotton and oil."[6]

Each new extension or self-alienation, is met with numbness in the individual and society.[7] McLuhan built his theory of extension around the Narcissus myth, in which Narcissus does not recognize himself in his extended reflection and thus becomes a "servomechanism" of his self-alienated being, or, as critical theorist Erich Fromm would say, a "slave of things."[8] McLuhan wrote,

> The extension of himself (Narcissus) by mirror numbed his perceptions until he became the servomechanism of his own extended or repeated image... Now the point of this myth is that men at once become fascinated by any extension of themselves in any material other than themselves.[9]

The theme of humans as slaves of technology also, though, has a dialectic within itself in which there is a positive force of enthusiasm. As McLuhan argued, "The capitulation of Western man to his technology, with its crescendo of specialized demands, has always appeared to many observers as a kind of enslavement. But the resulting fragmentation has been voluntary and enthusiastic."[10]

Yet each extension, instead of being a positive agent in controlling the environment, generates shock and numbness much as would the amputation of the limb. McLuhan drew the parallel between extension and amputation, as "...a theory of disease...goes far to explain why man is impelled to extend various parts of his body by a kind of auto-amputation."[11]

Transformation and Reversal

Against the negation of "being" in each extension and its concommitent "numbness" and "amputation," the media process is granted positive dynamics. To begin with, McLuhan argued that each extension stores and translates human knowledge because "...technologies are ways of translating one kind of knowledge into another mode... What we call 'mechanization' is a translation of nature, and of our own natures, into amplified and specialized forms."[12] In fact, extension and translation are treated as synonyms, as McLuhan suggested we have "...extended or translated our central nervous system into the electromagnetic technology."[13]

Also, each medium comes into being to release pressure created by former media. In other words, the media both create and relieve strain:

> Thus, the stimulus to new invention is the stress of acceleration of pace and increase of load. For example, in the case of the wheel as an extension of the foot, the pressure of new burdens resulting from the acceleration of exchange by written and monetary media was the immediate occasion of the extension or "amputation" of this function from our bodies. The wheel as a counter-irritant to increased burdens, in turn, brings about a new intensity of action by its amplification of a separate or isolated function (the feet in rotation). Such amplification is bearable by the nervous system only through numbness or blocking of perception...[14]

In this process, each alienation of being is truly met with alienation and the process is repeated with each new medium:

> [Narcissus'] image is a self-amputation or extension induced by irritating pressures. As counter-irritant, the image produces a generalized numbness, or shock that declines recognition. Self-amputation forbids self-recognition.
>
> The principle of self-amputation as an immediate relief of strain on the central nervous system applies very readily to the origin of media of communication from speech to computer.[15]

The seriousness of the alienated reaction becomes more pronounced, however, with more advanced media, specifically electronic media, because the auto-amputation has moved from the extremities of the body to the nervous system and consciousness. "The principle of numbness comes into play with electric technology, as with any other. We have to numb our central nervous system when it is extended and exposed, or we will die." [16]

Another indication of contradiction at work in McLuhan, after the self-alienation of media extension, is his notion that media totalities reverse themselves after a point in their development: "When all the available resources and energies have been played up in an organism or in any structure there is some kind of reversal of pattern."[17] He also calls this "reversal of pattern" a "break boundary." It is decisive in changing the entire media environment.

In any medium or structure there is what Kenneth Boulding calls a "break boundary at which the system suddenly changes into another or passes some point of no return in its dynamic process." Several such "break boundaries" will be discussed later, including the one from stasis to motion, and from the mechanical to the organic in the pictorial world.[18]

What initiates these "break boundaries" is hybridization or "cross-fertilization" of media environments, such as occurred when print crossed with the steam press, or radio with the movies.[19]

McLuhan's concept that all media are in a constant state of interplay with other media rests on the observation that all media are hybrids, except for the light bulb, which he used as an example of a medium that is pure transformational message without another medium for its content: "Except for light, all other media come in pairs, with one acting as the 'content' of the other, obscuring the operation of both... Media as extensions of our senses institute new ratios, not only among our senses, but among themselves, when they interact among themselves."[20]

McLuhan argued that the possibility of action, what Marxists call praxis, occurs at the intersection of the two media systems. It is an interaction of forms characterized by dynamic process, power and release.

The hybrid or the meeting of two media is a moment of truth and revelation from which new form is born. For the parallel between two media holds us on the frontiers between forms that snap us out of the Narcissus-narcosis. The moment of the meeting of media is a moment of freedom and release from the ordinary trance and numbness imposed by them on our senses.[21]

Critical Consciousness in McLuhan's Theory

The technological determinism inherent in this process has been the source of much of the criticism aimed at McLuhan. However, few critics appear to notice that McLuhan is mining the interstices of the media hybridization for openings that allow awareness and change. The media may be a force of nature with a life of its own, but society can "think things out before we put them out."

It has now been explained that media, or the extensions of man, are "make happen" agents, but not "make aware" agents. The hybridizing or compounding of these agents offers an especially favorable opportunity to notice their structural components and properties...These media, being extensions of ourselves, also depend upon us for their interplay and their evolution. The fact that they do interact and spawn new progeny...need baffle us no longer if we trouble to scrutinize their action. We can, if we choose, think things out before we put them out.[22]

As these environments interact, it is possible to perceive the hidden media environment, and in this sense, there is a process of negation that could be equated with Marxism's critical consciousness. However, in McLuhan's case, it is the artist rather than the revolutionary who helps raise critical consciousness in the masses by negating the existing system through the creation of a dialectical antithesis: "As our proliferating technologies created a whole series of new environments, men have become aware of the arts as 'anti-environments' or 'counter-environments' that provide us with a means of perceiving the environment itself."[23]

The "early warning system" of art helps make people aware of the impact of technology, as artists, the "antennae of the race," are several decades ahead of social and technological change.[24] As technology reaches beneath consciousness to alter sensory balance and perception, McLuhan endowed people with limited freedom. As extensions, the media deeply affect people, but media effects can be assessed before being introduced because of the artist. McLuhan's goal was to increase that freedom through art.

By focusing on the psychic and social effects of media instead of their content, McLuhan took the radical position that society should not look to content changes in any medium as a solution to the problems created by that medium. Rather, society should examine the media structure itself and change the media. As a result, he can inspire outrage over the rights that electronic media violate, as well as emphasize the need for action.

> Electric technology is directly related to our central nervous system, so it is ridiculous to talk of "what the public wants" played over its nerves. Once we have surrendered our senses and nervous systems to the private manipulation of those who would try to benefit from taking a lease on our eyes and ears and nerves, we don't really have any rights left.[25]

The Method is the Message

The point, McLuhan argued, is not to understand and submit to technological inevitability and its violation of rights, but to understand the media world in order to change the media and increase human freedom. "If we understood our older media, such as roads and written word, and if we valued their human effects sufficiently, we could reduce or even eliminate the electronic factor from our lives."[26] The central focus of that understanding is on conflict, both in media origins and in media futures. *Understanding Media: The Extensions of Man*, "in seeking to understand many media, the conflicts from which they spring, and the even greater conflicts to which they give rise, holds out the promise of reducing these conflicts by an increase of human autonomy."[27]

Understanding media is the key to controlling the media, but McLuhan does not endorse either strict historical study or a totalitarian utopianism. He favoured a study focused on the present, concrete, material facts. That study of the present, in Marxism called praxis, affects the future.

> The frequent and futile resort to futurism and archaism as strategies for encountering radical change… Yet these two uniform ways of backward and forward looking are habitual ways of avoiding the discontinuities of present experience with their demand for sensitive inspection and appraisal.[28]

The Four Laws of the Media

McLuhan's open-ended, relational, mosaic methodology of hybrid media, based on alienation, break boundary, transformation, reversal, understanding, and autonomy, had evolved into the more formalized four laws of media by the mid-1970s. By being more formal, the four laws gave McLuhan a methodological rigor growing out of his early more open mosaic system. The four laws, however, were developed not only after McLuhan's zenith of popularity but also after his book publishing had ceased and his critics had forgotten him. Except for a short academic journal article and a letter to the editor of another publication, the laws did not receive any in-depth treatment until the publication of two books co-authored by McLuhan nearly a decade after his death.

McLuhan biographer Philip Marchand reports that the laws of media were to have been part of *Take Today: The Executive as Dropout*, published in 1972, and that McLuhan agreed with Doubleday to write a book about the laws in 1973. However, he did not publish the laws until an article appeared in *Technology and Culture* in 1975.[29] And in fact, the "article" which was in the form of a letter to the editor, unfortunately did not explain the laws. Instead, the short letter described the purpose, the approach used in arriving at the laws, the scope of the laws beyond narrow communications media, and a request for feedback from readers.[30] McLuhan, without defining any terms or processes of the laws, introduced them by an example:

> A sample of my proposed "Laws" of the media follow [*sic*] (the four steps of the process are named in the first "law" and assumed for the rest):
>   I. Cable TV
>   A. Amplifies quality and diversity of signal pickup.
>   B. Obsolesces diffusion broadcasting.
>   C. Retrieves early transmission broadcasting pattern of point-to-point (ship to shore).
>   D. Reversal is flip to home broadcasting.[31]

Without further elaboration, McLuhan listed twenty-six samples of the laws of media, with the media resembling the diverse listing he developed in *Understanding Media*.

The laws did not surface again until McLuhan published an article in the general semantics journal *Et cetera* in 1977 where he discussed the process.[32] He explained that the laws arose from philosopher of science Karl Popper's principle that a scientific hypothesis is one that is capable of falsification. The laws made McLuhan aware that as artifacts, media are all "outerings and utterings of man," and, as words, each has a grammar and syntax.

> There seem to be only four features, and they are in analogical proportion to each other:
>   (a) What does it enhance?
>   (b) What does it obsolesce?
>   (c) What does it retrieve that had been obsolesced earlier?
>   (d) What does it flip into when pushed to the limits of its potential?[33]

McLuhan tied this tetradic unit to metaphor in what he called the discovery that all extensions are metaphoric in structure, and that they are all linguistic. Metaphor, he contended, bridges gaps rather than following connections, because the four parts of the metaphor are discontinuous yet in ratio. McLuhan cited Aristotle's four-part analogy of psychological operations in support:

> Let then C be to D as A is to B: it follows alternando that C:A::D:B. If then C and D belong to one subject, the case will be the same with them as with A and B; A and B form a single identity with different modes of being; so too will the former pair. The same reasoning holds if A be sweet and B white.[34]

McLuhan then argued that the parts of the tetrad have the same complementary character, so that, (C) retrieval, is to (B) obsolescence, as (A) amplification, is to (D) reversal. As a result, (C) retrieval, is to (A) amplification, as (B) obsolescence, is to (D) reversal. Although the meaning of the above description may appear unclear, comparison of the four parts of the tetrad with the earlier hybrid media model easily shows the lines of descent. Also, the editor's introduction to McLuhan's article, as well as later passages in the posthumous work relating to Aristotelian logic, are helpful in thinking through this process.

Comparison of the four parts of the tetrad with the earlier hybrid media model show clear lines of descent. The law of enhancement, or amplification, relates to the theory of extension. Media extend bodily and sensory functions, speeding up one function and creating a bias in favor of that function.[35] The law of obsolescence can be related to the idea that media come in pairs, or hybrids, and the former, becoming content of the latter, is diminished as a form. For example, electronic media obsolesce print media.[36] The fourth law, reversal, is an explicit part of the earlier hybrid method. When a media system reaches the limit of its energy, it tends to reversal into a form that will drive itself into obsolescence and enhance a conflicting characteristic.[37] The third law, retrieval, does not have any apparent antecedent in the former model, although it might be foreshadowed by McLuhan's notion that each new media environment turns the older environment into an art form.[38] Marchand notes that the third law of retrieval was developed in McLuhan's book, *From Cliche to Archetype* (1971), which demonstrated that clichés from the past are transformed into today's archetypes.[39] For example, print technology retrieved the entire world of antiquity, which had not been widely accessible in chirographic culture.[40]

Paul Levinson's introduction to McLuhan's article in *Et cetera* is helpful in terms of connecting the tetradic laws to Hegel's dialectics:

This categorization bears more than fleeting resemblance to Hegel's dialectic, and may be thought of as a modern, multidimensional update of Hegel's more "linear" system. Like Hegel's, McLuhan's laws postulate a cyclical evolution of human processes, encompassing both the trivial and the most profound.[41]

According to Marchand, McLuhan felt that the tetrad was better than Hegel's triad, which he considered a "truncated" tetrad that eliminated the third law: retrieval. McLuhan thought the triad was for "visual man."[42] In contrast, McLuhan wrote that Hegel was a proponent of "acoustic subjectivism": "Hegel simply flipped out of [David] Hume's visual determinism into acoustic subjectivism. All of their followers are still under the illusion that the acoustic world is spiritual and unlike the outer visual world, whereas, in fact, the acoustic is just as material as the visual."[43]

As Marxist historian Robert Tucker notes, turning Hegel's spiritual acoustic world into a material world was Marx's original uprighting of Hegelian philosophy,

In McLuhan's posthumous work, he wrote that Hegel's "great triad" is a connected rather than an interval-bridging form because of the "sameness-in-reverse" of the dialectical thesis, antithesis and synthesis.[44] He criticized the triad form, including the Hegelian dialectical triad, for eliminating the fourth element—McLuhan's "ground"—which "flips" the triad into a new form that is "resonant" and "metamorphic." The tetrad, he argued, is simultaneous rather than sequential, does not impose theoretical classifications as Hegel's triad does. In addition, the tetrad treats all four parts as processes. McLuhan believed that the tetrad moved well beyond Marxism. "The tetrad renders obsolete all groundless dialectical and systematic Marxist approaches to interpretation of social processes and technological transformations of culture by flipping the discussion into a kind of linguistic of real words."[45]

As a modified Hegelian triad, and as materialistic Hegelianism, McLuhan's tetrad would appear to fit the description of modified Marxism. McLuhan even attacked philosophy in discussing the tetrad, as Marx did in arguing for action, arguing that the "laws of media in tetrad form belong properly to rhetoric and grammar, not philosophy."[46]

The tetrad and its inner relationship are further explained in *The Global Village: Transformations in World Life and Media in the Twenty-*

first Century (1989) as embodying both a diachronic function—one of history and development—and a synchronic function—compressing past, present and future into one simultaneously.

> The action of any artifact…is diachronic as it undergoes progressive history and development from enhancement—which should be regarded as a form of amplification—to obsolescence (A to B to C to D). It is synchronic if one were to view the artifact mythically as a configuration (A/D = C/B and B/D = C/A).[47]

The tetrad also raises the hidden environment or ground, to visibility. And it reveals the double action of visual and acoustic properties in the life of a medium. In other words, enhancement and retrieval are figures; obsolescence and reversal are grounds.[48] The tetrad allows understanding of "and-both," the positive and negative results of the medium.[49] The alternative way of thinking to "both-and" is "either-or" thinking, which McLuhan relegated to an early stage of Aristotle's analysis in his expanded discussion of Aristotle's analysis of the four parts of metaphor.[50] McLuhan argued that Aristotle's essential point about metaphor is "both-and" thinking.[51]

Yet McLuhan considered the law of the excluded middle as the foundation for constrained, sequential Western logic in which "either-or," or A excludes non-A, is the only possibility. This logic eventually excludes the middle ground rather than "both-and" or "A and non-A" thinking. According to McLuhan, "both-and" thinking found in the tetrad is able to entertain two diametric possibilities at once, as evidenced by preliterate peoples.[52]

These judgments are made despite McLuhan's embrace of Aristotle, the father of the law of the excluded middle. By contrast, political theory scholar Patrick Peritore identified "either-or" thinking as Aristotelian logic, which demands annihilation of one being by another through the law of the excluded middle.[53] According to Marxist art historian Arnold Hauser, "both-and" thinking is the essence of Hegelian dialectic. The starting point for Hegelian dialectics, Hauser argued, is "the axiom that A was simultaneously non-A and that everything had a double, even conflicting meaning."[54] He argues that the key to dialectics are "two contrastive phases": on one hand, the "negation and surrender of a dominating view" and the "rejection of demands which are just coming into being," on the other; "the settlement of the antagonism…by means of a more complex unity" and a "new synthesis which embraces antitheses." "Contradiction" is the origin; "reconciliation" is the culmination. Of the whole process, its "decisive criterion is antagonism."[55]

The contrastive phases, each with two parts, could be envisioned in the form of a tetrad. The four parts would correspond to McLuhan's pairs of figures and grounds. "Negation" and "rejection" would be the figure and ground of "enhancement" and "obsolescence": respectively, a positive/negative pair of the process. New media extend until they encounter non-medium, and, at the end of their extension/enhancement, obsolesce the old medium. "Settlement" and "new synthesis" are comparable to "retrieval" and "reversal" as the other constitutive part of the process, retrieving elements necessary to settle into a new synthesis of old and new, or reversal, which means that it becomes something very different, not the opposite.

Hauser also disagreed with Hegel's position that dialectics demands a three-part process and believes that "Hegel's dialectic moves in a mechanical rhythm, a waltz rhythm, as people have not neglected to remark." Instead, dialectics can reveal more or fewer phases. The key, he argues, is "the global aspect under which the forces in question form a context."[56]

In her assessment of McLuhan's dialectical method, political scholar Judith Stamps contrasts her approval of McLuhan's dialectics in his early works, *The Mechanical Bride: Folklore of Industrial Man* and *The Gutenberg Galaxy: The Making of Typographic Man,* with her disapproval of his analytic technique and a crescendo of disapproval of the analysis beginning in *Understanding Media* and culminating in the tetradic laws of the media.[57] In his early "mosaic" approach—one similar to that of Theodor Adorno, Walter Benjamin, and Harold Innis, "constellation" metaphor—McLuhan differed only in that he did not use Marxist categories of analysis.[58] Yet theoretically, all four are linked by their use of juxtaposition instead of linear causality and by their refusal to reduce "social and historical processes to a string of billiard ball-like causal relations,"contributing to a lack of specificity.[59]

Stamps' analysis of this early negative dialectic suggested that McLuhan introduced the idea of "counter-environments" or "anti-environments"—most notably artists or new media—to provide marginal, or negative points of contact that offer the possibility of new levels of awareness.[60] Stamps noted that at this meeting place there is a "moment of freedom and release" and a "moment of truth and revelation."[61]

According to Stamps, in his later career, McLuhan received some much-deserved criticism for reducing his theoretical claims to fit specific types of media, making him appear to be a mechanistic thinker or technological determinist. She also noted that he began to forgo historical documentation, which made his later work sound dogmatic.[62] By the late 1960s, the mechanistic statements and reductionism was so visible in his work that Stamps asks: "What can one say? Something had clearly gone awry in the land of constellations."[63]

By the time of *Take Today,* in which Stamps found McLuhan's statements on Marx's concern for private property "visual" and thus obsolescent, McLuhan had become "a formerly lucid critic of modernity who had become a sign of it: a-historical, directionless, and tending to triviality."[64] The posthumous *Laws of Media* quickened the pace of this decline, offering a "monocausal theory of history" that left history behind in following the fool's mission of trying to prove McLuhan's theory scientifically.[65] Criticizing the attempt on a number of fronts, Stamps centred a large part of her critique on the four laws themselves, the first two being tautological, and the second pair too specific to be useful as a critical tool.

Stamps argued that the principle of extension in the first law and the principle of diminishment in the second, go without saying, although according to Hauser especially, the meeting of being and non-being is the core of dialectics. The law of reversal, which in the analysis above can be understood as the phase of new synthesis, confused Stamps because it lacked an element of necessity and required additional cultural contextualization. The fourth law, retrieval, also is meaningless without cultural context and identification of the hidden ground.[66]

Ignoring the dialectical process underneath the tetradic laws discussed above, Stamps called them a "desperate move... Indeed, the entire exercise seems to turn its back on the historical and cultural analysis that were so central to the works of Adorno, Benjamin, Innis, and the early McLuhan."[67]

This chapter argues, however, that McLuhan's early and later dialectics are closely related and, according to Hauser's open-ended concept of dialectics, McLuhan's tetrad accommodates the essential elements of dialectical thinking. Application may be another matter, but the theory itself should stand above McLuhan's pronouncements of its theoretical applications. More importantly, Stamps agreed that despite his protests against dialectics, McLuhan employed a variant of dialectics. According to the essence of dialectics discussed by Hauser, McLuhan was very close to the heart of dialectical thinking throughout his career.

Accepted on his own terms, then, McLuhan would reject being subsumed by Hegelian or Marxist dialectics. However, despite his protests to the contrary, McLuhan employed a version of dialectics. His explanation of dialectics is contradicted by the full-scale discussions offered by Hauser and Peritore. The critical media galaxy that comes to life by applying this dialectical theory, including its social, economic and political components, will be presented in the next chapter.

NOTES

1. Marshall McLuhan, *The Gutenberg Galaxy: The Making of Typographic Man* (Toronto: University of Toronto Press, 1962), 7.
2. Marshall McLuhan, *Understanding Media: The Extensions of Man* (New York: Mentor, 1964), 19.
3. Ibid., 39.
4. McLuhan, *Gutenberg Galaxy*, 7.
5. McLuhan, *Understanding Media*, 23-24.
6. Ibid., 35.
7. Ibid., 21.
8. Erich Fromm, *Marx's Concept of Man* (New York: Ungar, 1961), 49.
9. McLuhan, *Understanding Media*, 51.
10. Ibid., 74.
11. Ibid., 52.
12. Ibid., 63.
13. Ibid., 67.
14. Ibid.
15. Ibid.
16. Ibid., 56.
17. Ibid., 43.
18. Ibid., 49.
19. Ibid., 50.
20. Ibid., 60-61.
21. Ibid., 63.
22. Ibid., 57.
23. Ibid., ix.
24. McLuhan, *Understanding Media*, xi.
25. Ibid., 73.
26. Ibid., 93.
27. Ibid., 59.
28. Ibid., 75.
29. Philip Marchand, *Marshall McLuhan: The Medium and the Messenger* (New York: Ticknor and Fields, 1989), 241-242.
30. Marshall McLuhan, "McLuhan's Laws of the Media," *Technology and Culture* 16, no. 1 (January 1975): 74-75.
31. Ibid., 75.
32. Marshall McLuhan, "Laws of the Media," *Et Cetera* 34, no. 2 (June 1977): 175-178.
33. Ibid., 175

34. Ibid., 177, citing *The Basic Works of Aristotle*, ed. Richard McKeon (New York: Random House, 1941), 594.

35. McLuhan, *Understanding Media*, 52.

36. Ibid., 24.

37. Ibid., 43.

38. Ibid., ix.

39. Marchand, *Medium and Messenger*, 241.

40. Marshall McLuhan, with Wilfred Watson, *From Cliche to Archetype* (New York: Pocket Books, 1971), 189.

41. Paul Levinson, introduction to "Laws of the Media," by McLuhan, *Et Cetera* 34, no. 2 (June 1977): 173-174.

42. Marchand, *Medium and Messenger*, 241.

43. McLuhan, *Letters*, 489.

44. Marshall McLuhan, with Eric McLuhan, *Laws of the Media: The New Science* (Toronto: University of Toronto Press, 1988), 126-127.

45. Ibid., 127.

46. Ibid., 128.

47. Marshall McLuhan, with Bruce Powers, *The Global Village: Transformations in World Life and Media in the Twenty-first Century* (New York: Oxford University Press, 1989), 9.

48. Ibid., 10.

49. Ibid., 11.

50. Ibid., 29-31.

51. Ibid., 32.

52. Ibid., 39.

53. N. Patrick Peritore, "Radical Dialectics," unpublished paper (Department of Political Science, University of Missouri, Columbia, MO, 1985), 54.

54. Arnold Hauser, *The Sociology of Art*, trans. Kenneth J. Northcott (Chicago: University of Chicago Press, 1982), 337.

55. Ibid., 345.

56. Ibid., 346.

57. Judith Stamps, *Unthinking Modernity: Innis, McLuhan and the Frankfurt School* (Montréal: McGill-Queen's University Press, 1995), 97-150.

58. Ibid., 134.

59. Ibid., 135.

60. Ibid., 138-139.

61. Ibid., 142, citing McLuhan, *Understanding Media*, 63.

62. Ibid., 142.

63. Ibid., 143.

64. Ibid., 145.

65. Ibid., 146.

66. Ibid., 146-147.

67. Ibid., 149.

McLuhan's Critical Media and Culture Galaxies

Civilization and its Contents

Having measured McLuhan's approach for similarities with dialectics, a broad outline of the media and culture environments that McLuhan's methodology generates will help separate the significant historical phenomena from the mythology. This chapter will describe these media and culture galaxies. McLuhan's broad historical sweep—which matches those of his contemporaries, the Frankfurt School's Max Horkheimer, Theodor Adorno (although in less pejorative terms), and Walter Benjamin—moves from an initial stage of oral culture and tribalism to a second stage of print culture and nationalism, then into a third stage of electronic culture and retribalism.[1]

Civilization, according to McLuhan, is a process started by the introduction of the phonetic alphabet as a visual technology. By contrast, civilization is a process dissolved by acoustic electronic technology.[2] Technology, medium and extension are nearly synonymous in McLuhan's work. The message of any technology is the change in pattern that it brings about in society. The problem with electric technology is that the visual culture of mechanical technology is unable to recognize and cope with the electric world.[3] McLuhan argued that "electric technology is within the gates, and we are numb, deaf, blind and mute about its encounter with Gutenberg technology, on and through which the American way of life was formed."[4]

McLuhan's media mission was to understand media and the conflicts they cause in order to increase human autonomy from technology. This task is all the more difficult because the simple use of a technology involves embracing its perceptual field.[5]

> It is this continuous embrace of our own technology in daily use that puts us in the Narcissus role of subliminal awareness and numbness in relation to these images of ourselves. By continuously embracing technologies, we relate ourselves to them as servomechanisms... An Indian is the servomechanism of his canoe, as the cowboy of his horse or the executive of his clock.[6]

So while technology is itself visual or acoustic by being either mechanical or electric, the response to technology can be denial, which would characterize a visual response, or awareness, characterizing an acoustic response.

Ideology Concepts

McLuhan's media galaxies affect and are affected by sociopolitical and economic, philosophical and religious, and scientific and technical organization and institutions—in short, the world views that critical communication theory refers to as ideology.

To place McLuhan's universe in the context of critical theory, some ideas from cultural and critical scholars will provide a base for McLuhan, who did not appear to use the concept of ideology. First, cultural studies scholar John Fiske included as dominant ideological codes: individualism, patriarchy, race, class, materialism and capitalism.[7] For sociologist Todd Gitlin and cultural studies scholar Raymond Williams, hegemonic ideology penetrates everyday life and common sense, including playing, working and believing.[8] This concept shares with Fiske an assumption that society is divided along lines of class, sex, race, age, religion, occupation, education and politics. This also includes the notion that social relations are a struggle for power between dominant and subordinate groups as they create meaning "naturalized" by ideology.[9]

Marxist philosopher Louis Althusser, whose work forms a basis for British cultural studies, conceived of ideology as representations, including images, myths, and ideas. These ideological forms include religion, ethics and philosophy, art and "world outlook," including the "scientific world outlook." Ideology is an organic essential part of every society. Althusser asserted that ideological images and concepts are primarily unconscious; they are lived as if they were the world itself. In class-based society, the ruling class prevails but the ruling class is not above its ideology. The ruling class believes its own myth, according to Althusser, even though existence belies the ideology as an imaginary relation. For example, in bourgeois ideology the idea that all people are free mystifies those people who are exploited.[10] These categories taken together form a basis for a thematic organization that includes ideas and beliefs about working, playing, art, philosophy, religion, materialism, race, class, and science. This thematic structure for ideology includes different aspects of ideology as a lived system of beliefs and naturalizes them as "common" sense. Describing McLuhan's ideological galaxies in terms of politics and economics, philosophy and religion, science and technology, and popular culture will provide a critical context for his arguments relating media to culture.

Politics and Economics: Beyond Dollars and Sense

For McLuhan, the book encouraged individualism, nationalism, industrialism, mass markets and universal education beginning in the sixteenth century. The printed word eroded the corporate patterns of feudalism and introduced the idea of divide and rule in politics. Machiavellian politics became individualistic and quantitative in the application of the uniformity and repeatability of print to the control of the State.[11]

Western power, according to McLuhan, is driven by the idea of extension by homogenization. Print homogenized regional groups with the centralization of power and new nationalism. The idea of linear progress was born because print media were interpreted as "an engine of immortality" and leaders sought to act to benefit future ages. Nationalism emerged as print spread vernacular languages and replaced tribal communities with the association of individuals. Today, however, the electronic media are working against nationalism. McLuhan suggested the speed and breadth of the media make national groupings unworkable.[12]

In economics, the fragmentation and uniformity of print weakened the cooperative medieval craft guilds. Print developed market and commercial values as well as nationalism. McLuhan suggested that he book was a uniformly priced commodity, which initiated the idea of price systems in economics.[13] Economic markets needed literate culture to start and maintain them through the "visual technology of prices." Thus, in contrast to the bartering system in oral cultures, literate societies have to fragment inner life through price mechanisms in order to create price systems.[14]

According to McLuhan, money was preceded by commodities in oral cultures. In literate cultures, the notion of money as an abstract currency emerged, although circumstances such as war may bring back commodity money to a literate culture.[15] Like language, money stores collective work, but it also is a specialist medium like writing, which separates work from other activity. In the electronic age, money retains its power to specialize and fragment human functions as it stores and translates work. However, electronic media endanger the concept of money as the fragmenting print media yield to the inclusive electronic media, which brings people close to total involvement in their work. As in primitive society where the standard of living is similar for the wealthy and the poor, the ruling class in the electronic age has similar entertainment and other goods to the middle class. Automation replaces work with the movement of information and the credit card replaces money. Work does not exist in an acoustic world, McLuhan argued, comparing the primitive hunter with the contemporary painter. Where the whole person is involved there is no work; the job succumbs to dedication and commitment.

Philosophy and Religion: Sacred and Profane

According to McLuhan, a "sacred" universe is auditory, a "profane" universe is visual. Visual media fragmented the universe into visual segments producing non-religious modern philosophy and science.[16] The mechanical clock fostered the concept of a numerically quantifiable and mechanically driven universe.[17] Nature and scripture were separated by print culture. With René Descartes, animals became animal machines and nature was desacralized. Alexander Pope converted nature into the "chain of being" and in the nineteenth century man became the "missing link." "The great chain of being" was the eighteenth-century metaphor of philosopher John Locke and the industrial sewing machine stitch.[18]

The ability to conceive of time as something that happens between two points applies the visual, abstract and uniform values of print culture. The idea of time as durations created impatience unknown in oral cultures. Visual culture patterns all routine daily activities to the clock rather than to organic need.[19] Citing William Shakespeare, John Donne, and Andrew Marvell, McLuhan argued that the Renaissance reaction to the new mechanical time sense was ambiguous and resistant. He cited Shakespeare: "Tomorrow and tomorrow and tomorrow, creeps in this petty pace from day to day"; and "Like as the waves move towards the pebbled shore, so do our minutes hasten to their end."[20] Print produced the idea of repeatability needed to conceive of infinity.[21]

The detachment and individualism fostered by print was expressed in the ability to act without reacting. To separate thought and feeling, action and reaction, allowed the individual to emerge from the tribe.[22] Electronic and oral people who integrate thought, feeling and action are hesitant. Print culture teaches acting without thinking and is embodied in the attitude: "Damn the torpedoes. Full steam ahead."[23]

McLuhan argued that this "gift" of "disinterested" detachment has become "an embarrassment" in an electronic culture that values involvement.[24] Art and nature are united again in the acoustic space of Lewis Carroll and Werner Heisenberg's uncertainty principle as the basis of electricity and quantum mechanics. In acoustic space, the centre is dispersed as the age of discontinuity retrieves all cultures at once.[25] In electronic culture, space and time interpenetrate. Clock time becomes restrictive, its repeatability giving way to electronic multiplicity of rhythms.[26] Print culture reduces truth to matching of inner and outer, as lying is easy only when dealing with a medium like print. Truth is achieved by stress on visual matching. In the electronic age, a lie becomes a "credibility gap" and "truth" becomes "trust."[27]

McLuhan explored Eastern philosophy and religion where no phonetic alphabet split visual from acoustic space in order to illustrate the difference between Eastern and Western culture. He believed the Chinese ideogram did not upset sensory balance in the acoustic world, as is reflected in the electronic quality of Eastern thought. Asian cultures retain the richness of inclusive perception that literate cultures lose because the ideogram is a gestalt.[28]

Science and Technology: Newton to Einstein

According to McLuhan, Newtonian and Euclidian science are the mainstays of visual space, while Albert Einstein, Heisenberg and Niels Bohr are proponents of acoustic space in science. "Normal" and "common sense" space in the twentieth century is still Euclidean space, McLuhan writes, although Einsteinian space is retrieving the "normal" acoustic space of pre-literate Greeks.[29] Between the early Greeks and Einstein, Western civilization has understood the universe as a mechanistic container that consists of objects in linear, geometric order. This view is supported by visual technology. Euclid, and later Newton, placed objects in linear, sequential, geometric space.[30]

In the infinity of Galileo and Isaac Newton, critical historian Donald Lowe agrees with McLuhan that knowledge represented objects related in a homogeneous space discovered by mechanical sciences.[31] It was not until 1905, when Einstein published papers introducing what would become known as the special theory of relativity, that common concepts of space and time were challenged. Lowe argues that by 1916, the mechanistic universe of Newtonian physics fell to Einstein's relativity theories.[32] In the general theory of relativity, the space-time continuum is presupposed to be curved, not rigid or homogeneous: "Space-time ceases to be a stage…for the dynamics of nature; it becomes an integral part of the dynamic process."[33] McLuhan argued that Einstein's ideas of acoustic space call for "total reorganization of our imaginative lives" and provided that television has prompted that reorganization.[34]

The Method is the Message

Arts and Artists in the Media and Culture Galaxies

McLuhan may have tried to say little about politics and social theory in the belief he could be apolitical, but he had no reticence toward celebrating the arts and the artist in the activist social role he assigned them.[35] Arts and artists provide the backbone of his sensory balance theory and historical evidence. What human agency is granted in his media-technological determinism is granted to arts and artists as part of the advance guard—similar to Eastern Leninist Marxism—who are sensitive to changing sensory environments. Both the Gutenberg Galaxy and the global village, as well as the transitions between them, are aesthetically alive.

McLuhan's view of artists and the arts may be understood by looking at the transhistorical role he gives them; the historical shifts in that role from oral to typographic to electronic cultures; and the resultant blurring of distinctions between fine and popular arts and media. McLuhan granted the arts, in the all-encompassing sense that he used the term, a pivotal role in social formation.

Transhistorically, McLuhan's notion of media evolution is based on the idea that new media environments turn old media environments into art forms. For example, the alphabetic culture of Plato turned oral dialogue into an art form. As media environments succeed each other, art takes the role of an "anti-environment" or "counter-environment" to provide the majority of non-artists with the means of perceiving the new environment. The "early warning system" of art opens the "doors of perception." As media changes accelerate, technologies begin to perform the function of art in making human beings aware of the impact of technology. Using Ezra Pound's definition, the artist is the "antennae of the race" in anticipating social and technological changes by several decades. The artist enables consumers to prepare to cope with these changes.[36]

Art and technology are equated on one hand, but are opposed on the other. McLuhan believed that technology reaches beneath consciousness and alters sensory balance and perception without human awareness or resistance. The artist alone can counter technological effects because the artist is an "expert aware of the changes in sense perception."[37] McLuhan endowed human beings with limited freedom because the artist provides a map to adjust the psyche. The media deeply affect people because the media are human extensions; however, thanks to the artist, it is possible to assess media effects before media are introduced into society.[38] McLuhan's purpose was to serve that freedom of action through the arts as he ought to reduce the conflicts that media originate from and created and to increase "human autonomy."[39]

In broad historical terms, the arts have assumed many roles and definitions while society has tried to translate nature into art.[40] Electronic culture, which is becoming aware of media effects for the first time, senses that art can provide "immunity" to new technologies. Throughout history, only the "puny and peripheral efforts of artists" offer examples of conscious adjustments to new media. The artist understands the impact of technology decades before the impact, McLuhan claimed, and then builds models—"Noah's arks"—for adjusting to the impact.[41]

As technological change speeds up in electronic culture, the artist, who is ahead of the times, helps society keep pace with media that are ahead of their time and capable of destroying society. To prevent this destructive collision of media and society, "the artist tends now to move from the ivory tower to the control tower" as the central analyst of media forms and effects. McLuhan argued that the artist's role as res-cuer who can "sidestep the bully blow of new technology of any age" goes unnoticed as the "percussed victims" of technological violence are unaware of their need of the artist and dismiss the artist as impractical. On the other hand, making artists famous also can be a way of missing their prophetic message.[42]

The image invoked here is the artist as the suffering misunderstood genius with a solitary vision from a vantage point outside society. McLuhan considered that all scientists and humanists are artists. These artists and scientists, decades ahead of their time, can correct sense ratios before new technologies have traumatized and numbed the cul-ture. In a colorful phrase, McLuhan declared that art is "exact informa-tion of how to rearrange one's psyche in order to anticipate the next blow from our own extended faculties [that] show us how to 'ride with the punch,' instead of 'taking it on the chin.'"[43]

The Ideal, "We Have No Art," Lost and Found

Although the role of artists and the arts becomes more crucial in electronic culture, McLuhan assigned variations of the same role to the artist throughout history. As media fragment and specialize in visual culture, however, art also fragments and specializes from everyday life. The phrase from the Balinese, "We have no art; we do everything as well as possible,"[44] summarizes McLuhan's view of "primitive" art which, along with medieval art, has much in common with modern art.[45] Art remained part of the fabric of acoustic life through the Middle Ages and early Renaissance. The arts themselves were not separated. Written and printed works were read aloud and poetry was set to music. Speaking, music, literature and art were closely related. Even the visual aspect of this culture, the lettering of illuminated manuscript, was sculptural. The quality of letters as engraved icons, rather than visual abstractions, has returned in electronic culture in advertising. The same quality can be detected in symbolist poetry, cubist painting, and even in the newspaper headline that tends toward the iconic form that is auditory and tactile rather than visual.[46]

With these broad strokes, McLuhan connected the pre-print era with the electronic era. McLuhan also focused on transitional figures who straddle acoustic and visual cultures. German painter Hieronymus Bosch mixed medieval forms in Renaissance space to convey with "earnest nightmare intensity" what it felt like to live between the unique, discontinuous space of the Middle Ages and the uniform, connected space of the Renaissance. McLuhan believed that Bosch dreaded the modern world just as Shakespeare did in *King Lear*. At the other cultural juncture, Carroll in the nineteenth century entered a "fantasia" in the transition from visual back to acoustic. Carroll's discontinuous space-and-time anticipated Franz Kafka, James Joyce, and T. S. Eliot, yet only Carroll "greeted the electronic age of space-time with a cheer."[47]

For McLuhan, the key to art of the visual era of typography was the emergence of perspective and the vanishing point in Renaissance painting, which together give rise to a new concept of infinity. Perspective and the vanishing point, unknown in Greek and Roman times, are attributed to literacy by McLuhan. Printing extended the visual sense with definition and uniformity. The other senses were muted to create a new awareness of infinity.[48] The first printed musical scores in the sixteenth century separated words and music. This laid the groundwork for the visual musical developments of the eighteenth and nineteenth centuries, including the specialized and fragmented formation of symphony orchestras.[49] Looking at primitive and medieval art, literate people in whom the visual sense dominates as a universal principle of organization mistakenly think that such art fails to reproduce visually accurate representations.[50] McLuhan argued that the perception of time and space, visual or acoustic-tactile, is a learned perception.[51]

For more than a century artists have responded to the electric age. Abstract art, beginning with the breakup of the visual plane with Paul Cézanne, offers a "central nervous system" rather than a pictorial image.[52] Painters since Cézanne have recovered the image in which all the senses are unified. Each object creates its space rather than being contained in empty space either visually or musically.[53] By releasing objects from the uniform continuous space of typography as, for example, Salvador Dali did by juxtaposing a piano with a mountain, modern art and modern poetry were ushered in.[54]

One casualty in this mosaic of simultaneous items is the point of view. The art of impressionism in the late nineteenth century included the pointillism of Georges Seurat and the light studies of Claude Monet and Auguste Renoir. McLuhan compared Seurat's "stipple of points" to telegraphic transmission of photographs and to the television image. Electricity is only incidentally visual and auditory; it is primarily tactile.[55] The sense of touch, which organically unifies art, was popularized in the works of Paul Klee, Walter Gropius and others in Germany in the 1920s.[56]

According to McLuhan, the artistic response to the electronic age was epitomized by cubism, which decreed that "the medium is the message." McLuhan cited art historian E. H. Gombrich's view of cubism as a radical attempt to eliminate ambiguity and emphasize the painting as a human-made artifact.[57] McLuhan argued that cubism presents all aspects of an object at once instead of the "point of view" of linear perspective. Cubism demands a gestalt or instant awareness of the whole. The world of visual linearity turning into the world of acoustic mosaic also occurred in physics, poetry and communication.[58] Einstein's relativity theory in 1905 dissolved the uniform visual space of Newtonian physics, which was continuous and rational, and introduced Pablo Picasso, the Marx brothers, and MAD magazine.[59]

McLuhan found photography decisive in the transition between the mechanical age and the electronic age. The small dots of photography presage Seurat's pointillism.[60] Photography in the nineteenth century greatly affected painting, displacing the artist from representational work. Painting turned to inner creativity in expressionism and abstract art. Similarly, the realistic novelist competing with photography, newspapers, film and radio could no longer describe events for readers who already were informed. The poet and novelist turned inward.[61]

Fine and Popular Arts, Games and Media Merge

This shift from the mechanical to the electronic also shifted the fine arts in relation to the popular arts. The two reunited in a way that, according to McLuhan, existed before the fragmentation of the arts in the Gutenberg galaxy. Picasso, McLuhan noted, liked American comics. Fine artists have shown great interest in American popular art as an imaginative reaction to culture. High culture is a product of a specialized industrial culture, while popular art and artists such as Charlie Chaplin resist the mechanical routines of society.[62] Another popular art form, advertising, frames products as essential parts of social processes. Commercial artists develop ads into icons, which are unified, symbolic images rather than fragments.[63]

Games also are included by McLuhan as popular art. He called games extensions of society and collective responses to dominant cultural forms. They offer a way of adjusting to stress and a model of the universe.[64] Art, he argued, became a civilized substitute for games and rituals as literacy rose. More than play, however, art, is an extension of awareness in conventional patterns. Unlike sports and other popular arts, which are a reaction to society, high art profoundly reflects on culture. The function of art, McLuhan argued, is its social effects. Fine art, popular art and games as well as media, impose their own assumptions on audiences by setting up new patterns of perception. Also, art and games translate experience, into a new material that has already been felt or seen in cultural experience.[65]

Art merges with other expressive forms, reassuming its oral era relationships, when electronic media recreate a means of depth experience. The visual categories of "classical" and "popular," "highbrow" and "lowbrow" lose distinction. Recording technology has created a depth-participation approach to music. The recording media blurred the distinction between serious music and popular music because depth infers involvement instead of isolation. Insight rather than point of view demands involvement in process that makes content seem secondary. As an analogy, McLuhan argued that consciousness is an inclusive process independent of content; for example, it is not necessary to be conscious of anything in particular.[66]

The taped recording made available a musical spectrum covering many centuries and cultures, expanding the narrow selection of periods and composers.[67] McLuhan distinguished between stereo sound, which was new in his day, and monaural recordings, which reproduced visual culture's single point of view. Stereo recording, McLuhan concluded, did for music what cubism and symbolism had done for art and literature. Stereo sound accepts multiple layers and perspectives, becoming sound in depth, as television is the visual in depth.

The crowning effect of electronic media culture, for McLuhan, is "synaesthesia" or unified sensory and imaginative experience. He argues that synaesthesia has been the dream of artists throughout the typographic era as they bemoaned the fragmentation of literacy. This artistic dream was achieved by radio and television as all-enveloping extensions of the central nervous system. The way of life maintained for centuries by the separation of the senses and the dominance of the visual cannot withstand radio and television. McLuhan wrote that they erode the visual structures of "abstract Individual Man."[68]

Dialectic of Visual and Acoustic Arts

McLuhan's visual/acoustic dialectic of the arts challenges common sense when applied to the arts and popular culture. According to McLuhan, not all written poetry, novels and plays are visual, typographic or literate. Not all music is acoustic. Not all visual art is visual. The arts—visual, musical, literary—respond to the dominant medium, or technology, of the era to create acoustic literature and paintings in the electronic media age. In the past age of typography, music had visual characteristics. For example,

> In our age artists are able to mix their media diet as easily as their book diet. A poet like Yeats made the fullest use of oral peasant culture in creating his literary effects. Quite early, Eliot made a great impact by the careful use of jazz and film form... Artists in various fields are always the first to discover how to enable one medium to use or to release the power of another...
>
> The printed book had encouraged artists to reduce all forms of expression as much as possible to the single descriptive and narrative plane of the printed word. The advent of electric media released art from this straightjacket at once, creating the world of Paul Klee, Picasso, Braque, Eisenstein, the Marx Brothers, and James Joyce [69]

In other words, the poetry of Yeats is acoustic and resembles oral culture, Eliot's poetry is musical and filmic, and the paintings of Klee, Picasso and Braque, released from visual space of typography, also become acoustic.

Literature: All Books are not Books

As all forms are influenced by the dominant medium of an age, literary forms themselves bear marks of visual or acoustic content. All books are not books. McLuhan's categorization of poets, playwrights and novelists of the typographic era, however, is contradictory.

Regarding literature, the entire typographic era seems to shrink at both ends, from its inception in 1450 to its supersedence in 1844. McLuhan viewed early print culture authors such as Shakespeare, Donne, Marvell, Miguel de Cervantes and Francois Rabelais in the sixteenth century as using print to react against, and challenge the destructive changes brought about by print culture.[70] Poetry, according to McLuhan, escaped from the full impact of print culture until the late seventeenth century.[71] Other poets such as Pope also transcended print culture, despite their immersion in the height of the typographic era during the seventeenth and eighteenth centuries. They are perhaps imbued by McLuhan with the artistic "antennae" that allowed them to remain aloof from history.[72] Early nineteenth-century poets John Keats, Percy Bysshe Shelley and William Wordsworth are similarly examples of, yet exemptions to, typographic culture.[73] Mid-nineteenth-century writers, working at the onset of the electronic era (as signaled by the telegraph in 1844), are almost all categorized as electronic-acoustic examples, including Edgar Allan Poe, whose mystery genre is a key acoustic form in McLuhan's analysis.[74] Charles Dickens—whom McLuhan credits with the original form of stream of consciousness writing—and Gustave Flaubert also take on acoustic shades.[75]

Comparing McLuhan's categorization of print culture authors with the positions of humanities scholar Walter Ong and Lowe provides a fuller appreciation. Ong supports the latent orality of Shakespeare in the rhetorical pattern of speech-making in *Julius Caesar*.[76] The itinerant hero of the episodic novel of Cervantes, Daniel Defoe, Henry Fielding and to a degree, Dickens (as well as Dickens' fondness for reading aloud from his works), are cited by Ong as residual orality in a text-bound print culture.[77] While certain aspects of the approach taken by Ong and Lowe reaffirm McLuhan, Ong puts Poe's detective story genre, dating it from 1841, firmly in the print culture sphere as a "pyramidically structured narrative," of which an oral culture would be incapable. Ong does, however, follow McLuhan's observation that in the detective story the writer works from effect to causes in a non-linear fashion,[78] which for McLuhan, made the mystery a non-visual genre. Ong contrasts the "flat," iconic, universal characters of oral culture to the "round," individualized, psychological characters of literate culture. He notes that the plotless literature of the electronic age, including the writing of Kafka, Samuel Beckett and Thomas Pynchon, abandons the "round" character of the classical novel, except in "regressive" genres such as westerns.[79]

In his exploration of visual and typographic bourgeois society, Lowe credits the success of the historical novel pioneered by Walter Scott in the early 1800s with the time-consciousness of bourgeois society.[80] The structured perspectives in the typographic space of the bourgeois novel are characterized by Lowe as a "silent, detached, one-way address by a writer, using linguistic signs, which the reader receives through the eyes." This type of novel, which Lowe calls "narrative of estranged subjectivity," spans the late eighteenth to early twentieth centuries and begins with Samuel Richardson's epistolary novels of 1740. Visual bourgeois novelists include Laurence Sterne, Jane Austen, Stendhal, Honoré de Balzac, Dickens, Flaubert, George Eliot, Thomas Hardy and Émile Zola, and collapse with Henry James.[81] Lowe heralds the modern novel with Gertrude Stein's *Three Lives* in 1909, and includes in early form the works of Marcel Proust, and Joyce—who in different ways rejected objectivity, development in time, specific perspective, and chronological narrative.[82]

Music: For the Eye as Well as Ear

McLuhan argued that before the typographic era, music was closely related to the all the other arts.[83] He added that print culture in the Renaissance split poetry from song so that instruments were played without vocal accompaniment until the two converged in the twentieth century with Béla Bartok and Arnold Schoenberg.[84] The "tactile implosion" of electronic media has brought music and casual speech together in the works of Schoenberg, Igor Stravinsky, Carl Orff and Bartok. McLuhan compared Stravinsky and Bartok to the medieval composer Dufay.[85] Jazz also tends toward the discontinuous, participant and spontaneous, and was heard by McLuhan as a return to oral poetry. McLuhan translated the French *jaser* as "to chatter," calling jazz a dialogue among musicians and dancer.[86] Rock music, from the Twist to the Beatles and music videos, is granted acoustic power in McLuhan's musical universe.[87] The Twist, a dance of the 1960s, is called an "unanimated dialogue" of gestures that indicate depth involvement but no message.[88] The troubadour tradition returned with the Beatles and Joan Baez. Much modern poetry is put to music as the walls between the written and oral crumble.[89] The Beatles and jazz extend the speech of lower and middle classes.[90] And rock music videos are compared to Watusi mating dances.[91] For McLuhan, the experimental music of John Cage is a musical equivalent of poetry's ambiguities, splitting music from melody.[92]

McLuhan built an acoustic musical bridge from the Middle Ages to the electronic era and from high culture to popular culture. His analysis skipped the visual musical era, however, except for references to the waltz, the Charleston, Wolfgang Amadeus Mozart and the march, as well as to the separation of voice and instruments. He called the waltz a mechanical dance matching the industrial era. The waltz replaced feudal court and choral music.[93] The waltz is precise and militaristic, its dancers uniform, equal and freely moving.[94] McLuhan contrasted the Charleston and the Twist, likening the former to "a mechanical doll agitated by strings."[95]

Finally, the musical achievements of the eighteenth and nineteenth centuries are attributed to the separation of poetry from music. McLuhan paralleled fragmentation and specialization in print society with newspapers and symphony orchestras.[96] In a comparison between the symphony musician and the contemporary businessperson, McLuhan noted that both experience the musician's inability to hear the music as a whole and hear only noise. McLuhan inferred that electric production, like the symphony orchestra, demands rigorous harmonizing efforts but returns little satisfaction.[97] Nonetheless, the symphony player is fragmented and specialized. Of the few composers from the visual era named by McLuhan are Richard Wagner and Eric Satie, both of whom are given acoustic qualities. Wagner, McLuhan wrote, combined a mythic past in the simultaneous musical present and used ritual to organize his music.[98] He compared Satie's music to Picasso's art, evoking a sense of industrial-era melancholy.[99]

As with literature, McLuhan's shift in music from visual to acoustic blends backward into the nineteenth century. By comparison, Lowe marked the shift from linearity to multi-perspectivity in music with Schoenberg's works in 1909. These works broke with linear tonality and explored liberated dissonance. Between 1909 and 1913, Schoenberg, Alban Berg and Anton Webern produced an atonal system that focused on color, rhythm and phrasing rather than harmony. Lowe also included the early works of Stravinsky.[100]

Visual Arts: An Acoustic Side, Too

McLuhan's main artistic references apart from the literary realm were to painters. McLuhan allied primitive, medieval and modern visual art, which had been separated by the visual gulf of the print era. The rise of linear perspective is the critical technique in the development of visual space in painting, but McLuhan treated it as a learned rather than a natural form of perception.

The old belief that everybody really saw in perspective, but only that Renaissance painters had learned how to paint it, is erroneous. Our own first TV generation is rapidly losing this habit of visual perspective as a sensory modality...[101]

Beginning with Cézanne in the nineteenth century, the visual plane of perspective art began to dissolve. The point of view became untenable, leading to the multi-perspectival approach of cubism and the non-representational forms of abstract expressionism and beyond to postmodern art.

Visual-era art contains its own ideology. McLuhan argued that in seventeenth-century art, the portrait returns the gaze of the observer, creating a dualism. The portrait turns art into a mirror to involve the audience in reaction and share the point of view of the artist.[102] McLuhan wrote that, for example, a Rembrandt van Rijn self-portrait shows the self-consciousness created by the public environment of print culture and reveals the private dimension.[103] He added that Albrecht Durer's perspective drawings, made through a screen by matching dots in a scene in which nothing moves, reflect a geometric perspective that represents the "single vision" of Newton; a "single vision" that William Blake deplored.[104] The fixed position of perspective forces peripheral vision on the viewer, and the dualism of centre and margin parallels the dualism of subject and object. In McLuhan's work, only perspective permits a dispassionate, uninvolved survey of the world.[105] McLuhan wrote that in the visual landscape the outer world existed to end in a picture. He cited as an example Thomas Gainsborough's landscapes, which he compared with Wordsworth's "Solitary Reaper," in which the beautiful is in the foreground and the "sublime auditory" is in the background.[106]

Another visual art genre is the *memento mori*, such as Georges de la Tour's *The Repentant Magdalen*, which, according to McLuhan, treats the skull as a Baroque mirror contrasting darkness with the sight of the skull in the quest for depth through duality. The visual culture contrasts outer and inner and divides appearance and reality.[107]

Acoustic-era art offers a contrasting ideology, exemplified by Cézanne, who occupies a pivotal point in McLuhan's shift from visual to acoustic space. He was the first to abandon perspectival illusion in favor of multiple perspective and structure in painting.[108] Among acoustic artists, McLuhan compares James McNeill Whistler to Joseph Mallord William Turner, whose seascapes moved painting away from objects to the effects of light on color.[109] Whistler also popularized

Japanese art, which for McLuhan has never forsaken acoustic space. Edvard Munch's *The Scream* is described by McLuhan as an unstable universe. The "undulating swirl of landscape pulsates with the scream," while the "rational road" is an "orientation point" that intensifies the scream.[110] McLuhan declared that Seurat's pointillism reversed perspective and made the viewer the vanishing point. Beginning with Seurat, space was no longer neutral; it recovered the ancient portent form of space and time.[111] Seurat, for McLuhan, is the "prophet of TV," as he tips the balance from the visual space of the Renaissance to the acoustic space of the modern.[112] Georges Braque's work represents the type of cubist art that announced "the medium is the message." Commenting on one Braque painting, McLuhan wrote, "A point of view is a serious liability in approaching this canvas." The painting retrieves "primitive values in everyday objects" and recovers "the world of cave painters."[113]

The acoustic world also is alive in medieval art. As a transitional artist, Bosch inserted the medieval world into visual, rational Renaissance space. The disturbing shift from collective space to private space is clearly reflected in Bosch's phantasmagoric vision, which McLuhan compared to that of Kafka.[114] In modern abstract art, visual space is internalized in a way that is disturbing to audiences. McLuhan compared this process with the difficulty of perceiving pictorial space in the Renaissance because of its objectivity and alienation.[115]

Popular Culture: Expressive Forms

The dichotomy of popular culture and high culture, of fine arts and mass media, did not deter McLuhan. He treated Chaplin and King Lear, baseball and Greek drama, advertising and museum art, all as equals.[116] According to him, "classical" and "popular," "highbrow" and "lowbrow" were being outdated by the media, as television was realizing the "synaesthesia" that thinkers and artists had idealized for centuries.[117]

Postmodernist Charles Jencks—who argues that media shape postmodern culture—supports McLuhan in his blurring of fine art and popular art. So does art historian Janet Wolff, who included all cultural products as art. She noted that not all "fine" art was considered fine when it was being produced, and cited Mozart, post-impressionism and classical architecture as examples.[118] Art historian John Walker disagreed and insisted on a separation of the two, because popular culture serves the dominant ideology as an "opium of the people," while fine art has the power to critique mass culture. For Walker, mass media include radio, television, newspapers, advertising, comics, magazines, paperback books and recorded music.[119] Interestingly, McLuhan put pop art, one of Walker's examples of fine art, in the category of non-art.[120] Offering another contrasting opinion, critic John Berger argued that the tradition of oil painting reproduces the dominant ideology of capitalism, which has been extended and intensified through the publicity images of electronic culture. Images from the oil painting tradition are used in publicity in service of consumer culture.[121]

Marxist art historian Arnold Hauser and US cultural studies scholar James Carey have also wrestled with the popular art versus fine art problem. Hauser, defining the popular art of films, best-selling novels and radio, centred on popular art's purpose as entertainment, relaxation and play. Popular art is formulaic and produced for the economic consumption of the urban masses—jazz is "dance music" and utilitarian. For Hauser, mass art is an outgrowth of popular art, substituting the seriousness of fine art with the "happy ending" of Hollywood films.[122]

Hauser's analysis followed the mass culture debate of the 1950s that, according to Carey, was waged by sociologist C. Wright Mills and others. Mills attacked the popular arts from the left, advocating a democratic community free from academic elites and economics. The conservative side, represented by Dwight MacDonald, argued an anti-populist line to advance folk art and elite art.[123] In a brief history of the popular culture debate, Carey suggested that the subject matter was lost in the behaviorism of the 1960s or was trivialized. Popular culture then was absorbed into the problem of power and domination in critical theory. Carey argues for the original version of the mass culture debate, which clearly demarcated fine art from popular art.

> I have become more convinced that the protagonists in the mass culture debate were on the hunt for the real goods. If anything the pertinence of the arguments they set forth has grown over the years ... for they collectively grasped, however much they differed, how modern societies were put together and the major trajectories of their development.[124]

Carey suggests that popular art and fine art, high culture and mass culture are contained within a larger category of "expressive forms." Among specific forms of culture are art and journalism. The social scientist studies the cultural forms of religion, ideology and journalism; the literary critic the form of the novel, play and poem.[125]

For McLuhan, mass culture—both high culture and popular culture—also expressed the dialectic of visual and acoustic space. To differentiate, visual culture is associated with mechanical processes of sequence, uniformity, repeatability and fragmentation. Acoustic culture is associated with organic processes of simultaneity, depth involvement and participation. As McLuhan wrote,

> At present, the mechanical begins to yield to the organic under conditions of electric speeds. Man now can look back at two or three thousand years of varying degrees of mechanization with full awareness of the mechanical as an interlude between two great organic periods of culture... Printing, the first complete mechanization of a handicraft, breaks up the movement of the hand into a series of discrete steps that are ... repeatable... From this analytic sequence came the assembly-line principle, but the assembly line is now obsolete in the electric age because synchronization is no longer sequential. By electric tapes, synchronization of any number of different acts can be simultaneous.[126]

Combinations of the visual-mechanical and the acoustic-organic can be seen in McLuhan's analysis of mass culture forms, including movies, games, comics, and popular music. For example, the movie form combines the mechanical and organic, retaining a link with typography in its sequence of still images and its ability to generate fantasy in the audience. The movie also assumes the audience is literate, citing the difficulty oral cultures have in learning to see movie images. In addition, movie content derives from the narrative form of the novel.[127] According to McLuhan, film form is "the final fulfillment of the great potential of typographic fragmentation." He added that the modern literary technique of stream of consciousness used by Proust and Joyce is really a film technique, and offsets the visual culture elements found in film. So, film and stream of consciousness create a release from mechanization.[128] The movie pushed the mechanical into the organic, thus, not surprisingly, when the movie appeared, so did cubism.[129] Inasmuch, then, as these and other elements can be combined in movies, the form itself takes on either visual or acoustic properties. Therefore, each electric popular culture form can be differentiated by its visual or acoustic properties.

In McLuhan's discussion of television, the "television mosaic" departs qualitatively from the movie medium. McLuhan discussed the western, the soap opera, the detective and courtroom drama, and the quiz show. The western's quest for identity on the frontier between two worlds for the prototypic Western man, who is civilized and detached, illustrates visual space in television. The western genre, a natural form for the movie and television, is a "paradigm of the condition of man in a rapidly changing or growing society."[130] The soap opera is equated as a companion of the western.[131]

Three other genres are examples of acoustic style. According to McLuhan, the detective and the courtroom drama are typical examples of an intensely participational form of television. The courtroom drama demonstrates the television star's association with the role rather than the actor, in contrast to the movie's star system.[132] The television mosaic was prefigured in Poe's invention of the detective story with its deep participation in creativity and its movement from effect to causes.[133] McLuhan argued that the television quiz show also followed the pattern of deep participation.[134]

Fiske concurred with the notion that television is an acoustic—or oral—and not a literate medium, which differentiates it from film. The oral mode is dramatic, episodic, mosaic, dynamic, active, concrete, ephemeral and social, according to Fiske. In contrast, the literate mode is narrative, sequential, linear, static, abstract, permanent and individual. Fiske argued that television's textual forms are oral and that viewers who enter television's dialogue treat it as oral.[135]

Modern Mass Media in the Galaxies

McLuhan's interest was not in the mass media themselves, but in the broader historical and cultural issues and in the arts. This is most easily seen when attempting to catalog his comments about the modern forms of mass media: newspapers, magazines, radio and television. Within the media and culture galaxies these media are analyzed dialectically as sensory forms.

Newspapers: Literary and Telegraph Press

Contrary to what might appear as common sense, in McLuhan's media matrix the newspaper is not a "visual" typographic medium as is the book. For McLuhan, the newspaper tends toward the "mosaic" and the electric, resembling television.

Here I must repeat that the newspaper, from its beginnings, has tended, not to the book form, but to the mosaic or participational form. With the speed-up of printing and news-gathering, the mosaic form has become a dominant aspect of human association; for the mosaic form means, not a detached "point of view," but participation in process. For that reason, the press is inseparable from the democratic process, but quite expendable from a literary or book point of view.[136]

McLuhan made a distinction between the point of view of the "literary" press and the mosaic of the "telegraph" press as he described the change from the mechanical age of typography to the electric age of the telegraph.[137] As examples of the hybrid nature of media, literary newspapers like *The New York Times* and the *London Times* offer "columns representing points of view." In contrast, telegraph newspapers like the *Daily Express* and *New York Daily News* offer a "mosaic of unrelated scraps in a field unified by dateline." McLuhan noted that photographs transmitted telegraphically by news services resemble Seurat's pointillism. As creations of the telegraph and global news services then, the modern newspaper tends toward an "acoustic medium" rather than a "visual" medium. McLuhan even equated reading a newspaper with watching television.

The newspaper is pushed further toward the acoustic or electric by the reporter's use of the oral medium of the telephone, which McLuhan argued fosters an "inclusive authority of knowledge" and erodes the hierarchical, delegated authority of the chain of command.[138] The newspaper moves toward corporate, collective and communal acoustic culture, and is incompatible with private and exclusive book culture. The daily process of "making the news" creates the inside story of community action.[139] McLuhan also equated the newspaper with symbolist and surrealist art and poetry, calling it an inspiration for the latter's inclusive awareness and an approach that increases understanding of Joyce's *Ulysses* as well as other literature.[140]

Magazines: Mosaic and Pictorial

McLuhan found the same hybrid character in magazines that he found in newspapers. *Time* and *Newsweek*, McLuhan suggested, are mosaic in form, creating "corporate images of society in action" rather than "windows on the world like the old picture magazines." McLuhan wrote that these news magazine readers were involved, unlike "passive" picture magazine "spectators," and added that the news magazines were on the rise during television's early growth while pictorial feature magazines were declining.[141] "Mosaic news" eschews narrative, point of view, comment and explanation. Instead, it invites participation in the social process.[142] McLuhan identified *Life* as an example of a pictorial magazine that was forced by television to face the demand for in-depth audience participation and involvement.[143] He characterized the pictorial magazines as using features that present photographs and fragmentary points of view in the pictorial treatment of news.[144]

The photograph was treated ambivalently by McLuhan. He contrasted the photograph's fragmentary isolation of a moment in time—a visual-print characteristic—with television's continuous scanning that tends toward the iconic and timelessness—an acoustic-electric characteristic.[145] At the same time, he put the photograph on a plane of significance with movable type and the printing press, except that, for him, the photograph heralded the split between the typographic age and the graphic age, foreshadowing Seurat's pointillism.[146] On one hand, normal visual, photographic perception and the notion of the camera as a machine that cannot lie are both elements of typographic culture. On the other hand, the photograph's integral role in creating the modern newspaper and the movie align it with acoustic culture. McLuhan argued that the photograph can only be understood in its hybrid form with other media.[147] By intensifying the visualization of natural objects, photography had a reverse effect, he argued, but then allies the photographic and visual worlds as "secure areas of anesthesia" in America's literate culture.[148] Despite this rather unclear approach, it is evident that the photograph can be visual or acoustic, depending on its media mate. In this regard, the pictorial magazine tends toward the visual, while the newspaper tends toward the acoustic.

Radio: Book Bias in Electronic Form

McLuhan noted that the development of news since the telegraph was applied to journalism as a continuous process, whether in print or electronic form. He wrote that the telegraph shortened the sentence; radio shortened the news story; and television introduced the "interrogative mood" into journalism.[149] Within radio, however, he found that the same hybrid character divides the literary and telegraphic press. According to McLuhan, the British Broadcasting Corporation showed a "print and book bias," which made it "awkward and inhibited in radio and TV presentation." This network contrasts with the "hectic vivacity" of commercial radio in the United States.[150] McLuhan characterized radio—still on the continuum from visual to acoustic—as an acoustic medium that is intimate, person-to-person and private, retrieving "gestural qualities" that were denied by print media.[151]

Television: Extending McLuhan's Hybrid

Of all of the departures from common sense, McLuhan's consideration of television as an acoustic rather than a visual medium is perhaps the most challenging. McLuhan argued that visual space is a product of literacy and is the eye's perception of space without the other senses. Visual space is more a mental construct that is continuous, uniform, infinite and empty. In comparing visual space to the "mind's eye,"[152] McLuhan writes that visual space is connected logically and sequentially.

> If you think of every human sense creating its own space, then the eye creates a space where there can only be one thing at a time. The eye acts as a machine—like a camera. Light focused on the back of the eye ensures that two objects will not occupy the same place at the same time. The mind teaches the eye to see an object right side up, on a plane, and in perspective space.[153]

McLuhan argued that acoustic space is "natural space," like the "mind's ear" of oral and electronic cultures. Acoustic space is discontinuous, heterogeneous and simultaneous.[154]

Television, in this dichotomy, falls toward the acoustic and the tactile. McLuhan defined television as an extension of the sense of touch—the maximum interplay of all the senses.[155] McLuhan also cited broadcaster and author Tony Schwartz's contention that in watching television the eye acts like an ear.

> Watching television, the eye is for the first time functioning like the ear. Film began the process of fracturing visual images into bits of information for the eye to receive and the brain to reassemble, but television completed the transition. For this reason it is more accurate to say that television is an auditory-based medium. Watching TV, the brain utilizes the eye in the same way it has always used the ear. With television, the patterning of auditory and visual stimuli is identical.[156]

Schwartz's proposal of the auditory base of all electronic media, including television, film, radio, and recordings, argued that these media are processed by the human brain in the same way as aural information. The ear translates vibrations into electronic signals and sends them to the brain. The brain "hears" the vibrations and creates what does not exist as a whole in any single moment. Schwartz argued that this process held for electronically transmitted auditory and visual information. Film, for example, relies on immobile images divided by a darkness. The brain "sees" motion. He argued that television is more different than film when compared to the real-life visual experience of a continuous stream of visual input. He suggested an experiment to show that, visually, the television image never exists:

> If we were to set up a series of two thousand still cameras focused on a TV, each shooting at one two-thousandth of a second and firing sequentially (so that we could cover a one-second time span completely), no single camera would record a picture. The image we "see" on television is never there. A still camera, shooting at one two-thousandth of a second, will capture only a few dots of light or perhaps a single line across the television. In everyday visual experience, of course, a still photograph of a landscape shot at one two-thousandth of a second will capture a complete visual image of a landscape.[157]

Whether discussing the arts or the mass media, McLuhan's mosaic, or dialectical method, can be seen moving in his media galaxies of hybrid media and social form. Having described McLuhan's method and the phenomena under dialectical analysis, the next chapter will compare several concepts that McLuhan shares with his contemporary neo-Marxist scholars of the Frankfurt School, Benjamin, Adorno and Horkheimer, who all employed dialectical method.

NOTES

1. Marshall McLuhan, with Quentin Fiore and Jerome Angel, *The Medium is the Massage: An Inventory of Effects* (New York: Bantam, 1967), 44-45, 48, 63.
2. Marshall McLuhan, with Quentin Fiore and Jerome Angel, *War and Peace in the Global Village* (New York: Bantam, 1968), 24.
3. Marshall McLuhan, *Understanding Media: The Extensions of Man* (New York: Mentor, 1964), 23, 31.
4. Ibid., 32.
5. Ibid., 59, 55.
6. Ibid., 55.
7. John Fiske, *Television Culture* (London: Methuen, 1987), 5.
8. Todd Gitlin, *The Whole World Is Watching: Mass Media in the Unmaking of the New*

Left (Berkeley, CA: University of California Press, 1980), 10; Raymond Williams, *Marxism and Literature* (Oxford: Oxford University Press, 1977), 110, 112-113.

9. John Fiske, "British Cultural Studies," in *Channels of Discourse*, ed. Robert C. Allen (Chapel Hill, NC: University of North Carolina Press, 1987), 255-256.

10. Louis Althusser, *For Marx*, trans. Ben Brewster (New York: Pantheon, 1969), 231-235.

11. McLuhan, *Understanding Media*, 157, 160.

12. Ibid., 159-161.

13. Ibid., 161.

14. Ibid., 128.

15. Ibid., 124-132.

16. Ibid., 144.

17. Ibid., 135.

18. Marshall McLuhan, with Wilfred Watson, *From Cliche to Archetype* (New York: Viking, 1970), 37, 40.

19. McLuhan, *Understanding Media*, 135-136.

20. Ibid., 138-139.

21. Ibid., 112.

22. Ibid., 88, 158.

23. Ibid., 162.

24. Ibid., 157.

25. McLuhan and Watson, *Cliche to Archetype*, 39.

26. McLuhan, *Understanding Media*, 137-138.

27. McLuhan and Watson, *Cliche to Archetype*, 32, 34.

28. McLuhan, *Understanding Media*, 86-87.

29. Marshall McLuhan, with Eric McLuhan, *Laws of the Media: The New Science* (Toronto: University of Toronto Press, 1988), 22.

30. Marshall McLuhan, with Bruce Powers, *The Global Village: Transformations in World Life and Media in the Twenty-First Century* (New York: Oxford University Press, 1989), 118.

31. Donald Lowe, *History of Bourgeois Perception* (Chicago: University of Chicago Press, 1982), 13.

32. Ibid., 112.

33. Ibid., citing P. G. Bergman, "Relativity," *Encyclopaedia Brittanica*, 15th ed. *Macropaedia*, vol. 15 (1974), 586.

34. McLuhan, *War and Peace*, 24.

35. James M. Curtis, "McLuhan: The Aesthete as Historian," *Journal of Communication* 31 (summer 1981): 149-150.

36. McLuhan, *Understanding Media*, ix-xi.

37. Ibid., 33.

38. Ibid., 57.

39. Ibid., 59.

40. Ibid., 65.

41. Ibid., 70.

42. Ibid., 70-71.

43. Ibid., 71.

44. Ibid., 72

45. Marshall McLuhan, with Harley Parker, *Through the Vanishing Point: Space in Poetry and Painting* (New York: Harper and Row, 1968), 8.

46. McLuhan, *Understanding Media*, 147.

47. Ibid., 149; McLuhan and Parker, *Vanishing Point*, 10, 14.
48. McLuhan, *Understanding Media*, 112.
49. Ibid., 246.
50. Ibid., 290.
51. McLuhan and Parker, *Vanishing Point*, 9.
52. McLuhan, *Understanding Media*, 105.
53. Ibid., 137.
54. Ibid., 253.
55. Ibid., 219.
56. Ibid., 105.
57. Ibid., 27.
58. Ibid., 28.
59. Ibid., 150.
60. Ibid., 171.
61. Ibid., 174.
62. Ibid., 153.
63. Ibid., 201
64. Ibid., 208-209.
65. Ibid., 213-214.
66. Ibid., 247.
67. Ibid., 248.
68. Ibid., 274-275.
69. Ibid., 61-62.
70. Marshall McLuhan, *The Gutenberg Galaxy: The Making of Typographic Man* (Toronto: University of Toronto Press, 1962), 14-15, 194, 213; McLuhan, *Understanding Media*, 138-140.
71. Marshall McLuhan, *Letters of Marshall McLuhan*, eds. Matie Molinaro, Corinne McLuhan, and William Toye (Toronto: Oxford University Press, 1987), 246.
72. McLuhan, *Gutenberg Galaxy*, 309; McLuhan, *Understanding Media* 155-157.
73. McLuhan and Parker, *Vanishing Point*, 22-23, 41, 119, 155.
74. McLuhan, *Understanding Media*, 282.
75. Ibid., 258-259.
76. Walter Ong, *Orality and Literacy: The Technologizing of the Word* (New York: Methuen, 1982), 45.
77. Ibid., 149-150.
70. Ibid.
79. Ibid., 153-154.
80. Lowe, *Bourgeois Perception*, 41.
81. Ibid., 74-79.
82. Ibid., 115-116.
83. McLuhan, *Understanding Media*, 147.
84. Ibid., 159.
85. Ibid., 286.
86. Ibid., 245.
87. Marshall McLuhan, with Harley Parker, *Counterblast* (New York: Harcourt, Brace and World, 1969), 33. McLuhan and Powers, *Global Village*, 45; McLuhan, *Understanding Media*, 40.
88. McLuhan, *Understanding Media*, 285.
89. McLuhan and Watson, *Cliche to Archetype*, 83.

90. Ibid., 145.
91. McLuhan and Powers, *Global Village*, 45.
92. McLuhan and Watson, *Cliche to Archetype*, 77; McLuhan, Fiore and Angel, *War and Peace*, 135.
93. McLuhan, *Understanding Media*, 36, 40.
94. Ibid., 245.
95. Ibid., 40.
96. Ibid., 246.
97. Ibid., 308.
98. McLuhan and Parker, *Counterblast*, 113.
99. McLuhan, *Understanding Media*, 243.
100. Lowe, *Bourgeois Perception*, 114-115.
101. McLuhan, *Understanding Media*, 251-252.
102. McLuhan and Parker, *Vanishing Point*, 13.
103. Ibid., 105.
104. Ibid., 16.
105. Ibid., 20.
106. Ibid., 119, 121.
107. Ibid., 101.
108. McLuhan, *Understanding Media*, 280.
109. McLuhan and Parker, *Vanishing Point*, 24.
110. Ibid., 177.
111. Ibid., 24-25.
112. Ibid., 181.
113. Ibid., 209, and McLuhan, *Understanding Media*, 28.
114. McLuhan and Parker, *Vanishing Point*, 76-77.
115. Ibid., 28.
116. McLuhan, *Understanding Media*, 153, 201, 208-209.
117. Ibid., 247, 275.
118. Charles Jencks, *What is Post-Modernism?* (New York: St. Martin's Press, 1986), 50; Janet Wolff, *Aesthetics and the Sociology of Art* (London: George Allen and Unwin, 1983), 11, 18.
119. John A. Walker, *Art in the Age of Mass Media* (London: Pluto Press, 1983), 18-21.
120. McLuhan and Parker, *Vanishing Point*, 29.
121. John Berger, *Ways of Seeing* (London: BBC and Penguin Books, 1972), 134.
122. Arnold Hauser, *The Sociology of Art*, trans. Kenneth J. Northcott (Chicago: University of Chicago Press, 1982), 580, 583, 589, 607-609.
123. James Carey, *Communication as Culture: Essays on Media and Society* (Boston: Unwin Hyman, 1989), 37, citing C. Wright Mills, *The Power Elite* (New York: Oxford University Press, 1959).
124. Ibid., 37-39.
125. Ibid., 43-44.
126. McLuhan, *Understanding Media*, 141.
127. Ibid. 249-250.
128. Ibid., 257-258.
129. Ibid., 27.
130. McLuhan and Watson, *Cliche to Archetype*, 90; McLuhan, Fiore and Angel, *War and Peace*, 126-127.
131. McLuhan and Watson, *Cliche to Archetype*, 91.

132. McLuhan, *Understanding Media*, 272, 277.
133. Ibid., 282.
134. Ibid., 216
135. Fiske, *Television Culture,* 105-107.
136. McLuhan, *Understanding Media*, 188.
137. Ibid., 219.
138. Ibid., 239.
139. Ibid., 189.
140. Ibid., 193.
141. Ibid., 183.
142. Ibid., 202.
143. Ibid., 152.
144. Ibid., 201.
145. Ibid., 169.
146. Ibid., 171.
147. Ibid., 172-175.
148. Ibid., 180-181.
149. Ibid., 192.
150. Ibid., 268.
151. Ibid., 261.
152. McLuhan and Powers, *Global Village*, 45.
153. Ibid., 38.
154. Ibid., 45.
155. McLuhan, *Understanding Media*, 290.
156. Tony Schwartz, *The Responsive Chord* (New York: Anchor Books, 1974), 16, cited in McLuhan and McLuhan, *Laws of Media*, 158, and McLuhan and Powers, *Global Village*, 63.
157. Schwartz, *Responsive Chord*, 14.

McLuhan and the Frankfurt School

A Critical Theory Perspective on the Media

Although contemporaries, the Frankfurt School theorists and McLuhan apparently never made reference to each other. Yet as dialectical theorists, McLuhan, Max Horkheimer, Theodor Adorno and Walter Benjamin share central comments in their seminal works on the media. This chapter will present points of convergence between McLuhan, Adorno, and Benjamin, focusing primarily on their dialectical analysis of media and of visual society, or the Enlightenment.

Critical theorists could have helped McLuhan formulate a social theory in linking the mass media to cultural and social change. The works of Horkheimer, Adorno, and Benjamin, as well as that of Erich Fromm and Herbert Marcuse, suggest positive and negative roles for the arts and media as social forces of domination or liberation and the reproduction of ideology. A review of some of their basic ideas and their use in recent media studies provides a more solid means to link media to ideology and thus enhances McLuhan's theory.

Political theorist Scott Warren argued that critical theory and Western Marxism counter the failed orthodox Marxism of the Soviet Union's anti-democratic political system. Critical theory also responds to capitalism entering a post-liberal State with an "increase of monopoly structures and growing government intervention in the economy." The theory of a revolutionary working class became unworkable and Marxists had to face the decline of that class.[1] Critical theory, Warren contended, opposes technological society's ideological defense of the capitalist status quo.[2] A major goal of critical theory is the liberation of reason from use as an instrument of domination.[3] Critical theory assaults ideology and false consciousness in order to assist the growth of critical self-awareness.[4] As critical theorists became concerned with cultural and ideological forces that thwarted revolutionary movements and furthered the system of domination, they turned to the problems of authority and mass culture.[5]

Literary scholar Patrick Brantlinger suggested that the Frankfurt School critical theorists were faced with the fact that monopoly capitalism and imperialism produced fascism and Nazism rather than a workers' revolution.[6] Civilization had produced its opposite: barbarism. The Frankfurt thinkers argued that the dominated classes had been bought off by mass media. Their goal was to create radical philosophical consciousness against instrumental reasoning, reification, commercialization, and mass culture and mass media, all viewed as forms of political domination.[7]

In Marcuse's critical theory, the media and mass culture are one factor that prevents the realization of utopia, where life is art. The media and mass culture justify the status quo and divert attention from the oppression exerted by the ruling class. Brantlinger argued that this domination is largely psychological in Western democracies, where the media internalize false needs and false consciousness. The media and the culture industry threaten human liberation; newspapers, film, radio and television cut off communication, co-opt culture, and destroy subjectivity and privacy. Media also co-opt the aesthetic realm by making works of intellectual culture seem familiar, and high culture disappears. The media make radical thought and practice impossible. Genuine art is inaccessible to the public, which is suffering from reified false consciousness, but genuine art also has historical importance as the expression of dialectical negativity. Brantlinger contended that genuine art mirrors society's opposite, shadowing the liberation it has failed to achieve.[8]

The negative assessment of the media doesn't waver in Horkheimer and Adorno. Brantlinger wrote that Horkheimer also believed that "mass communication is non-communication," and that the movie, book and radio destroy personal life. Adorno accused the culture industry of impeding the growth of independent individuals. He also found that the culture industry transforms the critical negativity of art into shallow affirmation. The world is filtered through the culture industry and is deadened as mass media produce a retreat from enlightenment into myth. Again, the media, which promise to universalize culture, lead instead to the regression of civilization into barbarism.[9]

Horkheimer attributed intellectual passivity to television and expressed resignation toward technology. Adorno found that television follows totalitarian creeds, even though the surface message is anti-totalitarian. According to Brantlinger, the Frankfurt School emphasized the problems of the nearly-universal false consciousness that is seen as the main product of media.[10]

Brantlinger suggested that Benjamin, a German literary essayist, offered a more positive role for the media. Benjamin thought that mechanical reproduction freed art from ritual to political expression and that liberation may come partly through media. In his dialectic, art becomes a reified commodity through media, but it also is democratized by media. The media politicize art, making the media a revolutionary force that could free mass culture. According to Brantlinger, younger Marxists have picked up on the hopeful side of Benjamin's analysis. Enzensberger faults Marxists for not being aware of the media's socialist possibilities as a challenge to bourgeois culture.[11]

Comparing McLuhan and the Frankfurt Theorists

Political theorist Judith Stamps' thesis that McLuhan, as well as Harold Innis, shared a dialectical approach with Benjamin and Adorno argues that the use of Marxist terminology by the Frankfurt School provided a divergence of thinking between them.[12] However, this discussion will attempt to show that McLuhan, Benjamin, and Adorno focused on the same social phenomena with similar dialectical analyses. Stamps argues that all four theorists moved beyond Marxism, but in different ways, while providing a historical and material-based analysis.[13] They also shared approaches: a focus on the margins of dominant institutions and a negative reading of history. All four also used constellations, mosaics or galaxies at the centre of their dialectical method.[14] Yet in her comparisons, Stamps looks at their approaches to political economy and oral culture but not to media and mass culture.[15]

Other discussion comparing McLuhan and the Frankfurt School has been sporadic.[16] Cultural studies scholar James Carey issues a disclaimer that he is not trying to "resurrect" or "restore" McLuhan's "tarnished reputation." His interest is in focusing attention on a problem central to both McLuhan and Benjamin, that of "visual society." Carey includes Benjamin because Benjamin was currently of academic interest.[17] An explicit comparison of the two theorists is compressed in just three paragraphs, using them more as a springboard to Carey's own discussion of visual society.[18]

Carey finds the four links between McLuhan and Benjamin. Both McLuhan and Benjamin studied the evolution of the human sensorium. However, Carey noted that Benjamin had a more inclusive sense of an entire mode of modern existence, unlike McLuhan who limited his scope to technology. Both selected the transformation of sound into sight as the critical moment historically, although McLuhan focused on the conversion of oral and written tradition into print culture.

Benjamin, by contrast, focused on the erosion of tradition by the repro-ducibility of visual images, from the woodcut to movies. Both associ-ated this shift to the visual with the destruction of tradition, the reduc-tion of communication, and the loss of authentic experience. Finally, both romanticized the process and included a reversal effect: a moment in history when the lost tradition, communication and authenticity will be restored. In this regard, Benjamin looks to politics while McLuhan looks to technology.

For Carey, the sum of these similarities was this: "What Benjamin and McLuhan in their better moments realize is that the study of the mass media is the study of this actual constitution of a mode of life in which the media play a central role, not simply as technologies, but as part of a project at once technical, social and epistemological."[19]

In a seldom-cited article Carey wrote that McLuhan's theories have redeeming qualities and, indeed, should form the basis of an agenda for cultural studies:

> McLuhan's work, for all the arguments I have leveled against it elsewhere, is an important part of this more general body of writing and ought to be reconsidered in its light... McLuhan caught this project on a large scale, despite the politics and romance which stopped him short of an adequate analysis. But to take up his challenge anew and re-situate the analysis of the media at the hinge of the oral and the visual remains an important item he left on the agenda of contemporary cul-tural studies.[20]

In another little-cited journal that ceased publication after several issues, literary theorist Pamela McCallum found that although it would be "intriguing" to argue that Benjamin and McLuhan's critical theories are linked, the "structural affinities" may be superficial and the two the-ories and methods are only "tangentially related."[21] These similarities she allows: both use an "ideogrammatic method"—what McLuhan called his "mosaic approach"—and both "ransack the junkyard of mass cultural banalities."[22] She also noted that Benjamin's aural and post-aural cultures are "strikingly similar" to McLuhan's visual and acoustic culture.[23] Yet McCallum dismissed McLuhan by saying that he "rechan-nel(s) Benjamin's fondness for concrete historical details in the direc-tion of a pure technological determinism."[24] Citing literary scholar John Fekete's critique of "McLuhanacy," she found that McLuhan's the-ory is pervaded by reification of technology.[25] And she called his mosaic approach, or his dialectic, rigid, one-dimensional and detached from history. Although McLuhan suggested that he could reconstruct the social totality from juxtaposed images, McCallum argues that he fails to represent the "dialectical temporality of history."[26] Both Benjamin and McLuhan were limited by their technological determinism, but Benjamin inseparably linked technology with social organization and production, while McLuhan follows a one-dimensional technological model. In addition, McCallum asserts that Benjamin's use of aphorism and ideogram as a way of accessing the social totality contrasts with "the naive empiricism of McLuhan's system of thought."[27]

McCallum's negative analysis of McLuhan is rebutted by Stamps, especially McCallum's criticism of his technological determinism.[28] Summarizing McLuhan's media galaxy in *The Gutenberg Galaxy: The Making of Typographic Man,* Stamps argued that he analyzes the historical unfolding of different modes of social interaction, principally teaching and social discourse.[29] McCallum fails to consider the social relations McLuhan does discuss; in arguing that he does not address the relation between social universals and history she overlooks his discussion of political-economic relations, and she fails to see McLuhan's distinctive epistemological method.[30]

Stamps argues that although McLuhan and Benjamin shared an attempt to understand and critique modernity, they should not be compared point by point. She distinguishes the differences between the Frankfurt School's development of Marxism, and Innis and McLuhan's variant of political economy and communications. Both the Canadians and the Europeans undertook critiques of Western rationalism, psychologies, epistemologies and economic relations, although McLuhan set an "unreflective" and "mechanistic" course with *Understanding Media: The Extensions of Man.*[31]

Stamps elucidates a number of similarities between Benjamin and McLuhan, especially in the relatively contemporary work of McLuhan's, *The Mechanical Bride: Folklore of Industrial Man.* They dealt with similar themes of fascism, narcissism, mechanism and individualism, and also shared an interest in the banal surface of mass culture. In addition, their images of the Middle Ages and the oral reader and storyteller, and their use of mystical traditions, were similar. Both were anti-elitists who saw the changing media's effects as a way of ending domination. Both saw the camera and the moving image as key historical moments.[32]

The key difference Stamps finds is in schools of political economy: Benjamin following a European Marxist tradition and McLuhan a "self-styled, eclectic, highly improvised mode." Benjamin extended the

Marxist framework, while McLuhan both rejected and misunderstood Marxism's basic ideas. However, at the same time, McLuhan leaned toward dialectical formulations.[33] Benjamin used the standard Marxist categories of class, McLuhan did not. Despite this, Stamps argued, McLuhan did not forgo the study of cultural histories, including differentiating Western from colonial and non-Western cultures and exploring centre-margin relations. What McLuhan gains that Benjamin and Marxism lacks, is a grasp of multiple cultural histories and an escape from ethnocentrism.[34]. Stamps' critique of Marxism, however, ignores a wealth of studies in dependency theories of centre-periphery political economy relations, including Armand Mattelart's media analysis.

McLuhan and Benjamin

Marxist art historian Arnold Hauser compared McLuhan to Benjamin, writing that McLuhan popularized Benjamin's idea of "technical reproducibility." In Benjamin's seminal essay, "The Work of Art in the Age of Mechanical Reproduction," there are more shared concepts between McLuhan and Benjamin than Hauser indicated. A reading of *Dialectic of Enlightenment,* the major work on mass media by Frankfurt School critical theorists Horkheimer and Adorno, also shows evidence of central similarities in methodological and media analysis in relation to McLuhan's writings, including their contention that radio created Hitler.

The goal of Benjamin's essay was to determine what form capitalist modes of production had taken in the half century between Marx's time and his own—during which capitalist production had become fully manifested in the superstructure. He was interested in the dialectics of the development of art under capitalism.[35] Unique to this project, Benjamin wrote, is the mechanical reproduction of art, which has been increasing in intensity since the ancient Greeks practiced stamping coins. He discussed the woodcut, printing, engraving, etching and lithography, although he overstepped printing as "merely a special, though particularly important case," in order to focus on the "new stage" in reproduction techniques introduced by lithography, photography, sound recording and which all culminate in film.

> Around 1900 technical reproduction had reached a standard that not only permitted it to reproduce all transmitted works of art and thus to cause the most profound change in their impact upon the public; it also had captured a place of its own

among artistic processes. For the study of this standard nothing is more revealing than the nature of the repercussions that these two different manifestations—the reproduction of works of art and the art of film—have had on art in its traditional form.[36]

Benjamin argued that the age of mechanical reproduction has "eliminated" art's "aura" of "authenticity" because a reproduction lacks "its presence in time and space, its unique existence at the place where it happens to be."[37] He further suggested that this "shattering of tradition" by removing the work of art from this existence—he includes landscapes reproduced in photography and movies as examples—destroys "the historical testimony" and "authority of the object." Dialectically to this negative, the reproduction "reactivates the object reproduced" as it brings the object into the observer's own situation.

This resembles two ideas in McLuhan's terminology. First, media extend sensory and bodily functions, widening their scope, and second, the electronic media abolish time and space.[38] But Benjamin appeared even more like McLuhan as he discussed sensory perception:

> During long periods of history, the mode of human sense perception changes with humanity's entire mode of existence. The manner in which human sense perception is organized, the medium in which it is accomplished, is determined not only by nature but by historical circumstances as well.[39]

McLuhan also argued that sense ratios—the relationship between the dominant sense and those senses that are suppressed—change as media change and as the entire society changes.[40] In other words, echoing Warren's discussion of dialectics, the totality is contained in the individual, and the individual in the totality.[41]

Benjamin equated changes in perception brought about by mechanical reproduction with the "decay of the aura." He related them to the concurrent and contradictory desires of "contemporary masses" to "bring things 'closer' spatially and humanly," while "overcoming the uniqueness of every reality by accepting its reproduction."[42] These desires are manifest in the increasing social perception of "the universal equality of things" and in the increasing importance of statistics in the "theoretical sphere."

McLuhan equated the ideas of individual equality and statistical reasoning with the typographic media: the alphabet and printing.[43] Yet he would have agreed with the idea that electronic media increase the desire for closeness and intimacy in the "global village."[44]

For Benjamin, the central insight of the age of mechanical reproduction is that it liberates the work of art from dependence on ritual and its cult value, as exemplified in cave paintings and the cult of beauty developed during the Renaissance. With mechanical reproduction, art becomes designed for reproducibility and is based on the practice of politics and its exhibition value. He cited photography and film as the best examples of the latter.[45] He argued that the change occurs around 1900, when photography's exhibition value waxed and its cult value waned. The change, he argues, went unnoticed even by those in the nineteenth century who debated the value of painting versus photography.

> The dispute was in fact the symptom of a historical transformation the universal impact of which was not realized by either of its rivals. When the age of mechanical reproduction separated art from its basis in cult, the semblance of its autonomy disappeared forever. The resulting change in the function of art transcended the perspective of the century; for a long time it even escaped that of the twentieth century.[46]

The notion that media effects are met with a lack of awareness, shock and numbness is, as discussed earlier, central to McLuhan's thesis.

Considering film, Benjamin argued that the audience's position vis a vis the performance is different than in the theater. Because the camera mediates in film, the audience "takes the position of the camera" and its identification is with the camera. For its part, the camera continuously changes its position, thus the movie becomes multiperspectival. In contrast, the stage performance is presented in person; the actor can adjust to the audience and the audience must "respect the performance as an integral whole."[47]

McLuhan—who also argued that in film the audience takes the position of the camera and that movies are multiperspectival—was interested in the same dialectical interplay of media pairs such as theater and movies as well. For example, McLuhan compared the movie, which heralded a world of "growth" and "organic interrelations" of "configurations" and "the inclusive form of the icon," to cubism, which destroyed the point of view with "all facets of an object simultaneously." Suggesting dialectical interplay, McLuhan argues that all media come in pairs. As such, television restructured the movies and "the newspaper killed the theater."[48]

Benjamin presaged another of McLuhan's ideas when he noted that the new print media of the daily press were changing the book era's writer-reader, or producer-consumer, relationship. McLuhan heralded photocopying technology as making everyone a publisher.[49] Benjamin considered this process in literature as analogous to Soviet cinema's use of people who portray themselves instead of actors. Benjamin wrote that

> For centuries a small number of writers were confronted by many thousands of readers. This changed toward the end of the last century. With the increasing extension of the press ... an increasing number of readers became writers... And today there is hardly a gainfully employed European who could not, in principle, find an opportunity to publish somewhere or other comments on his work, grievances, documentary reports... Thus, the distinction between author and public as about to lose its character... At any moment, the reader is ready to turn into a writer.[50]

According to Benjamin, mechanical reproduction also causes other relational changes. It changes the role of the artist, he argued, drawing the analogous ratio or metaphor, that the painter is to a magician as the cameraman is to a surgeon. The painter-magician keeps his or her distance from the reality-patient, while the cameraman-surgeon penetrates deeply with mechanical equipment.[51] McLuhan would agree that perspective painting puts the viewer outside the painting, at a distance, while cinema and abstract painting involve the viewer in depth.[52]

Benjamin argued that mechanical reproduction also changes the reaction of the masses toward art. Because of the nature of the medium, painting can be viewed by one or a few, thus individual reaction is enhanced. In contrast, individual responses to film are controlled by the collective experience and "the individual reactions are predetermined by the mass audience response they are about to produce."[53] McLuhan would also have agreed that print era media such as representational painting, foster individualism, while film and electronic media foster participation.[54]

Benjamin might even be said to agree with McLuhan's assertion that the electronic media cause an implosion that wipes out print media's compartmentalization and abstraction.[55]

Our taverns and our metropolitan streets, our offices and fur-
nished rooms, our railroad stations and factories appeared to
have us locked up hopelessly. Then came the film and burst
this prison-world asunder by the dynamite of the tenth of a
second, so that now, in the midst of its far-flung ruins and
debris, we calmly and adventurously go traveling. With the
close-up, space expands; with slow motion, movement is
extended... The camera introduces us to unconscious optics
as does psychoanalysis to unconscious impulses.[56]

And McLuhan's notion of the cross-bred media recreating in their own
forms the messages of the emerging dominant form also is found in
Benjamin. McLuhan detected that literary and artistic forms resonated
with the new perceptions created by electronic technology ahead of
their time.[57] Benjamin also reflected this theme:

One of the foremost tasks of art has always been the creation of
a demand which could be fully satisfied only later. The history
of every art form shows critical epochs in which a certain art
form aspires to effects which could be fully obtained only with
a changed technical standard, that is to say, in a new art form...
Dadaism attempted to create by pictorial—and literary—
means the effects which the public today seeks in the film.[58]

McLuhan and Benjamin would appear to agree that audience participation changes as media change, and both find positive lessons in
popular, or lowbrow, culture. McLuhan argued that the popular electronic media, which academicians had ignored, were important cultural indicators.[59] Benjamin pursued the idea that changing media
forms result in change in the nature of participation

The fact that the new mode of participation first appeared in
a disreputable form [movies] must not confuse the spectator.
Yet some people have launched spirited attacks against pre-
cisely this superficial aspect... Clearly this is at bottom the
same ancient lament that the masses seek distraction whereas
art demands concentration from the spectator. That is a
commonplace.[60]

Evocative of McLuhan's sensory balance dialectic, Benjamin defined
the "polar opposites" of distraction and concentration. Distraction

involves absorbing the work of art, while concentration involves *being* absorbed by the work of art, or contemplation. Benjamin then compared "use" and "perception" to touch and sight, as two ways of appropriating art.

> On the tactile side there is no counterpart to contemplation on the optical side. Tactile appropriation is accomplished not so much by attention as by habit... Habit determines to a large extent even optical reception... For the tasks which face the human apparatus of perception at turning points of history cannot be solved by optical means, that is, by contemplation alone. They are mastered gradually by habit, under the guidance of tactile appropriation.[61]

Benjamin argued that at this century's historical turning point distraction-tactility provided by the mass art of film is a "covert control" that shows how much new tasks are solved by apperception. For Benjamin, "reception in a state of distraction, which is increasing noticeably in all fields of art and is symptomatic of profound changes in apperception, finds in the film its true means of exercise."[62]

McLuhan contended that all multi-sensory media, with television at the apex, are by virtue of that fact essentially tactile and unconscious and echo Benjamin's terms "tactile" and "distracted."[63] Contemplation, a rational, visual response fostered by print technology, is the opposite of tactile, for McLuhan, and thus clear parallels can be drown.

The final parallel between Benjamin and McLuhan is one of tone rather than specific content. Benjamin has been noted as the one Marxist theorist who alone developed a liberatory function for the media.[64] And McLuhan is well-known as a herald of new technology.[65]

In stark contrast to all these parallels, though, are striking differences. As a Marxist, Benjamin interjected the concepts of private property relations and class struggle. He saw his theory of art as a "weapon" against fascism, which he noted makes use of mechanical technology, and for "the formulation of revolutionary demands in the politics of art." Benjamin held that the ritual value of art is analogous to fascism in its attempts to aestheticize politics. Conversely, communism's response is to politicize art.[66] Mechanical reproduction, with its own dialectics, contributes to both the politicization of art and the aestheticization of politics.

The aesthetics of today's war appears as follows: If the natural utilization of productive forces is impeded by the property system, the increase in technical devices, in speed, and in the sources of energy will press for an unnatural utilization, and this is found in war... The destructiveness of war furnishes proof that society has not been mature enough to incorporate technology as its organ... Mankind, which in Homer's time was an object of contemplation for the Olympian gods, now is one for itself. Its self-alienation has reached such a degree that it can experience its own destruction as an aesthetic experience of the first order. This is the situation of politics which fascism is rendering aesthetic. Communism responds by politicizing art.[67]

The ideas that technical "speed" and technology itself demand an outlet; that technology is society's "organ"; that mankind has reached an extreme "self-alienation," and become its own art form; and that the electronic media present an opening for fascism in creating the mass, all resonate in McLuhan. Yet McLuhan cannot be said to count private property or the class struggle in his analysis. In fact, he argued that by virtue of extending the human nervous system in electronic media, society has no rights left.[68] Regarding fascism, McLuhan simply stated that radio is a medium that retribalizes masses and which allows for collectivization regardless of whether the collectivization is fascist or Marxist in nature. Radio's propensity toward retribalization—for good or ill—has gone unnoticed, according to McLuhan.[69] And he reported that Hitler owed his rise to radio:

That Hitler came into political existence at all is directly owing to radio and public-address systems. This is not to say that these media relayed his thoughts effectively to the German people. His thoughts were of very little consequence. Radio provided the first massive experience of electronic implosion, that reversal of the entire direction and meaning of literate Western civilization.[70]

McLuhan, Horkheimer, and Adorno

However, this observation about radio, fascism and Hitler had been made in the period following Benjamin's death in 1940. Unlike Benjamin, Horkheimer and Adorno focused on the dark side of the media in their negative dialectics.[71] Their thoughts on radio resonate deeply with McLuhan's:

> The radio becomes the universal mouthpiece of the Fuhrer... The National Socialists knew that the wireless gave shape to their cause just as the printing press did to the Reformation. The metaphysical charisma of the Fuhrer invented by the sociology of religion has finally turned out to be no more than the omnipresence of his speeches on the radio, which are a demoniacal parody of the omnipresence of the divine spirit. The gigantic fact that the speech penetrates everywhere replaces its content... The inherent tendency of radio is to make the speaker's word, the false commandment, absolute.[72]

In both passages, the medium of radio is more important than the message content in creating Hitler. But if one contrast may be made between McLuhan, Horkheimer and Adorno in these two passages, it could be between the lack of moral tone in the former and the strong moral condemnation lacing the latter. This may indicate the larger contrast noted by Brantlinger that Horkheimer and Adorno condemned mass communication as non-communication while McLuhan cheerfully welcomed the new media.

Yet despite the seeming moral differences, the content of the two passages is similar. More important, a reading of the deeper social process observed by Horkheimer and Adorno concerning the dialectic of Enlightenment, although interpreted from a different moral ground, matches McLuhan's process in what McLuhan would have called the dialectic of visual culture, or the dialectic of the Gutenberg Galaxy.

The task Horkheimer and Adorno set out was

> nothing less than the discovery why mankind, instead of entering into a truly human condition, is sinking into a new kind of barbarism... [I]n the present collapse of bourgeois civilization not only the pursuit but the meaning of science has become problematical.[73]

In this excerpt, the new barbarism is a reminder of McLuhan's "retribalization" and the questioning of science echoes McLuhan's doubt that scientific method could exceed its historical environment.

Horkheimer and Adorno continued:

The dilemma that faced us in our work proved to be the first phenomenon for investigation: the self-destruction of the Enlightenment. We are wholly convinced ... that social freedom is inseparable from enlightened thought. Nevertheless, we believe that we have just as clearly recognized that the notion of this very way of thinking, no less than the actual historical forms—the social institutions—with which it is interwoven, already contains the seed of reversal universally apparent today.[74]

Here "bourgeois civilization" is equated with the Enlightenment, which is destroying itself. Without enlightenment, however, the authors' values cannot exist. McLuhan, by contrast, posited that the new barbarism will create its own values, which are perhaps like the superior values of oral culture. Whatever the outcome of this area of disagreement, McLuhan, Horkheimer and Adorno agree that a way of thinking and living is passing in a process of reversal.

Technology fits into this primary phenomenon as a dialectic of "social progress" and the "fallen nature of modern man." Material productivity offers the conditions for "a world of greater justice," but allows a minority to control and administer the technology, while most people are devalued.[75] The authors described their theses as: Myth is already enlightenment and enlightenment reverts to mythology. The role of the "culture industry" or the new media, is to aid the regression of enlightenment into myth and ideology.[76]

Beginning in ancient Greece, the goals of enlightenment were the end of human fear, the establishment of sovereignty, the "disenchantment of the world, the dissolution of myths and the substitution of knowledge for fancy."[77] The Enlightenment identified anthropomorphism—the projection of subjectivity onto nature—as the principle of myth.

In this view, the supernatural, spirits and demons, are mirror images of men who allow themselves to be frightened by natural phenomena... "It is man!" is the Enlightenment stereotype repeatedly offered as information, irrespective of whether it is faced with a piece of objective intelligence, a bare schematization, fear of evil powers, or hope of redemption.[78]

McLuhan described the same process, when man traded an eye for an ear and left the dark terror of acoustic space armed with the logical, rational, empirical alphabet to create three thousand years of enlightenment.[79] Horkheimer and Adorno did not attribute a cause to the emergence of enlightenment from myth. Certainly they did not attribute it to the alphabet. They did agree, however, that the transition occurred between the pre-Socratic cosmologies and the absorption of the Olympic gods in Plato's logos.[80] Enlightenment, however, is equally dialectic in an admixture of positive and negative; science lacks some of the advantages of myth and magic.

> Myth turns into enlightenment, and nature into mere objectivity. Men pay for the increase of their power with alienation from that over which they exercise their power. Enlightenment behaves toward things as a dictator toward men. He knows them insofar as he can manipulate them.[81]

The authors contended that the enlightenment reverts into mythology because it is a totalitarian system. "For enlightenment, the process is always decided from the start."[82] The return to myth is the result of enlightenment's confounding of truth and thought with mathematics, so that mathematics is made into an absolute.

> Nature, before and after the quantum theory, is that which is to be comprehended mathematically; even that which cannot be made to agree, indissolubility and irrationality, is converted by means of mathematical theorems... Thinking objectifies itself to become an automatic, self-activating process; an impersonation of the machine that it produces itself so that ultimately the machine can replace it. Enlightenment has put aside the classic requirement of thinking about thought... Mathematical procedure became, so to speak, the ritual of thinking... [It] turns thought into a thing, an instrument which is its own term for it.[83]

With the medium of number, cognition and thought are turned into repetition and tautology. They argued that

> The more the machinery of thought subjects existence to itself, the more blind its resignation in reproducing existence. Hence enlightenment returns to mythology, which it never really knew how to elude. For in its figures mythology had the essence of the status quo: cycle, fate, and domination of the

world reflected as the truth and deprived of hope... The world as a gigantic analytic judgment, the only one left over from all the dreams of science, is of the same mold as the cosmic myth which associated the cycle of spring and autumn with the kidnapping of Persephone.[84]

The reversal from enlightenment to myth is not propelled by media extensions any more than the reversal from myth to enlightenment. Other than linking radio to the rise of Hitler and fascism, the authors treated electronic media as without redeeming value as agents of domination in mass culture:

Modern communications media have an isolating effect... The lying words of the radio announcer become firmly imprinted on the brain and prevent men from speaking to each other; the advertising slogans for Pepsi-Cola sound out above the collapse of continents; the example of movie stars encourages young children to experiment with sex and later leads to broken marriages. Progress literally keeps men apart.[85]

The unremitting gloom is in stark contrast to McLuhan's retribalization. The electronic media of Horkheimer and Adorno do not revive the mythology of the old barbarism, but seem to extend the domination of nature that was the goal of the enlightenment, only in nightmare fashion.

Despite these contradictions, the overall cyclic movement of history from myth to reason, and its return to myth, is shared by McLuhan, Horkheimer, and Adorno—in other words, the operation of dialectics. It should be noted, however, that political theory scholar Patrick Peritore cites Adorno's "negative dialectics" as non-dialectical, and argues against a philosophy of dialectics. In the final chapters, McLuhan's place in communication research will be assessed in light of this methodological study. A place will be sought for McLuhan on the critical theory side of the paradigm, amid conflicts between administrative and critical communications research. First, the understanding of McLuhan by cultural studies and postmodernist scholars will be addressed.

NOTES

1. Scott Warren, *The Emergence of Dialectical Theory: Philosophy and Political Inquiry* (Chicago: University of Chicago Press, 1984), 145.
2. Ibid., 146.
3. Ibid., 152.
4. Ibid., 154.
5. Ibid., 156-157.
6. Patrick Brantlinger, *Bread and Circuses: Theories of Mass Culture as Social Decay* (Ithaca, NY: Cornell University Press, 1983), 223.
7. Ibid., 228.
8. Ibid., 230-234.
9. Ibid., 235-237.
10. Ibid., 244-247.
11. Ibid., 238-240.
12. Judith Stamps, *Unthinking Modernity: Innis, McLuhan and the Frankfurt School* (Montréal: McGill-Queen's University Press, 1995), 134.
13. Ibid., 18, 19.
14. Ibid., 20-21.
15. Ibid., 154-167.
16. James Carey, "Walter Benjamin, Marshall McLuhan, and the Emergence of Visual Society," *Prospects: An Annual of American Cultural Studies* 12 (1987): 29-38; Pamela McCallum, "Walter Benjamin and Marshall McLuhan: Theories of History," *Signature: A Journal of Theory and Canadian Literature* 1, no. 1 (1989): 71-89; Judith Stamps, "The Bias of Theory: A Critique of Pamela McCallum's 'Walter Benjamin and Marshall McLuhan: Theories of History,'" *Signature: A Journal of Theory and Canadian Literature* 1, no. 3 (1990): 44-62; Stamps, *Unthinking Modernity*. Paul Grosswiler, "A Dialectical Synthesis of Marshall McLuhan and Critical Theory," (paper presented at the annual meeting of the International Communication Association, Chicago, Ill., May 1991); Paul Grosswiler, "The Dialectical Methods of Marshall McLuhan, Marxism, and Critical Theory," *Canadian Journal of Communication* 21, no. 1 (1996): 95-124.
17. Carey, "Visual Society," 29.
18. Ibid., 34-35.
19. Ibid., 36.
20. Ibid., 37.
21. McCallum, "Theories of History," 71.
22. Ibid., 74-75.
23. Ibid., 78.
24. Ibid., 79.
25. Ibid., 82-83.
26. Ibid., 85.
27. Ibid., 86.
28. Stamps, "Bias of Theory," 44-62.
29. Ibid., 50.
30. Ibid., 51.
31. Ibid., 52-53.
32. Ibid., 54-57.
33. Ibid., 55.

34. Ibid., 57, 59-61.
35. Walter Benjamin, "The Work of Art in the Age of Mechanical Reproduction," in *Illuminations*, ed. Hannah Arendt, trans. Harry Zohn (New York: Schocken Books, 1969), 218.
36. Ibid., 219-220.
37. Ibid., 220-221.
38. McLuhan, *Understanding Media*, 19.
39. Benjamin, "Work of Art," 222.
40. McLuhan, *Understanding Media*, 33.
41. Scott Warren, *The Emergence of Dialectical Theory: Philosophy and Political Inquiry* (Chicago: University of Chicago Press, 1984), 108.
42. Benjamin, "Work of Art," 223.
43. McLuhan, *Understanding Media*, 104-105.
44. Ibid., 20, 46.
45. Benjamin, "Work of Art," 223-225.
46. Ibid., 226-227.
47. Ibid., 228.
48 McLuhan, *Understanding Media*, 27-28, 60-61, 249-251.
49. Marshall McLuhan, with Quentin Fiore and Jerome Angel, *The Medium is the Massage: An Inventory of Effects* (New York: Bantam, 1967), 123.
50. Benjamin, "Work of Art," 232.
51. Ibid., 233-234.
52. Marshall McLuhan, with Harley Parker, *Through the Vanishing Point: Space in Poetry and Painting* (New York: Harper and Row, 1968), 12-13; McLuhan, *Understanding Media*, 27.
53. Benjamin, "Work of Art," 234.
54. McLuhan, *Understanding Media*, 36-38; 251-257.
55. Ibid., 58.
56. Benjamin, "Work of Art," 236-237.
57. McLuhan, *Understanding Media*, 61-62.
58. Benjamin, "Work of Art," 237.
59. McLuhan, *Understanding Media*, 247.
60. Benjamin, "Work of Art," 239.
61. Ibid., 240.
62. Ibid.
63. McLuhan, *Understanding Media*, 272-273.
64. Hans Enzensberger, *The Consciousness Industry* (New York: Seabury Press, 1974), 116, 120-122.
65. Brantlinger, *Bread and Circuses*, 269.
66. Benjamin, "Work of Art," 218, 241-242.
67. Ibid., 242.
68. McLuhan, *Understanding Media*, 73.
69. Ibid., 265.
70. Ibid., 262.
71. Brantlinger, *Bread and Circuses*, 235-237.
72. Max Horkheimer and Theodor Adorno, *Dialectic of Enlightenment*, trans. John Cumming (New York: Continuum, 1987), 159.
73. Ibid., xi.
74. Ibid., xiii.

75. Ibid., xiv.
76. Ibid., xvi.
77. Ibid., 3.
78. Ibid., 6-7.
79. McLuhan, Fiore and Angel, *Medium is Massage*, 45, 48.
80. Horkheimer and Adorno, *Enlightenment*, 6-7.
81. Ibid., 9.
82. Ibid., 24-25.
83. Ibid., 25.
84. Ibid., 27.
85. Ibid., 221.

McLuhan and Cultural Studies

Rejection of McLuhan Transformed

British cultural studies scholars, in contrast to their predecessors, the Frankfurt theorists, responded to McLuhan's media and social theories in their work. McLuhan did not cite cultural studies research in his own published work, although his published letters included a response to US cultural studies and several references to French semiotician Roland Barthes and French structuralism.[1] One of the founders of British cultural studies, Raymond Williams, set the tone for this research area with his initially ambivalent response to McLuhan, which subsequently turned into a continual and hostile interpretation of his work.[2] Another cultural studies founder, Stuart Hall, followed this interpretation.[3] US cultural studies, reflected in the work of James Carey, also responded to McLuhan negatively, although the initial response was more positive than later assessments.[4] The work of a prominent semiotician, Umberto Eco, also put McLuhan in a negative light early on.[5]

Despite these early developments, as a rapidly evolving and theoretically diverse approach to communication issues, cultural studies has come nearly full circle in its response to McLuhan. Currently, his work is met with a more positive reception.[6] Of these scholars, cultural sociologist John B. Thompson uses the ideas of Harold Innis and McLuhan together to form the three foundations of his study of media and social practices,[7] and British sociologist Nick Stevenson has strongly called for a historical reappraisal of McLuhan.[8] Canadian cultural studies scholar Jody Berland has incorporated McLuhan's spatial analysis into her research on cultural technologies.[9] Another scholar in Canada, John Fekete, has transformed his all-out attack on what he previously termed "McLuhanacy," into a passing acceptance.[10] This chapter will chart this crescendo of negative responses that later reverses itself into a positive reassessment.

Williams Rejects McLuhan

It is a paradox, literary scholar Donald Theall points out, that Cambridge gave rise to both McLuhan's interest in the New Criticism and

Williams' interest in cultural studies. Analyzing culture through the social role of mass media, British cultural studies was strongly committed to a Marxist position and believed it was the only plausible theory around which a new society could be created.[11]

Initially, Williams gave *The Gutenberg Galaxy: The Making of Typographic Man* a mixed review, agreeing with McLuhan's emphasis on the media as a social factor and their effect on perception.[12] Williams thought McLuhan "was ahead of all other scholars in analyzing print culture," but he criticized McLuhan for isolating print as a causal factor in social development. Ironically, Williams accused McLuhan of doing what McLuhan, in his mosaic method, argued that he is avoiding: isolating the media. First, Williams acknowledged that McLuhan recognizes causal factors in history other than the means of communication—which he compared to Marx's focus on capital. Williams advocated exactly what becomes McLuhan's project: to return history to "the whole man" after the nineteenth-century isolation of political and economic factors.

> The study of the relations of culture and communications leads us by sheer weight of evidence to thinking in terms of fields of forces rather than in terms of linear cause and effect. That is to say, the perception of the great importance of print and its institutions commands us not to isolate them, but to return them to the whole field.[13]

McLuhan's mosaic method attempted to provide a field approach, although Williams argued that he failed in this attempt. Despite this, Williams cited McLuhan's "real originality" and called him "one of the very few men capable of significant contribution to the problems of advanced communication theory."[14] And Williams looked forward "with exceptional interest" to the analysis of the changes of the end of print culture which McLuhan promised in a forthcoming book.[15]

However, in later works that respond more globally to McLuhan, Williams completely dismissed him by claiming that he is a technological determinist; which later cultural studies works have tempered. Williams' *Television: Technology and Cultural Form* (1992) is viewed as a response to McLuhan's media and social theories about television. According to a new introduction to the book, television scholar Lynn Spigel points out that Williams, who rarely cited his contemporary scholars, attacked McLuhan for his "ahistorical" formalist analysis of media which prefaces psychic rather than social processes.[16] McLuhan's "technological determinism" reduces everything in history outside of media to an effect and naturalizes capitalist media institutions. In such a system, cultural and political argument and action are pointless. Williams noted that time erased the early interest in McLuhan's attention to differences among speech, print, radio, television and other media.[17]

But by treating media as psychic adjustments rather than human practices, McLuhan made intention and content irrelevant. Media are "desocialized" in an "abstracted sensorium."[18] McLuhan's image of society—the global village for example—was "ludicrous" as a description of existing social states because it elevated instant communication from a technical to a social level, and thus ignored the fact that the electronic media are controlled and shaped by social institutions. By eliminating social controls as a cause in media effects, McLuhan's position made the only possible response to "let the technology run itself."[19] McLuhan's formalism, then, had become social theory and practice "in the heartland of the most dominative and aggressive communications institutions in the world."[20]

Arguing for the "radically different" view that conceives of technology as an effect of the social order,[21] Williams predicted that McLuhan's communication theory would not survive for long, but again returned to him briefly in order to dismiss him as a technological determinist for whom the "medium is (metaphysically) the master" with the power to shape social relationships and content.[22] Williams called such theories reifications of human activity and social practice. Later, according to Spigel, Williams spoke against McLuhan even after he had lost his popularity.[23]

In one of the introductory texts in cultural studies, Williams' view of McLuhan has been taken and completely reduced to the charge of technological determinism leveled in *Television: Technology and Cultural Form*.[24] According to author Graeme Turner, Williams saved his most vehement criticism for the theory that the medium itself has a causal effect on behaviour, its "psychic" effects.

> Consequently, Marshall McLuhan's work is dismissed as "ludicrous" and Williams treats his privileging of technologies of television with contempt: "If the effect of the medium is the same, whoever controls or uses it, and whatever apparent content he may try to insert, then we can forget ordinary political and cultural argument and let the technology run itself."[25]

Another founding scholar of cultural studies, Stuart Hall, also identifies McLuhan as the "precursor-prophet of postmodernism" who
turned away from his critique of new technologies in *The Mechanical
Bride:Folklore of the Industrial Man* toward a "celebration" of "the very
things he had most bitterly attacked. This is a response Hall finds common among postmodernist "ideologues" like Jean Baudrillard.[26]

Carey Rejects McLuhan

US cultural studies also began with a largely negative but mixed
assessment of McLuhan. This is especially evident in the writings of
James Carey, whose later assessment of McLuhan became solely negative. Carey's rejection of McLuhan has been argued to have set the tone
for McLuhan's rejection by US communication scholarship as a whole.[27]
It also appears to have set the tone within the loosely grouped discipline
of US cultural studies, of which Carey is an often-cited proponent.

Implying that McLuhan was a "hard" technological determinist, in
contrast to Innis, whom he calls a "soft determinist," Carey contrasts
the mentor and his disciple by arguing that McLuhan took a minor
theme from Innis—that media affect sensory organization and
thought—and made it his central argument, while ignoring Innis' central argument that media affect social organization and culture.[28]
Carey finds Innis' argument superior to McLuhan's, although he notes
that both theorists treat both psychic and social effects. McLuhan considered media effects on nationalism, science and education.[29] Carey
does not reject the overall argument, but he rejects the making of the
psychology of perception into the mainstay of the theory. His main
criticism of McLuhan has been that his theories and analyses can be
better explained by Innis.[30] However, Carey appears to agree with
McLuhan and disagree with Innis when he analyzes the role of the
media in the 1960s generational conflict. He asserts that the spatial
bias of television and other electronic media has eliminated space, a
claim that seems to oppose McLuhan's contention that electronic
media reverse the spatial bias of print media. Innis argued that film
and radio extend print's spatial bias.[31]

Carey appears even more like McLuhan as he links the generation
gap to the rate of media change:

> The spread of a worldwide urban civilization built upon rapid
> and ephemeral means of communication ultimately mean that
> individuals of the same age in Warsaw, Moscow, Tokyo, and

New York sense a membership in a common age group and feel they have more in common with one another than with individuals older and younger within their own societies.[32]

Carey ultimately embraced Innis' theory that the main effect of media is on social organization, although he was careful to note that the causes of generational conflict include factors other than the media "but to which the media are linked in a syndrome."[33] Despite this, the attack on McLuhan is resolute—noting that his "daring and exquisite insights" are negated by his "style of presentation, his manner, and his method." He casts McLuhan as a "poet of technology" who offers a "secular prayer to technology," and who represents a "secularized, religious determinism."[34]

Carey's reading of McLuhan appears to harden over time, despite the fact that McLuhan wrote to him in 1974 to disavow being a technological utopian who was "for or against" the media structures he was studying.[35] Yet it is Carey's reading of McLuhan as a celebrant of technological determinism that is used as the framework by cultural studies scholars and other contemporary communication theorists who continue to comment on McLuhan.[36]

Semiotics Rejects McLuhan

Semiotic analysis, often applied in cultural studies, would be expected to be hostile to McLuhan and Innis, as well as other formalists, because semiotics focuses on individual and social decoding of media content. Semiotics' hostility to McLuhan was evident early on. Writing in the 1960s, Umberto Eco called McLuhan an "apocalyptic" who implies that the "mass media do not transmit ideologies; they are themselves an ideology."[37] The content becomes irrelevant because it is the constant immersion in messages that erode different contents and strip them of meaning. Eco suggested that this position leads to "tragic consequences" as the audience member receives only a "global ideological lesson, the call to narcotic passiveness. When the mass media triumph, the human being dies."[38] Eco disagreed vehemently with McLuhan's position that, as Eco put it, "when the mass media triumph, the Gutenbergian human being dies, and a new man is born, accustomed to perceive the world in another way."[39]

Echoing Williams' interest in political action, Eco offered a "guerrilla solution" if activists cannot gain control of the source and the channel. This solution involves groups communicating outside of the mass media that receive messages and discuss them in terms of the codes of the addressee and the codes of the source.[40] The focus is on the interpretation of messages:

> The battle for the survival of man as a responsible being in the Communications Era is not to be won where the communication originates, but where it arrives… I am proposing an action to urge the audience to control the message and its multiple possibilities of interpretation.[41]

According to Eco, scholars and educators should "fight a door-to-door guerrilla battle" as the "only salvation for free people."[42] These "communications guerrillas" would restore a critical response to McLuhan's passive reception, at which point "the threat that 'the medium is the message' could then become, for both medium and message, the return to individual responsibility."[43]

On a more technical level, Eco argued against the idea that "the medium is the message" based on the "residual freedom" of the audience to "to read it in a different way."[44] Detailing the mechanics of communication, Eco elaborated on the "communication chain" that includes the source, the transmitter, the signal, the channel, and the receiver who transforms the signal into a message for the addressee. This process requires a shared code between the source and the addressee.

At the heart of the argument, Eco charged McLuhan with overlooking the various links in the chain, and using the term "media" to mean at times channel, code or the form of the message. Eco argued that calling the alphabet and the street "media" mixes a code with a channel. Light can also be many things, but not a medium:

> To say that light is a medium is a refusal to realize that there are at least three definitions of "light." Light can be a Signal of information (I use electricity to transmit impulses that, in Morse code, mean particular messages); light can be a Message (if my girlfriend puts a light in the window, it means her husband has gone out); and light can be a Channel (if I have the light on in my room I can read the message-book.)[45]

Eco further attacks McLuhan's terms and definitions. He first stated that McLuhan was wrong in arguing that media are metaphors that translate experience into new forms. Instead, he asserted that a medium translates experience into new forms because it carries a code. A metaphor, by contrast, is a substitute term for another term within one code. Thus for Eco, the problem rests on the confusion over the definition of "medium," which McLuhan claimed can be used to describe extensions of the body, but which also as confuses channels, codes and messages. The formula that "the medium is the message" proves ambiguous and contradictory.[46] Eco offered several alternative formulas:

(1) The *form* of the message is the real content of the message (which is the thesis of avant-garde literature and criticism);

(2) The *code,* that is to say, the structure of the language ... is the message (which is the famous anthropological thesis of Benjamin Lee Whorf...);

(3) The *channel* is the message (that is, the physical means chosen to convey the information determines either the form of the message, or its contents ... (which is a familiar idea in aesthetics ...)

All these formulas show that it is not true, as McLuhan states, that scholars of information have considered only the content of information without bothering about formal problems.[47]

In this analysis, McLuhan wasn't presenting a useful, or even a new theory. In contrast, it would be useful to understand whether technology is imposing changes in the channel, code, messages or receivers. In challenging McLuhan's thesis Eco offered a different proposition: "The medium is not the message; the message becomes what the receiver makes of it, applying to it his own codes of reception, which are neither those of the sender nor those of the scholar of communications."[48]

In addition to muddling links in the communication chain, Eco also charged McLuhan with ignoring "discordant interpretations," which he called the "constant law of mass communications," as messages are sent to diverse social situations where diverse codes are applied.[49] Yet even adapting "the medium is the message" to the "message depends on the code" does not, for Eco, solve the problem because of the variability of interpretation. Even if television transmits the ideology of advanced capitalism, the "addressee" receives the ideology according to his or her social situation, education, and mood.[50]

Eco also argued that McLuhan's mosaic method undermined his own thesis. Because McLuhan is writing a book, he cannot help but present logical proofs of his "affirmations" and oppositions, which are to him "co-presence" rather than "contradiction," and which lead him back to rational, linear thought.[51] According to Eco, if McLuhan is arguing for a total and radically new dimension of thought, then books can no longer be written. Instead, the problem is to integrate these "new dimensions of intellect and sensibility" with existing media, the book. The critic, as a moderator, must translate the global reach of communication into the language of a "Gutenbergian rationality, specialized and linear."[52]

Eco playfully noted that McLuhan offers some benefit, "as there is in banana smokers and hippies," and poked fun at McLuhan by saying that his "perpetual intellectual erection" led him from the "plane of heuristic happiness," where he asserted the disappearance of linear thinking, to the "realm of the imponderable," where he speculated on the disappearance of vertical lines in nylon stockings.[53]

With the leading scholars of critical cultural approaches to communication and mainstream communication research in the United States in line against McLuhan, it is somewhat remarkable that his theories, as well as his name, have crept slowly back into cultural studies. Attempts to recover McLuhan have moved from the invisible to the more tentative, and have culminated in the more recent appearance of several extensive efforts to reclaim McLuhan for cultural studies.

McLuhan Reappears in Cultural Studies

After McLuhan was summarily rejected by one of the founding members of British cultural studies, in addition to the scholars most associated with US cultural studies, as well as those studying semiotics, it is no surprise that the label of "technological determinism" continued to tarnish McLuhan's theories. This is true even as cultural studies has evolved in Britain and Europe, Australia and North America, and even as McLuhan's general concepts found their way into cultural studies through the work of scholars such as John Fiske.[54] More recently, cultural studies has begun to reassess McLuhan more openly, especially in Europe,[55] Australia,[56] and Canada,[57] as well as the United States.[58] Even one of his harshest critics in Canada, John Fekete, has partially rehabilitated McLuhan.[59]

Fiske employed humanities scholar Walter Ong's orality-literacy typology (which was also adapted by historian Donald Lowe) to his study of television, arguing that television is an oral medium, which makes it different from film. The oral mode is dramatic, episodic, mosaic, dynamic, active, concrete, ephemeral and social—all terms analyzed in formal terms by McLuhan, as well as Ong. The literate mode is narrative, sequential, linear, static, permanent and individual—again, a category resembling those of McLuhan. Fiske suggested that television's textual forms are oral, and viewers who enter television's dialogue treat it as oral.[60]

Even more similarly to McLuhan, Fiske found that within the oral form of television, programs tend toward more literate or oral content. *Magnum, P. I.*, for example, represents male-bonding action adventure in social roles identified with the literate mode.[61] In contrast, *Max Headroom* is an example of television reality in the program itself— Max is a true television character.[62] Fiske did not cite McLuhan in terms of the general typology, or in terms of Max Headroom—whom McLuhan also has called a "discarnate man" because satellites and computers put the audience in Max's position as one "who could orig- inate anywhere in the net system and trace his 'location' faster than he can be traced."[63]

Beyond unattributed adaptation, this reassessment of McLuhan can be seen in literary scholar Patrick Brantlinger's juxtaposition of McLuhan with Williams. Brantlinger asserted that "Williams seems to be expressing a version of technological determinism qua utopianism like Marshall McLuhan, whose theories Williams explicitly repudi- ates."[64] Also, Williams' view of communication as a cure for history's ills "seems to land in just the sort of facile optimism that ... Williams himself accuses McLuhan of expressing."[65] In contrast, though, Williams found communication to have an emancipatory potential, but without the "simplistic optimism" of McLuhan's technological deter- minism, and he viewed all social practices as language-based, as opposed to McLuhan's "media mystique."[66] Brantlinger also connects McLuhan to postmodernist Baudrillard, saying that Baudrillard has fol- lowed "his mentor" from a cultural critique of media to become "one of its celebrants and high priests," although he also adds that Baudrillard is a "pessimistic inversion" of McLuhan.[67]

While this comparison is without the exposition that Brantlinger offers between McLuhan and the Frankfurt School theorists, it does bring McLuhan and one of the founders of cultural studies under the same rubric of optimistic determinism. However, it offers no new read- ings of McLuhan to counteract the label that has followed him for almost thirty years. Brantlinger's linking of McLuhan and Williams within the same family is a step along the way to John Hartley's inclu- sion of McLuhan as an "institutional ancestor" of cultural studies. Williams, of course is one of the founders of British cultural studies, but in North America the names are different: "Harold Innes [*sic*] and

Marshall McLuhan would figure in any Canadian genealogy."[68] Although Hartley mentioned neither Innis nor McLuhan again, merely including McLuhan as a cultural studies progenitor is a step toward recognition.

In the works of media studies scholar Roger Silverstone and communications scholar Ien Ang, McLuhan's stature has grown but he still remains a minor intellectual player in their thinking. Discussing the place of television "reach" in the construct of the home, Silverstone comments on communications scholar Joshua Meyrowitz's theories of the changes wrought by electronic media, and in particular those changes attributable to television.[69] He notes that Meyrowitz's arguments involve McLuhan's idea of the global village, although the conclusions reached by both theorists are criticized as excessive and erroneous. Both Meyrowitz and McLuhan address media effects, but the "scale of the generalizations and profligacy of the conclusions" are unacceptable because greater media "reach" does not necessarily mean greater control. Also challenged are the claims that television can shift "deeply engrained values and habits." Silverstone argues that such a position contains "elements of plausibility" but is "untenable as it stands."[70]

After this qualified response to McLuhan, Silverstone credits McLuhan for identifying the technical media system as a global village. The convergence of electronic and computer media "are offering the promise (or the threat) of an integrated information and communication environment through which McLuhan's vision of the global village may yet become a reality."[71] In a discussion of McLuhan, Innis, Meyrowitz, and Ong in terms of technological determinations of media globalization, Silverstone calls these "contentious" theories "highly suggestive," but notes that many of them ignore social and cultural influences.[72] He asserts that the four theorists insist that media transform "human sensibilities and social structures" in an unqualified way. Silverstone finds this thesis intriguing yet misguided.

> McLuhan's infamous (and actually often misunderstood) catchall, "the medium is the message," acts now more as a symptom of a misguided generalization—of how not to think about the media—than as a statement which has any serious claim to empirical relevance. Yet the potential, a potential often, if not always evenly, realized, of media to reach down to the roots of social life and individual psychology is...not so easily dismissed. Nor is this potential, even in these accounts,

always pursued in isolation from a consideration of the political and economic context in which the technologies emerge and on which they are argued to have such powerful effects.[73]

Silverstone also considers whether electronic media differ in their biases to print—as McLuhan and Meyrowitz believed—or whether electronic media extend a spatial, imperial bias, as Innis suggested. Silverstone takes a dialectical stance to this question, similar to that of McLuhan, Meyrowitz, and Ong:

> Maybe one would need to see the emergence of electronic technologies as offering a new synthesis: operating within deeply entrenched political and economic systems, but acting in a number of different ways to shift the balances within contemporary culture away from the more or less clearly defined stabilities of a print-based society towards a new kind of orality, powerful in its implications, above all insofar as it affects the basic character of communication in the modern world.[74]

Silverstone acknowledges only Ong as holding this view, but a closer reading of McLuhan's dialectical theory shows a similarly complex process. Silverstone also extends the misconception that McLuhan, as a determinist, argued that the audience was an effect of the medium. Technology based theories of communication, particularly McLuhan's and Ong's, assert that television's power stems from technological characteristics that generate an "intrusive environment—an electronic space—which is universal and irreversible in its consequences."[75] Silverstone finds Ong's version of this argument more subtle. He argues that this type of theory can be viewed as technological determinism, or it can be read as if new demands are made by new technologies on senders and receivers.[76] Although Silverstone criticizes this theory for leaving out audiences, he does find it has value for describing "imperceptible but cumulative and fundamental changes" that occur between the audience and the media:

> They take place as a result of a more or less total immersion in a technologically shifted and shifting culture. When we talk about the influence of television and other media in our everyday lives, this is an important dimension, one often overlooked by empirical investigations ... or misunderstood.[77]

Silverstone also connects McLuhan's theories to Baudrillard, who offered a "post-McLuhan critique of the effect of electronic technologies on culture."[78] Baudrillard reformulates McLuhan's analysis of the effects of electronic media on social and psychic life. For Baudrillard the rise of television introduced a form of reproduction that he called "simulation," leading to a collapse between media and reality, and the arrival of postmodernism. This critique, Silverstone contends, shares an analysis but not an evaluation with McLuhan, because Baudrillard is pessimistic rather than optimistic. Baudrillard shares both an analysis and evaluation with the Frankfurt School.[79]

The connection between McLuhan, cultural studies and postmodernist thought is more fully illustrated in the work of Ien Ang, who posited the "global village" as a metaphor describing capitalist postmodernity.[80] Ang notes that the usual assumption underlying the metaphor is that world progress takes place through communication. She then describes a dialectical media universe that resembles McLuhan's: "In other words, the global village, as the site of the culture of capitalist postmodernity, is a thoroughly paradoxical place, unified yet multiple, totalized yet deeply unstable, closed and open at the same time."[81]

Citing Carey's critique of transmission models of communication, which are models McLuhan also strongly opposed, Ang followed Carey's projection of Innis' notion that modern capitalist culture is "space-binding." Ang does not differentiate between the analyses of electronic culture of Innis, Carey, and McLuhan:

> McLuhan's "global village," a world turned into a single community through the annihilation of space and time, represents nothing other than (the fantasy of) the universal culmination of capitalist modernity ...the making of the "global village" can be rewritten as the transformation, or domestication, of the non-Western Other in the name of capitalist modernity, the civilization which was presumed to be the universal destiny of humankind: global spatial integration is equated with global social and cultural integration.[82]

Ang argued dialectically from Baudrillard's focus on the fundamental failure of communication in contemporary culture and called for an inversion of the emphasis of communication theory to focus on meaningful communication as the basis for the global village.

This theoretical inversion, which is one of the tenets of post-structuralist theorizing, allows us to understand the global village not as a representation of a finished, universalized, capitalist modernity characterized by certainty of order and meaning, but as a totalized yet fundamentally dispersed world-system of capitalist postmodernity characterized by radical uncertainty, radical indeterminacy of meaning.[83]

This description, which forms the basis of Ang's critical theory, strikes a chord with McLuhan's analysis of electronic media culture because it threatens capitalism and modernism. Other postmodernists who are not also identified as cultural studies theorists have taken up this theme vis a vis McLuhan, but those arguments will be addressed in the next chapter.

Saving the Baby From the Bath Water

Even as McLuhan's theories and ideas are incorporated into cultural studies analyses, he is still understood within these cultural studies analyses through the original critiques of Williams or Carey. Moving beyond this label of technological determinism, the analyses of Innis and McLuhan make up one of three foundations used by cultural sociologist John B. Thompson,[84] and an entirely new reading of McLuhan has been undertaken in British cultural studies by Nick Stevenson.[85]

Analyzing the ways media have changed social interaction and experience in modern societies, Thompson credits McLuhan and Innis for emphasizing the effects of media forms on social interaction.

These theorists argued, rightly in my view, that different technical media help to create different environments for action and interaction; they argued that the form of the medium itself, quite apart from the specific content of the messages it conveys, has an impact on the nature of social life.[86]

Thompson finds the theme more interesting than the ways McLuhan and Innis develop it, casting his doubts on Innis' idea of communication bias. Rather than pursue the broad conclusions drawn by Innis and McLuhan, Thompson examines how technical media have "transformed the nature of social interaction, have created new contexts for action and interaction and new arenas for self-presentation and the perception of others." Focusing on television, Thompson describes the impact of media on interaction across time and space. He looks at the ways individuals act "for" and "in response" to others who are distant, and the ways that media affect social organization in everyday life.[87]

Stevenson's exploration of the relationship between mass communication and social theory boldly calls for a re-evaluation of McLuhan to appraise both his contributions and his shortcomings:

> I am to move against the grain of his most vocal detractors and forcibly suggest that his work be critically re-evaluated by students of the media. I will defend a version of McLuhan's writing that does not rest well with culturalism or postmodernism: that McLuhan's emphasis on technical media is important for distinguishing between different modes of cultural transmission (oral, literate, electric) and that these media structurate intersubjective social relations.[88]

Stevenson argues that McLuhan and social philosopher Jurgen Habermas were the only theorists to consider the impact of media other than television. In this regard, he noted that social theory neglected the importance of the media until the television age was well under way.[89] Looking at theories that focus on the technological means of communication as one of three paradigms of communication research—in addition to critical approaches of British Marxism and the Frankfurt School, and audience research—Stevenson suggests that McLuhan's "distinctive analysis" has been neglected by social theorists. Three of McLuhan's ideas, including implosion, hybridity and time and space restructuring, offer a substantial contribution to social theory.[90]

McLuhan is also seen as paving the way for postmodernism in the work of Baudrillard and literary scholar Fredric Jameson. Stevenson mentions Baudrillard and McLuhan together several times, as though their theories were identical, diverging mainly in McLuhan's "optimism" and Baudrillard's "pessimistic reading."[91] Stevenson argues that both contend that instant communication has made the public sphere obsolete; that the move from print to electronic culture is a factor in this change; and that individuals are unable to critically reflect on this media-induced change.[92] Further, the concept of implosion in the work of Baudrillard and McLuhan is identified as a postmodern idea worthwhile for its descriptiveness. Media cultures do reverse modernity's processes of specialization, and the increasing speed of media events, commercialization and political imagery all change "our perception of the real." In criticism, however, McLuhan and Baudrillard both abstract the media from their social and economic context, as well as neglect the ability of the audience to make meaning.[93]

In his richly textured analysis of McLuhan, Stevenson offers this historical summation:

> The radical impact of new forms of communication upon the dimensions of space, time and human perception are the dominant motifs of Marshall McLuhan. His work was, initially at least, widely recognized as articulating some of the most profound changes that the new media technologies were ushering in. But although McLuhan made an initial impact in the early 1960s ... he currently has few followers or admirers... In cultural and media studies, his ideas were at first warmly welcomed as making a major breakthrough in articulating some of the dimensions of the emergent electric culture. But the bubble of enthusiasm was soon to burst, and McLuhan's propositions were widely dismissed as exhibiting a form of technological determinism.[94]

Stevenson rephrases "the medium is the message" nearly as awkwardly as art historian Arnold Hauser, calling it "the provocative thesis that the most important aspect of media is not to be located within issues connected to cultural content, but in the technical medium of communication."[95] In *The Mechanical Bride,* Stevenson found McLuhan critical of media manipulation and control in a critique similar to that of Williams and the early Frankfurt School. This "critical-literary disposition," however, was abandoned for a "more celebrative mode" that eschews "cultural content."[96]

Despite a minor misinterpretation Stevenson stated that McLuhan does not view modern technologies as "alienating"[97]—the connection of McLuhan to critical, cultural, and postmodern theorists is strongly made. For example, Stevenson links McLuhan to Michel Foucault and feminism, comparing his claim of the ubiquity of media to theirs of the ubiquity of power.[98] Stevenson also makes the important observation that McLuhan argues that media audiences determine content, not media producers.[99] The audience's need for participation shapes the mass communication process as space, time, and ownership become irrelevant and audiences are able to "travel through time and space" without leaving home.[100] This leads Stevenson to a discussion of what he identified as one of McLuhan's main themes: implosion, in which "cultural hierarchies" and public and private spheres have merged. In Stevenson's interpretation, "The globe has imploded vertically, temporally and horizontally. McLuhan continues to state that humanity has collapsed on itself, returning to the village-like state characteristic of oral societies."[101]

Stevenson also emphasizes McLuhan's concept of hybrid media or "hybridized cultural forms."[102] This concept favours "spatial constellations" rather than "linear patterns of development," enabling researchers to study media effects on other media. As McLuhan "fruitfully suggests," a medium's historical development should be compared to other types of cultural production.[103] This shows a clear appreciation of McLuhan's mosaic or field approach.

Stevenson saw the media in a way similar to McLuhan's use of the maelstrom as a metaphor for media effects. But for Stevenson, the media are less like a maelstrom than "like a hurricane that has torn apart stable relations of time and space, while the hybridized and imploded culture of post-literate societies are continually shifting the contours of modern experience."[104]

Stevenson also works through the rejection of McLuhan in media and cultural studies as he argues for the need in media and social theory to discuss the issues of time and space in terms of media effects. He rebuts two critiques that propose reasons for rejecting McLuhan. The first criticism is Williams' claim that McLuhan's technological determinism naturalizes the current state of media institutions, which "desocializes" media analysis.[105] According to Stevenson, author Sidney Finkelstein, sociologist Tom Nairn and Hall repeat this criticism. He also calls Nairn one of McLuhan's sternest critics. But Nairn actually finds much to reclaim in McLuhan.[106] Hall compares McLuhan's uncritical stance to that of French postmodernism, which Hall says has abandoned cultural critique. In the second criticism, Williams and Hall fault McLuhan for insisting that sense ratios are determined by technical rather than linguistic forces.[107]

Although these two charges have substance, Stevenson would save McLuhan from abandonment:

> And yet, while all this is true up to a point, I am left with the impression that the baby is being thrown out with the bathwater. While the cultural critics are correct to point to the limitations of McLuhan's analysis, their own concerns also contain certain allusions. Critical analysis within mass communication—since McLuhan—has paid very little attention to those

questions which could be deemed central to his engagement. This might, for the sake of convenience, be compressed into a single question: How has the development of the media of communication reshaped the perceptions of time and space within contemporary society? This issue, under charges of technological determinism, has been dismissed from mainstream cultural theory. The way McLuhan addresses these issues is certainly open to question, and in this respect the charges of technological determinism carry a good deal of force. Yet I would argue, along with Carey (1989), Meyrowitz (1985) and J. B. Thompson (1990), that cultural media, regardless of their actual content, have had a radical impact on the nature of social life. The above authors, like McLuhan, argue that media of communication restructure time and space and thereby help shape intersubjective social relations. In this way, viewed less deterministically than McLuhan often presented himself, his writing remains full of insight.[108]

Offering his own view of McLuhan, Stevenson identifies four critical points: McLuhan's misleading analysis on the nature of time and space; the dialectic of unification and fragmentation in the media; the ways media can be used for social control; and McLuhan's relevance for the future of public space.[109] In Stevenson's analysis, McLuhan argued that electronic media have destroyed time and space constructs, which he called "essentialistic and highly exaggerated."[110] In rebuttal, I would argue that McLuhan took a more comprehensive, historical view that media shape time and space, or change the experience of time and space. In his third point, Stevenson cautions against McLuhan's optimism about the democratizing potential of electronic media, noting Foucault's notion of disciplinary power, which can be adapted to the media in much the same way as those of historian Mark Poster can be.[111] In minor disagreement with this view, I would suggest that McLuhan felt that the effects of electronic media were neither inherently good or bad, although he did link democracy to the influence of print culture rather than electronic culture. Stevenson's fourth point credits McLuhan with drawing attention to the relationship of media to the public sphere, suggesting that the global media provide new possibilities and dangers for public space.[112]

In the point about dialectics and the overview of McLuhan's analysis, Stevenson argues that the effects of television to promote democracy and erode hierarchy would "best be represented through a dialectic of unification and fragmentation." As an example, Stevenson mentions how the marketing strategies of toy makers affect children, or are resisted by both children and parents. A dialectical method would help "develop some of the more fruitful insights" of McLuhan.[113] Children, he notes, use television to become familiar with the adult world, but they are also a crucial market for manufacturers. Stevenson does not recognize that McLuhan's media, social and political analysis is dialectical, and therefore conforms with Stevenson's own suggestion that the dialectic should be expanded beyond media and individuals to include social, economic and political groups.

In summary, Stevenson finds that McLuhan "continues to offer challenging perspectives to those who are concerned to map out the contours of our culture."[114]

> McLuhan's analysis retains a contemporary relevance by introducing issues of space and time, implosion, and hybridity into media studies. His writing, emerging out of the context of Canadian social theory, has often been dismissed under charges of technological determinism and political conservatism. These arguments carry a good deal of analytic bite, but have been overstated by the supporting literature. McLuhan's contribution ... remains suggestive as to how media of communication have played a central part in the development of modernity... Despite the limitations of McLuhan's approach, supporters of future more democratic cultures will need to reconsider the implications of the changing technological landscape for the future of the public sphere.[115]

Canadian Cultural Studies and McLuhan

This reconsideration is well under way in Canadian cultural studies, and includes the work of Jody Berland, David Crowley and David Mitchell. Even longtime and fierce McLuhan critic John Fekete has reclaimed something of McLuhan in his recent writing. Berland argues that social theorists—except for Innis and thinkers influenced by him—have long thought of space as "static and secondary" as a cultural and social force.[116] Berland notes that recent social theory is challenging this view but it remains the case that for more than four decades since Innis, Canadian communication theory has focused on the media's space and time effects.

She calls the mediation between the production of texts, spaces and listeners of popular music "cultural technologies." In this term, Berland presents popular culture as a mediation between technologies, economics, spaces, and listeners.[117] Drawing on Innis' space-biased media theory and McLuhan's focus on technology, Berland argues that by examining audiences and media effects in terms of technological and social changes, Canadian communication theory diverges from mainstream media research. Mainstream research configures the audience as a group of individuals with different moods, tastes and choices. McLuhan, on the other hand, argued that the media produce "a continuous sensory and spatial reorganization of social life." Broaching the content issue brought up against McLuhan, Berland recognizes that for McLuhan "each new medium adopts the 'content' of its predecessor... Another way of putting this is that cultural hardware precedes software that will constitute its content."[118] The long-misunderstood issue of "the medium is the message" criticism is resolved quite simply.

Berland moves easily between McLuhan's long-rejected theory and the cultural studies founder who charted that rejection, Raymond Williams, by incorporating Williams concept of the "mobile privatization" of modern media.[119] Although Berland is not drawing a comparison, this concept is similar to McLuhan's notion that the media have usurped individual privacy. McLuhan's media dialectic also finds a place in Berland's discussion of the audience's interest in ever-newer technologies and the obsolescence of vinyl records and simple television sets. The older records and sets have become obsolete, which turns their content into art. That art is then retrieved by the new technologies.[120]

Berland notes that this approach to communication theory is distinctly Canadian because of Canada's media and political history, and its dialectic: "These issues reaffirm the paradoxical powers of technology, whose complex effects of emancipation and domination in the (re)formation of marginal political and cultural identities have formed the principle critical object of Canadian communication theory."[121]

One last Canadian cultural studies theorist can help illustrate how McLuhan's ideas, which were held in such high disregard by the branch of communication research with which they had the most in common, rose from complete disfavour to guarded acceptance. Fekete, who coined the term "McLuhanacy" and has been stridently critical of McLuhan,[122] has modified his criticism to paint McLuhan as a harbinger of postmodernism and poststructuralism,[123] and has dropped the critical rejection.[124] Fekete incorporated McLuhan's thinking as he describes the concept of "moral panic":

Anxiety information today travels at electronic speeds—what Marshall McLuhan once called the speed of angels—and creates instantaneous communication and community. A community of electronic panic... Contagion, assisted by our new media, is as much a feature of contemporary panic as delusion. It is clearly possible to live this panic mythically and in depth, as McLuhan also said; indeed, it is nearly impossible not to, given the speed with which it spreads out its patterned net. What people come to share is less and less based on exchange of immediately personal stories, and more and more on mythic participation in a common fate captured in numbers.[125]

Arguing against "numbers" research on violence against women for escalation and expansion of the statistics paradigm, Fekete suggests the academically risky but more productive approach of introducing a new paradigm. "McLuhan calls this the 'reversal of the overheated medium.'"[126] This modern research culture, he argues, works like the detective story from effects back to cause. "McLuhan, Buckminster Fuller, and other visionaries thirty years ago stressed this as an achievement of modern capability. But it clearly has its pathological dimensions as well."[127] He later repeats the theme of living mythically and in depth in speeded-up information, tying the idea to Baudrillard. Finally, Fekete lists McLuhan among a rarefied group, as one of the best contemporary cultural theorists of postmodern, technological culture. These include Barthes, Baudrillard, Heidegger, Nietzche, George Grant, McLuhan, and Arthur Kroker.[128]

Although Fekete's acceptance of McLuhan is done in passing while discussing issues well beyond communication theory and the media, it represents a shift for a staunch critic who called McLuhan "the major bourgeois ideologue of one-dimensional society."[129] The early Fekete argued that McLuhan accepted "the rule of technology, and suppresses the consciousness of alienation by insisting that technology is really ourselves and denying that the objectified praxis has really been alienated from us."[130]

Perhaps it is entering the realm of postmodernism that accounts for the greater acceptance of McLuhan and his theories. After all, postmodernist theorists from Baudrillard to architect Charles Jencks have found much insight in McLuhan that cultural studies has taken decades to begin to see, and is only now doing so through new readings such as Stevenson's and Berland's. The next chapter will explore McLuhan's relationship to postmodernism.

NOTES

1. Marshall McLuhan, *Letters of Marshall McLuhan*, eds. Matie Molinaro, Corinne McLuhan and William Toye (Toronto: Oxford University Press, 1987), 491-492, 506, 529, 539.

2. Raymond Williams, "Paradoxically, If the Book Works It to Some Extent Annihilates Itself," in *McLuhan Hot and Cool*, ed. Gerald E. Stearn (New York: Dial Press, 1967); Raymond Williams, *Television: Technology and Cultural Form* (Hanover, NH, and London: Wesleyan University Press, 1992); Raymond Williams, *The Year 2000* (New York: Pantheon, 1983).

3. Stuart Hall, "On Postmodernism and Articulation: An Interview with Stuart Hall," ed. Lawrence Grossberg, in *Stuart Hall: Critical Dialogues in Cultural Studies*, ed. David Morley and Kuan-Hsing Chen (London: Routledge, 1996), 131-132.

4. James Carey, "Harold Adams Innis and Marshall McLuhan," in *McLuhan: Pro and Con*, ed. Raymond Rosenthal (Baltimore, MD: Penguin, 1968), 270-308; James Carey, "McLuhan and Mumford: The Roots of Modern Media Analysis," *Journal of Communication* 31 (summer 1981): 162-178; James Carey, "Walter Benjamin, Marshall McLuhan, and the Emergence of Visual Society," *Prospects: An Annual of American Cultural Studies* 12 (1987): 29-38; James Carey, "Space, Time, and Communication: A Tribute to Harold Innis," in *Communication As Culture: Essays on Media and Society* (Boston: Unwin Hyman, 1989), 142-172; James Carey, with John J. Quirk, "The Mythos of the Electronic Revolution," in *Communication As Culture: Essays on Media and Society* (Boston: Unwin Hyman, 1989), 113-141.

5. Umberto Eco, *Travels in Hyper Reality*, trans. William Weaver (San Diego: Harvest/Harcourt Brace Jovanovich, 1990).

6. Nick Stevenson, *Understanding Media Cultures: Social Theory and Mass Communication* (London: Sage, 1995), 114-143; John B. Thompson, *Ideology and Modern Culture* (Stanford, CA: Stanford University Press, 1990), 225-226. Jody Berland, "Angels Dancing: Cultural Technologies and the Production of Space," in *Cultural Studies*, ed. Lawrence Grossberg, Cary Nelson, and Paula Treichler (New York: Routledge, 1992), 38-51; John Fekete, *Moral Panic: Biopolitics Rising* (Montréal-Toronto: Robert Davies Publishing, 1994), 16, 33, 38, 39, 336, 337, 355; Ien Ang, "In the Realm of Uncertainty: The Global Village and Capitalist Postmodernity," in *Communication Theory Today*, eds. David Crowley and David Mitchell (Stanford: Stanford University Press, 1994), 193-213; Roger Silverstone, *Television and Everyday Life* (London: Routledge, 1994); John Hartley, *The Politics of Pictures. The Creation of the Public in the Age of Popular Media* (London: Routledge, 1992

7. Thompson, *Ideology*.

8. Stevenson, *Media Cultures*.

9. Berland, "Angels Dancing."

10. John Fekete, "McLuhanacy: Counterrevolution in Cultural Theory," *Telos* 15 (spring 1973): 75-123; Fekete, *Moral Panic*.

11. Donald F. Theall, *Understanding McLuhan: The Medium is the Rear View Mirror* (Montréal: McGill-Queen's University Press, 1971), 18.

12. Williams, "Paradoxically," 188-191.

13. Ibid., 190.

14. Ibid., 190-191.

15. Ibid., 191.

16. Lynn Spigel, introduction to *Television: Technology*, by Williams, xv-xvi.

17. Williams, *Television: Technology*, 121.
18. Ibid.
19. Ibid., 122.
20. Ibid.
21. Ibid.
22. Raymond Williams, *Marxism and Literature* (London: Oxford University Press), 159.
23. Spigel, *Television: Technology*, xvi, citing Raymond Williams, *The Year 2000* (New York: Pantheon, 1983), 142-143.
24. Graeme Turner, *British Cultural Studies: An Introduction* (Boston: Unwin Hyman, 1990).
25. Ibid., 64, citing Williams, *Television: Technology*.
26. Hall, "Interview," 131-132.
27. Liss Jeffrey, "The Heat and the Light: Towards a Reassessment of the Contribution of H. Marshall McLuhan," *Canadian Journal of Communication* 14 (winter 1989): 1-29.
28. Carey, "Harold Adams Innis," in *McLuhan: Pro and Con*, 272, 281.
29. Ibid., 292, 293.
30. Ibid., 296.
31. Ibid., 298.
32. Ibid., 301.
33. Ibid., 299, 302.
34. Ibid., 303-305.
35. McLuhan, *Letters*, 491-492.
36. Ang, "Realm of Uncertainty," 194-195; Mattelart, *Mapping*, 127, 128. Stevenson, *Media Cultures*, 116.
37. Eco, *Hyper Reality*, 136.
38. Ibid., 136-137.
39. Ibid., 137.
40. Ibid., 142.
41. Ibid., 142-143.
42. Ibid., 143.
43. Ibid., 144.
44. Ibid., 138.
45. Ibid., 139.
46. Ibid., 233-234.
47. Ibid., 234-235.
48. Ibid., 235.
49. Ibid., 141.
50. Ibid.
51. Ibid., 230.
52. Ibid., 231.
53. Ibid., 236-237.
54. John Fiske, *Television Culture* (London: Methuen, 1987); John Fiske, "British Cultural Studies," in *Channels of Discourse*, ed. Robert C. Allen (Chapel Hill, NC: University of North Carolina Press, 1987).
55. Thompson, *Ideology*; Silverstone, *Everyday Life*; Stevenson, *Media Cultures*.
56. Hartley, *Politics of Pictures*: Ang, "Realm of Uncertainty."
57. Berland, "Angels Dancing."
58. Patrick Brantlinger, *Crusoe's Footprints: Cultural Studies in Britain and America*, (New York: Routledge, 1990).

59. Fekete, *Moral Panic*, 1994.
60. Fiske, *Television Culture*, 105-107.
61. Fiske, "British," 261-266.
62. Ibid., 252.
63. Marshall McLuhan, with Bruce Powers, *The Global Village: Transformations in World Life and Media in the Twenty-first Century* (New York: Oxford University Press, 1989), 118.
64. Brantlinger, *Crusoe's Footprints*, 55.
65. Ibid., 185.
66. Ibid., 180-183.
67. Ibid., 175.
68. Hartley, *Politics of Pictures*, 17.
69. Silverstone, *Everyday Life*, 29, 30.
70. Ibid., 30.
71. Ibid., 82.
72. Ibid., 92.
73. Ibid., 92-93.
74. Ibid., 94.
75. Ibid., 134.
76. Ibid.., 135.
77. Ibid., 136.
78. Ibid., 112.
79. Ibid., 113, 114.
80. Ang, "Realm of Uncertainty"; Ang, *Living Room Wars: Rethinking Media Audiences for a Postmodern World* (London: Routledge, 1996), 150-180.
81. Ang, "Realm of Uncertainty," 194.
82. Ibid., 195.
83. Ibid., 196.
84. Thompson, *Ideology*.
85. Stevenson, *Media Cultures*.
86. Thompson, *Ideology*, 225.
87. Ibid., 226-227.
88. Ibid., 115.
89. Ibid., 2.
90. Ibid., 5.
91. Ibid., 116.
92. Ibid., 174.
93. Ibid., 185.
94. Ibid., 114-115.
95. Ibid., 117.
96. Ibid., 118.
97. Ibid.
98. Ibid., 121.
99. Ibid., citing McLuhan, *Understanding Media*.
100. Ibid., 122.
101. Ibid., 123.
102. Ibid.
103. Ibid., 124.
104. Ibid.

105. Ibid., 125.
106. Tom Nairn, "McLuhanism: The Myth of Our Time," in *McLuhan; Pro and Con*, ed. Raymond Rosenthal (Baltimore, MD: Penguin, 1968), 140-152.
107. Stevenson, *Media Cultures*, 126.
108. Ibid., 126-127.
109. Ibid., 134.
110. Ibid.
111. Ibid., 138-139.
112. Ibid., 142.
113. Ibid., 138.
114. Ibid., 142.
115. Ibid., 142-143.
116. Berland, "Angels Dancing," 39.
117. Ibid.
118. Ibid., 43.
119. Ibid., 40.
120. Ibid., 46.
121. Ibid., citing Arthur Kroker, *Technology and the Canadian Mind: Innis/McLuhan/Grant* (Montréal: New World Perspectives, 1984).
122. Fekete, "McLuhanacy"; John Fekete, *The Critical Twilight: Explorations in the Ideology of Anglo-American Literary Theory from Eliot to McLuhan* (London: Routledge and Kegan Paul, 1977).
123. John Fekete, ed. *The Structural Allegory: Reconstructive Encounters with the New French Thought* (Minneapolis: University of Minnesota Press, 1984).
124. Fekete, *Moral Panic*.
125. Ibid., 32.
126. Ibid., 38.
127. Ibid., 39.
128. Ibid., 336, 337.
129. Fekete, "McLuhanacy," 121.
130. Ibid., 105.

9
McLuhan and Postmodernism

A Natural Affinity

As several new works in cultural studies rediscover McLuhan's theories and reclaim them for contemporary media and social theory, some postmodernists have consistently regarded McLuhan and his theories with more warmth.[1] Others have applied his theories under others' names.[2] Still, within the postmodern critique, McLuhan often retains the stigma of a technological determinist.[3] Although cultural studies and postmodernism—as well as poststructuralism—are often intertwined in contemporary media and social theory, they have been separated here in order to more lucidly shape the discussion thematically and historically.

In McLuhan's published work, the term postmodernism is not found. His writing discusses none of the prominent postmodernists except to assert that pop-art was non-art, denying art's definition as a special object being inserted in a special space.[4] Yet postmodern thinkers have rallied around, adapted and drawn from McLuhan. This chapter will look at how McLuhan has been incorporated into the work of several postmodernists and will compare McLuhan's media and social theories with elements identified by some postmodernists as essential to the postmodern condition.

Postmodernists themselves disagree about the nature of postmodernism, its origins and its history, but McLuhan and postmodernism appear fused by many critical theorists. Brooding about a decisive, global change—the fading of modernism and the emergence of a postmodern era in the mid-1970s—Fredric Jameson called "MacLuhanism" (*sic*) one of the "straws in the wind" along with postmodern literary and art theory and the rise of computers and information theory, that "seem to confirm the widespread feeling that 'modern times are now over' and that some fundamental divide ... or qualitative leap now separates us decisively from what used to be the new world of the mid-twentieth century."[5] In Jameson's critique, postmodernism coincides with the global multinational capitalism that emerged after World War II, following the "modernism" of the era of monopoly capitalism or imperialism. Postmodernism then, is seen as a cultural "dominant" that affects social arenas beyond those of aesthetics or culture alone.[6]

Professor of Russian James Curtis identifies "McLuhan and other postmodernists" as thinkers who shocked scholars because they considered mass culture an area worthy of serious thought.[7] For Curtis, modernism is equated with art movements of the first half of the twentieth century, while postmodernism, although continuous with modernism, differs in one of several ways by focusing on popular culture.[8] Other postmodernist scholars, such as architect Charles Jencks and philosopher Jean Baudrillard herald McLuhan as a harbinger of postmodernism and both adapt and extend his work. Perhaps the most celebrated and vilified of these is Baudrillard.

More negatively, sociologist Stanley Aronowitz and education scholar Henry Giroux describe McLuhan with the one-dimensional caricature that characterizes so much of cultural studies.[9] Arguing that "radical democracy" and its postmodern discourse have enthralled intellectuals for several decades, Aronowitz and Giroux contend that some of the "new prophets of hyperreality," including McLuhan, envision the computer as a force of individual freedom that obviates the need for political action and the struggle for power as it allows individuals to "create our own worlds, to escape the straitjacket of linear text and to make of thought a collage of insight. In this new world, Marshall McLuhan's most radical fantasy, the global village, is on the brink of realization."[10] Another discussion of postmodern theory addresses McLuhan in reductive terms as the author of a model of "implosion" adopted by Baudrillard, as a strict technological analyst who treats medium as pure medium, and as a technological determinist. This critique was framed within the context of the reproduction and interpretation of his work by Baudrillard.[11]

More positively, historian Mark Poster envisioned his own thesis of the mode of information, in part, as an extension of McLuhan's sensory extension theory[12] although in other works Poster neglects McLuhan.[13] Poster regards McLuhan's notion of the global village as feasible because time and space are no longer restricting the movement of information. The theory itself "has important consequences that call into question the adequacy of existing theories and positions."[14]

However, according to Poster, the notion that "the medium is the message" falls short even though McLuhan's aphorism intimates the mode of information. This is primarily because McLuhan focuses on the individual as a perceiving rather than an interpreting subject. McLuhan, he argues, treats humans as "sensing animals" that are acted upon by the media. Poster believes that his theory of the mode of information goes beyond McLuhan:

> What the mode of information puts into question, however, is not simply the sensory apparatus but the very shape of subjectivity: its relation to the world of objects, its perspective on the world, its location in that world. We are confronted not so much by a change from a "hot" to a "cool" communications medium, or by a reshuffling of the sensoria, as McLuhan thought, but by a generalized destabilization of the subject. In the mode of information the subject is no longer located in a point in absolute time/space, enjoying a physical, fixed vantage point from which rationally to calculate options. Instead it is multiplied by databases, dispersed by computer messaging and conferencing, decontextualized and reidentified by TV ads, dissolved and materialized continuously in the electronic transmission of symbols.[15]

Although claiming to exceed McLuhan, this description of "multiplied" man has much in common with McLuhan's concept of the "discarnate" individual, like Max Headroom, who is nowhere and everywhere. The notion of a subject located in a fixed position from which to think rationally is not McLuhan's electronic culture subjectivity, but his print culture subjectivity. There is little here that McLuhan has not already put forth.

Another misreading of McLuhan concerns Poster's comments on McLuhan's concept of the global village, which, because of distant communications through electronic media, has set up new frameworks of discourse. According to Poster, electronic media do not just "expand" or "multiply" the relationships fostered by oral or print media. He argues that electronic media change the structure and the conditions underlying communication so that while "anyone may talk with anyone else at any time," the words themselves "no longer mean exactly the same thing."[16] This assertion also resembles McLuhan's often criticized position that takes into account the enormousness of the change, and considers the qualitative change in electronic media that shakes individuals to their foundations and which results in profoundly deep shock.

The Method is the Message

As postmodernists vary their readings of McLuhan, descriptions and evaluations of modernism and postmodernism also vary from theorist to theorist. As Jencks notes, even the argument over the definition of "postmodernism" is an example of postmodernism, as no authority is positioned to make a definitive ruling that will go without challenge.[17] Art historian John Walker, contrasting positive and negative responses to the notion of postmodernism, notes that on the positive side postmodernism recognizes a rich diversity and pluralism of cultural styles and forms globally and it accepts a multitude of pasts and embraces tradition and history. It acknowledges that "at any one moment in time various generations are alive" and "the present contains within it a multitude of pasts." Conversely, negative interpretations include "stylistic anarchism," "unhealthy obsession with the past," "a mannerist phase," "shallow and superficial," and "the sign of a divided, decadent society."[18]

Perhaps postmodernism is most easily discussed in relation to modernism, in part because characteristics of both are tied to the media and the mode of communication. Modernism, as examined by art historian Timothy J. Clark and art sociologist Janet Wolff, may be seen as an outgrowth of the influence of photography and mechanical reproduction.[19] Walker offers a thematic typology of modernism as an aesthetic ideology that dominated Western culture for 125 years until its eclipse in the 1960s. He then compares thematic typologies of modernism and postmodernism.

According to Walker, modernism in the arts and mass media has the following elements: first, modernism embraces the new age of machines and technology and develops new forms of expression. Second, modernism completely breaks with the past to advocate the "tradition of the new," which values novelty and originality. Third, modernism rejects decoration and ornamentation, preferring geometric forms that suggest simplicity, uniformity, order and rationality. Fourth, modernism rejects local styles, favouring a single universal style. And fifth, modernism describes itself as art of the future, frequently inspired by socialism. Artists perceive themselves as engineers of a "brave new world."[20]

Walker describes postmodernism in the arts as a "half-way house" between the past and an unclear future. First, postmodernism rejects one universal style in favour of a plurality of styles and hybrids. Next, postmodernism revives historical and traditional styles in quotations and parodies. Third, postmodernism permits ornament and decoration. Fourth, postmodernism values complexity, contradiction and ambiguity while rejecting simplicity, order and rationality; the blending of high and low culture or fine and popular art is favoured in offering multi-layered readings. Finally, postmodernism values references in art to other works.[21]

McLuhan's arts and media theory straddles these categories of modernism and postmodernism. McLuhan was opposed to the modernist desire for a modern style that reflects a new age of technology, but he does embrace a new age of technology in which form determines function rather than form following function. He would also reject the modernists' desire for a "complete break with the past" and the value of novelty and originality. Within his dialectic, the deeper past is always being retrieved as the recent past is being obsolesced. Modernism's values of simplicity, clarity, uniformity, order and rationality quite strongly with McLuhan's concept of visual or typographic culture, a historically bounded culture that is being discontinuously changed by electronic or acoustic culture. Modernism's rejection of national styles in favour of an international style is similar to McLuhan's idea that nationalism has become irrelevant in electronic culture because a global village is being created. He does find, though, that in this global village minority voices are difficult to ignore. The modernist idea that the artist knows best and is producing the art of the future is an idea that McLuhan pursues in calling the artist the "antenna of the race" who is the sole guard against the onslaught of media technology.

McLuhan shared more assumptions and themes of postmodernism. He embraced a "plurality of styles" and "hybrid styles." In fact, McLuhan assumed that the pluralism of acoustic space is textually richer; the whole notion of "hybrids" is central to the creative power of McLuhan's critical media universe. The retrieval of history and tradition, through "retro-style," "quotations," "collage," "recyclings," "parodies" and "pastiches of old styles," is a theme that permeates McLuhan's mosaic thinking, and which is most clearly articulated in *From Cliche to Archetype* and *Through the Vanishing Point: Space in Poetry and Painting* (1968). Another strongly stated postmodern theme in McLuhan's work is the value of "complexity and contradiction," as well as ambiguity, which replace simplicity, purity and rationality. This is the centrepiece of acoustic space in McLuhan's thought. Also, McLuhan strongly favoured the postmodern "mixtures of high and low culture, fine art and commercial art" that are "capable of yielding multi-layered readings" and which again are central to acoustic space. The postmodern concern with design as "languages" resembles McLuhan's concern with media forms as "languages" through which different statements and meaning are constructed. And, finally, the postmodern idea of "intertextuality," that "every literary text or work of art relates to, alludes to, or comments on ... various other texts or works" also brims with McLuhan's mosaic method of looking at media in relation to other media, and seeing social and media change as interrelated.[22]

Although Walker made no allusions to McLuhan, Jencks, one of postmodernism's major proponents and defenders, finds McLuhan's theories useful in distinguishing between modernism and postmodernism which, he says, began in 1960.[23] Jencks defined postmodernism as a "paradoxical dualism, or double coding, which its hybrid name entails: the continuation of Modernism and its transcendence." The "double coding" of combining modern techniques with traditional techniques in order to reach the public as well as a high-culture minority is at the centre of Jencks' notion of postmodernism. Jencks contended that transcending modernism through the double coding of irony or humor symbolizes a loss of innocence and a desire to move beyond modernism's stylistic restrictions, as well as representing the failure of modernism. His thirty indicators of postmodernism emphasize symbolism, ornament, humor, technology and the relation of the artist to current and past cultures.

Postmodern art has been influenced by the "world village," as Jencks calls McLuhan's global village, through the international media.[24] Postmodern art can been seen emerging in about 1960 in a variety of art styles, including pop art, hyperrealism, photo realism, new image painting and other forms. At that same time, modernism in architecture had been international, progressive, optimistic and pro-industrial. This architectural style was at odds with the modernism of other arts and philosophy, including the works of James Joyce, Ezra Pound, T .S. Eliot, Stéphane Mallarmé, Picasso, and Werner Heisenberg, all of whom McLuhan holds up as examples of electronic culture. Jencks claims these modernists opposed industrial ideologies, and agreed only in the value of abstraction and the primacy of aesthetics.

Jencks called Eliot's attempts to overcome the dualism between emotion and cognition "Heroic Modernism." Further, he calls the idea of the subversive role of the artist, an idea supported by McLuhan, "Agonistic Modernism." This idea is based "on the myth of the romantic advance guard setting out before the rest of society to conquer new territory, new states of consciousness and social order."[25] Jencks claims that one area of art that many critics term postmodernism is actually late-modernism and includes the works of composer John Cage and writer William Burroughs. They are late-modern, he argued, because they are committed to the tradition of the new and they neglect the past and pluralism.[26]

The shift to postmodern culture, Jencks argues, is evidenced by other shifts which compare favourably to McLuhan's analysis of cultural change. Mass production shifts to segmented production while mass culture shifts to fragmented cultures. According to Jencks, McLuhan made the statement that it is as easy to manufacture one-of-a-kind tailpipes instead of mass-produced tailpipes, but public taste is not refined enough to demand custom tailpipes.[27] In the media, Jencks points out the same trend toward fragmentation, as network television's mass audience is giving way to cable television's fragmented audiences. Jencks also notes a shift from centralized authority to decentralized pluralism in the realm of politics and the family.

In Jenck's analysis, this pluralism logically leads to a shift from few styles to many genres as another offshoot of the global village. Stylistic pluralism and historical revivalism, he argues, create a cultural framework that resembles the pre-modern era with the rejection of the idea of "one true style."[28] He adds that the postmodern era denotes an age of discontinuity and collision, which he traces to cubism and Joyce, before mentioning McLuhan's notion that the modern newspaper page's "bizarre" organization by date line alone prefigured the postmodern sensibility shaped by television's disjointedness. Postmodern artists, Jencks argues, naturally incorporate incongruities and non sequiturs in their work because these elements appeal to their sense of reality.

All of these elements and others combine to create the "information society."[29] In this society, Jencks sees the growth of a new class to replace the proletariat, which he calls the "cognitariat," a "paraclass" that creates and passes on information. This social formation can be compared to Frankfurt theorist Erich Fromm's and Poster's concerns about the mode of information rather than production.

Jencks devises a three-era historical chart that is similar to McLuhan's and historian Donald Lowe's.[30] The first era, the pre-modern, extends from prehistory to the Renaissance. This era was slow-changing, with a sense of "reversible" time that was repetitive and cyclical. Small-scale agriculture and handicrafts characterized production in a hierarchically structured peasant-priest-king social system. The second era, the modern world, arrived with the rise of capitalism and the industrial revolution, and created a large working class dominated by the bourgeoisie. By the nineteenth century the system had centralized, codified and regularized mass production and mass consumption. In this era, time is vertical and sequential, replacing reversible time with the linear time of history. In the postmodern world from 1960 onward, the manufacturing and servicing of information supersedes the manufacturing of products. Information reverses the class relations of the modern era so that no class or group controls the postmodern world. He argued that the "cognitariat paraclass" is the closest to a position of power. He also argued that in the traditional political models of liberal and conservative two-party systems, capitalist and working class become obsolete in the postmodern world. Time ceases to be linear as world events speed up in a chain reaction; cultural systems change so fast they become identified as fashion as more and more information is processed in less and less time.

This historical charting appears to identify McLuhan as a postmodernist even though his sources can be clearly identified in Jencks' "Heroic Modernism" and "Agonistic Modernism" categories. Whether this is true, it at least shows that McLuhan resonates thematically with postmodern art theories.

Bridging postmodern art theory and cultural studies, art sociologist Janet Wolff, who includes all cultural products from paintings to music and film, argues that aesthetics are historical and ideological, although aesthetic value is not reducible to its social, political or ideological elements.[31] Wolff argues that a sociological approach to art finds its rough beginnings in Marx's writings, and credits the early Frankfurt school, including Walter Benjamin's work, and the more recent British cultural studies with advancing this perspective.[32] However, she neglects to mention McLuhan, even as she discusses theories of the impact of technology on artistic production.[33]

For his part, McLuhan did not acknowledge the role of class and ideology in the arts or in the work of artists, even as he lifted artists from their historical context to take the mantle of the "genius artist" and ignored the content of the form. Still, McLuhan agreed with some sociologists of art by refusing to treat the fine arts and popular arts as separate categories. Merging the two, however, takes place through a technological rather than an intellectual process. Also, McLuhan avoided any discussion of objective aesthetic judgment by insisting that the function of art is in its psychological and social effects.

Postmodernism in Cultural Studies

Cultural studies approaches to postmodernism are probably as varied as approaches to cultural studies itself. But a number of themes that are central to postmodern theory can be identified in reviewing cultural studies theorists' writing about postmodernism. Sociologist Nick Stevenson contrasts the postmodern theories of Baudrillard, whose "rejection of ideology, truth, representation, seriousness, and the emancipation of the subject" embrace many issues of postmodernism, with the postmodern theories of Jameson, whom Stevenson finds to be the "most sophisticated" postmodernist today.[34] In general, Jameson calls postmodernism the "cultural expression" or "logic" of "late capitalism." Fine and popular arts have been merged as the economic sector takes over the cultural sphere. Modernist culture has lost its subversiveness and contemporary cultural forms, like punk rock, are co-opted by the capitalist economic system.

For Jameson, the main themes of postmodernism include the absence of context and the uncertainty of interpretation; a growing concern with discourses; the end of the notion of individual style or the "death of the subject"; and a fragmentation of social meanings yielding "discursive heterogeneity" that best represents modern culture through parody or "pastiche." Jameson goes on to call pastiche a "blank parody" because the fragmenting of cultural styles has eroded social norms.[35]

The relevance of dialectical theory and McLuhan to postmodernism can be seen as Stevenson discusses the media's role in the postmodern era:

> Jameson ... argues that the electronic media generally, through its rapid turnover of news and events, quickly relegates recent experiences to a distant past... Jameson suggests that the ideological effect of the media comes through its form rather than its content. The conversion of reality into autonomous regimes of signification and the electronic speed of information circulation deprive the subject of a sense of historical process. However, as a dialectician, Jameson argues that the media and modern culture also contain a more critical potential... The new communication technologies contribute both to a pervasive historical amnesia and occasionally to more collective forms of communion.[36]

The themes of postmodernism identified by Jameson and some other themes that rise among a group of cultural studies scholars include: the death of individualism, as well as the end of Enlightenment thinking; fragmentation leading to parody and beyond to pastiche, with the loss of text and context, and, more positively, the gaining of inter-textuality; and the focus on discourse and codes.[37] Several other themes also bear mentioning in a cultural studies context. These are the retrieval in postmodern thought of pre-modernism; the pointlessness of political action; and the concept of the "other." Several authors who describe Baudrillard as an extreme postmodernist, and with whom McLuhan is associated, contrast Baudrillard with Jameson whom they consider a moderate postmodernist.

Theme 1: The Death of the Subject and the Enlightenment

Like Jameson, literary scholar Patrick Brantlinger pointed out the dis-appearance of the individual subject in postmodern theory. Brantlinger links that claim to a question of whether reason resides in individuals or is the result of history or society.[38] Brantlinger also noted that a central premise underpinning postmodern thought is that a paradigm shift has reversed a number of themes that arose from modernism's Enlightenment:

> The subversion ... of the Enlightenment faith in reason and science are themes underlying much recent theoriz-ing about a sweeping, fundamental shift in the cultural organization or "paradigm" of western civilization. The heralds of "postmodernism" often claim to know that we have moved beyond the "philosophy of the subject" to new forms of knowing. The "dialectic of enlightenment," the "twilight of individualism," the "death of the subject" or of reason—these themes obviously also announce the present crisis, at once academic and grandly historical.[39]

Arguing from a postmodern perspective, Ien Ang contends that modernism assumes a "universal destination for the whole world" that considers history to be a "linear development" in which the modern is the endpoint—"literally the End of History." Traditional or less-devel-oped societies must aspire toward that modern condition.[40] In contrast, postmodernism challenges this notion by undercutting the opposition of the modern, Western subject and the pre-modern, non-Western "other." Ang argues that

> the modern and the Western do not necessarily coincide, and the present has many different, complex and contradictory forces, projecting many different, uncertain futures. It is this ... heterogeneity of the present—characterized by a multiplicity of ... conflicting cultural self/other relationships—which is foregrounded in postmodernity.[41]

Other scholars also equate postmodernity with post-Enlightenment. Communications theorist James Collins notes that an accepted idea in postmodern theory is that partial rather than total processes are the ground for cultural critique—rejecting the "transcendentalist, universalistic dimensions of Enlightenment thinking."[42] Arguing against postmodernism, media economist Nicholas Garnham sees postmodernism, along with neoconservatism, as a replacement for Marxism, which has been withdrawn because of a "deep intellectual crisis." He claims that "Nietzchean postmodernists" are attacking the Enlightenment and its heritage.[43]

Also reacting negatively to postmodernism, John Hartley suggests that postmodernist theories are challenging scientific truth and promoting the notion that the belief in scientific truth is as "mystical" as religious revelation. These theories also contend that notions of "order, coherence and unity" are "totalizing fictions."[44] While pursuing his central theme of the politics of pictures, Hartley asserts the continuation of a modern world and dates it to the Renaissance: "The politics of pictures is not a newfangled symptom of a postmodern world, but a continuing and central feature of modernity, taking 'modern' to refer to post-medieval western history."[45]

However, Brantlinger argues that modernism also embraces at least the nineteenth century. Discussing moderate versions of postmodernist theory, he suggests that the Hegelian, Marxist, historicist "metanarratives" that tried to explain all social experience, yielded to "relative, partial, 'local' truths, perhaps best expressed in 'fragments,' 'evocations,' fictions, and Nietzchean aphorisms." In its extreme versions, as represented by the work of Baudrillard, postmodernism argues that the modern discourse of reason and individual subjects has been destroyed. Truth is inaccessible and representation of reality is impossible. The moderate postmodernist Jameson, however, retains Marxist analysis but relates the crisis of postmodernism to late capitalism.[46]

Brantlinger suggests that the concept of Marxist social totality is dismissed by extreme postmodernists such as Baudrillard, who argue that the dialectics of social totality relies on Hegelian "metanarratives" based on the failed Enlightenment goal of fulfilling history through modernization. However, Brantlinger claims that postmodern theorists substitute mostly "negative and anarchistic" visions of history for Marx's and Hegel's models.[47]

Theme 2: Fragmentation, Loss of Text, Context

Inherent in the death of the subject and the Enlightenment is the concept of fragmentation, textlessness and lack of context, although some cultural studies scholars such as John Fiske argue that postmodernism is intertextual. According to Hartley, who regards postmodernism with hostility and humor, postmodernist culture is conceived of as "fragmenting, localizing, becoming suspicious of totalizing metaphors of unity."[48] He adds that postmodernism has "abandoned" textual issues and postmodern scholars who critique television texts are interested in "performing feats of postmodernist criticism" that engage in "a form of textual display that celebrates fragmentation, difference, the dissociation of sign from reference, text from readership."[49]

Writing about channel surfing on television, Fiske says the process allows viewers to create a "postmodern collage" characterized by "fragments," "discontinuity," "juxtaposition" and "contradictions."[50] According to Fiske, postmodernism also rejects meaning, affirming "the image as signifier with no final signified," and an "infinite chain of intertextuality." Postmodern style consists of "parody" and "pastiche" that "asserts its ownership of all images."[51] For example, "Music video plunders old films, newsreels, avant-garde art: it parodies romances, musicals, commercials. Nothing is inappropriate, all is appropriated, excorporated; the exclusive is included, distinctions and categories dissolved into coequal fragments."[52]

Theme 3: Discourse and History

The work of Michel Foucault pursued this theme. He proposed that social discourse, much like a paradigm, is unconsciously founded in epistemic rules that change from era to era without a universal logic or continuity.[53] Lowe applies Foucault's discourse theory to the periodic, discontinuous historic changes in perception—the rise and fall of bourgeois perception—in combination with the communication-era theory of humanities scholar Walter Ong, a direct descendant of McLuhan's critical media and cultural galaxy.

One of the major notions of postmodernism is the "globalization of culture and society," which media studies scholar Roger Silverstone explores.[54] Citing writer Mike Featherstone, Silverstone defines post-modernism as a movement away from looking at global culture in terms of homogenization, such as claims of cultural imperialism and Americanization of the media, to "terms of diversity, variety and richness of popular and local discourses, codes and practices which resist ... order."[55]

Other Themes

Several related themes such as the retrieval of pre-modernism, the futility of political action, and the notion of the "other" bear mentioning because they also draw parallels to McLuhan. Regarding the retrieval of pre-modernism, Brantlinger identifies within postmodernism a reversal to "older, perhaps pre-modern cultural forms," citing Terry Eagleton's argument that rejoining literary criticism with political and social criticism restores eighteenth-century forms of criticism.[56] Brantlinger also argued that extreme postmodern theory renders political action "tame and illogical," unless it moves to anarchy at which point the media and consumer capitalism contain it.[57]

Finally, in a theme related to the death of the subject, Brantlinger finds "difference"—which he defines as "the threat or promise of 'the Other'"—to be the major theme of postmodernism. He cites a dialectic that needs to occur between one extreme version of ideas about "otherness," which leads to cultural isolation, and the other extreme, which leads to the universality of "human nature."

> Only through charting and understanding the ground between these positions ... as a questioning, a dialectic, can the humanities disciplines be genuinely human, engaged and engaging. As I have been arguing, cultural studies works to open sites or spaces where this dialectic can occur."[58]

McLuhan and Cultural Studies' Postmodern Themes

By mediating the identity of the individual as well as social forms, political and economic systems, and the media and arts themselves, and with technology acting as a dialectical interplay of the human and media extensions in history, McLuhan's theories posit an extremely fluid and changing concept of "human nature" that leaves identity largely as a construct of the dominant media and society. As an effect of the technologies of printing and the alphabet, which removed the individual from the corporate community, the subject has a historical beginning that is being challenged by the rise of electronic media culture. In McLuhan's analysis the individual has been socially organized as a construct by print culture and is being dissolved by electronic culture, which is leading to the death of the subject.

The concomitant death of the Enlightenment has been set forth as a basis for comparing McLuhan's dialectic to that of the Frankfurt School. McLuhan clearly challenged print culture logic, reason, linearity and its very mode of consciousness, which again are historically bound within the rise and fall of print culture. Along with postmodernists, McLuhan argued of the passing of modernism, of the Enlightenment and visual culture.

Fragmentation is a concept that McLuhan, unlike most postmodernists, associated with visual culture. For McLuhan, continuity, homogeneity, mechanization and fragmentation are all aspects of writing and print culture. However, if fragmentation is understood more in terms of McLuhan's mosaic of unrelated elements in interplay, then fragmentation is really a different idea more along the lines of synaesthesia, discontinuity and anti-linearity. Of course, McLuhan relied heavily on parody as well as humor and intertextuality. He, too, as a formalist, moved beyond the text or content of media, although as an interdisciplinarian he contextualizes this low-content analytic tool.

If "discourse" means a way of thinking, a paradigm, or a logic that characterizes a period and then discontinuously halts and is replaced by an unrelated way of thinking, then McLuhan did focus on discourse. To McLuhan, the modes of consciousness created by oral culture, print culture and electronic culture—and deriving from an unconscious system of rules as in Foucault's epistemes—are periodic discourses that change radically from period to period.

Other themes also reflect McLuhan's ideas. The concept of retrieving pre-modern forms strongly resembles the phase of McLuhan's mosaic method and his tetradic law of retrieval. For McLuhan, the cultural capital of accumulated eras is by definition brought into play in postmodernism as the media make previous cultural products available and as the new media environment retrieves aspects of earlier environments. This occurs even as it obsolesces some aspects of the most recent media environment. Even as this retrieval occurs, another postmodernist characteristic of McLuhan's thought is the merging of mass and high culture, a point also made by Jameson.

McLuhan was ambivalent with regard to political action. On the one hand, he argued that the new electronic media stripped individuals of many of their rights and that the effects of the media were beneath consciousness, and as a result political action would be futile. On the other hand, he argued that the artist represented the best response to new media as a make-aware agent instead of a make-happen agent. Through art then, action is possible. Finally, the concept of the "other" can be seen reflected in McLuhan's contrast of Western and traditional cultures, as well as the collision between the visual culture of the Enlightenment and postmodern electronic media culture. For the alienated and fragmented visual culture, the alien "other" is the acoustic culture. However, this otherness is supposed to be resolved by the emergence of an acoustic electronic culture.

McLuhan and Baudrillard

Although McLuhan shares many general themes with a wide range of postmodernist theorists in the arts and cultural studies, the closest comparison may be drawn between McLuhan and Baudrillard. Baudrillard meditates on McLuhan both admiringly and menacingly in his critique of Marxism's analysis of mass media.[59] Baudrillard himself has been labeled a "new McLuhan" who "out-McLuhans McLuhan" in describing the importance of the medium and the irrelevance of content as Baudrillard revises McLuhan in postmodern terms.[60]

Baudrillard biographer Douglas Kellner called the media "all-powerful" and "autonomous social forces" in Baudrillard's thesis on the media's role in the postmodern world.[61] But before McLuhan became a "guiding principle" for Baudrillard, Kellner reported that Baudrillard's mid-1960s review of *Understanding Media* followed the Marxist view of McLuhan as a technological determinist who naturalized the existing media structure. Baudrillard said the notion that "the medium is the message" was "the very formula of alienation in a technical society."[62] By the time of "Requiem for the Media," Kellner found Baudrillard expressing "technophobia" about the media—which is "bad" communication—and "nostalgia" for oral communication—which is "good" communication.[63]

In "Requiem," Baudrillard both lauds and laments McLuhan's theory that "the medium is the message" as he criticizes Marxist analysis of the means of communication as offering no analysis at all. McLuhan is first mentioned in a negative sense for treating the "media revolution" as empirically and mystically as his opponents, although he did recognize that Marx had excluded the means of communication from the realm of productive forces.[64] As Baudrillard rejects Marxism's dialectical analysis, he argues that simply adding the definition of productive forces to include communication is an inadequate alternative. Baudrillard claims the alternative is to discard the notion of the forces of production as "irredeemably partial" or "non-transferable ... to contents that were never given for it in the first place."[65] This rejection is based on the limitations of dialectical theory to the analysis of material production:

> The dialectical form is adequate to certain contents, those of material production: it exhausts them of meaning, but unlike an archetype, it does not exceed the definition of this object. The dialectic lies in ashes because it offered itself as a system of interpreting the separated order of material production ... [Marxism] is incapable of responding to a social process that far exceeds material production.[66]

For this reason, the article titled "Requiem for the Media" is also, for Baudrillard, "the Requiem for the dialectic."[67] Baudrillard contends that in Marxist analyses from Marx to Frankfurt School theorist Herbert Marcuse and Marxist media scholar Hans Enzensberger, the media are seen, as are all productive forces, as the promise of human liberation but the media are distorted and made into forces of domination by capitalism. The problem is that "media ideology functions at the level of form," a contention he shares with McLuhan. In a theme shared with Frankfurt School theorist Max Horkheimer, Baudrillard maintains that the media foster non-communication, a speech without response, or a "responsibility" that he defines as a "personal, mutual correlation in exchange." The media prevent response, except for what he calls "response simulation," and provide the base of social control and power.[68]

The solution Baudrillard puts forth is to restore the possibility of response to the media, "but such a simple possibility presupposes an upheaval in the entire existing structure of the media."[69] The social control of the media stems not from censorship or using the media as a means of spying on everyone. It stems from "the certainty that people are no longer speaking to each other, that they are definitively isolated in the face of a speech without response."[70] In other words, as with McLuhan, the social effect of media is caused by the media's formal characteristics.

Baudrillard draws McLuhan into the argument, saying that his theorem that "the medium is the message" is "closer to a theory" than Marxism. Baudrillard criticizes McLuhan at the same time, asserting that "in his total blindness to the social forms discussed here, he exalts the media and their global message with a delirious tribal optimism," and his theorem is "not a critical proposition."[71] For McLuhan, the media "are the revolution, independently of their content, by virtue of their technological structure alone," which is never questioned as McLuhan "views the medium only in its aspect of medium."[72]

While Baudrillard agrees with McLuhan, his outlook is grim rather than optimistic. Baudrillard's media have become a "total system of mythological interpretation ... from which no event escapes." In his unremitting pessimism, he finds "mass mediatization" to be the "quintessence" of the media, which consists of "the imposition of models."[73] McLuhan's "medium is the message" formula, he argues, transfers meaning onto the medium as technological structure. It is not the content of the press, television or radio that is "mediatized"; rather it is the "forced socialization as a system of social control."[74] Harking back to the near-revolution in France in May 1968, Baudrillard suggests that the revolutionary media were not the mass media:

> The real revolutionary media ... were the walls and their speech, the silk-screen posters and the hand-painted notices, the street where speech began and was exchanged—everything that was an immediate inscription, given and returned, spoken and answered, mobile in the same space and time, reciprocal and antagonistic The street is, in this sense, the alternative and subversive form of the mass media, since it isn't, like the latter, an objectified support for answerless messages, a transmission system at a distance. It is the frayed space of the symbolic exchange of speech—ephemeral, mortal: a speech that is not reflected in the Platonic screen of the media. Institutionalized by reproduction, reduced to a spectacle, this speech is expiring.[75]

According to Kellner, Baudrillard follows McLuhan by interpreting modernity, or McLuhan's print culture, as the explosion of commodities, mechanization, technology, and market relations. Postmodern society, or McLuhan's acoustic culture, is the implosion of all boundaries, regions and distinctions between high and low culture, appearance and reality.[76]

Baudrillard's mixed acceptance and rejection of McLuhan is followed later by further elaboration that collapses the medium and the content into the "simulations" and "simulacra" of "hyperreality," as illustrated in *Simulations*—and which draws McLuhan into its base. This work also briefly introduces other major themes of McLuhan's in addition to the merging of medium and message. First, he compared the ideas of Benjamin and McLuhan, especially their emphasis on reproduction and their respective notions of distraction and participation. This difference lead him to elaborate on McLuhan's notion of tactility and the media in electronic media culture, as well as McLuhan's distinction of "hot" and "cool" media. But these ideas are in themselves reductionist and either reverse or adapt beyond recognition some of McLuhan's key concepts.

Kellner notes that by the late 1970s, Baudrillard saw media, especially television, as "key simulation machines which reproduce images, signs and codes which in turn come to constitute an autonomous realm of (hyper)reality."[77] The media comprise a "hyperreality" that is "more real than real," subordinating the "real" to representation and leading to a "dissolving of the real."[78]

This collapsing of medium and message goes beyond the grammatically linked predicate nominative to argue that the media themselves have been dissolved. In *Simulations* Baudrillard makes this dissolution clear, and strangely credits McLuhan:

> The medium itself is no longer identifiable as such, and the merging of the medium and the message (McLuhan?) is the first great formula of this new age. There is no longer any medium in the literal sense: it is not intangible, diffuse and diffracted in the real, and it can no longer even be said that the latter is distorted by it.[79]

Kellner also suggests that Baudrillard expands on the idea that "content implodes into form" and adopts and extends McLuhan's idea to include not only the end of the message, but also the end of the medium.[80] In another work cited by Kellner, Baudrillard expands on the idea that the media and messages have collapsed, as have content and form:

> There are no longer media in the literal sense of the term ... that is to say, a power mediating between one reality and another, between one state of the real and another—neither in content nor in form. Strictly speaking this is what implosion signifies: the absorption of one pole into another ...

the effacement of ... the medium and the real... It is use-
less to dream of a revolution through content or through
form, since the medium and the real are now in a single
nebulous state whose truth is undecipherable."[81]

As Baudrillard collapses the dualism of message and medium, he
also negates the difference between sender and receiver, and heralds the
"disappearance of all the dual, polar structures" in a "circular" discourse
that also dissolves power and domination. The end of linearity and the
rise of "circular" discourse blurs the differences also between all polarities involving the media:

> "Circular" discourse ... no longer goes from one point to
> the other but describes a circle that indistinctly incorpo-
> rates the positions of transmitter and receiver... Thus
> there is no longer any instance of power, any transmitting
> authority—power is something that circulates and whose
> source can no longer be located, a cycle in which the posi-
> tions of dominator and the dominated interchange in an
> endless reversion which is also the end of power in its
> classical definition.[82]

It is also in *Simulations* that Baudrillard links Benjamin and
McLuhan in their analyses of technological form and the principle of
reproduction, which both go beyond Marxist analysis. He also finds
similarities in their notions of distraction—which is opposed to contemplation—and participation. This linking comes at least five years
before Carey compares McLuhan and Benjamin, and also comes before
the comparison is drawn in Canadian communication studies by literary theorist Pamela McCallum and political theorist Judith Stamps.

> Benjamin ... shows that reproduction absorbs the process
> of production ... altering the status of product and pro-
> ducer... We know that now it is on the level of reproduction
> (fashion, media, publicity, information and communication
> networks), on the level of what Marx negligently called the
> nonessential sectors of capital ... that the global process of
> capital is founded. Benjamin first (and later McLuhan)
> understood technique not as a "productive force" (wherein
> Marxist analysis is locked) but as a medium, as form and
> principle of a whole new generation of sense.[83]

Baudrillard further links Benjamin's and McLuhan's interest in the media-fostered end of reason and equates Benjamin's concept of "no contemplation" with McLuhan's idea of "participation"[84]:

> No contemplation is possible (in film). The images fragment perception into successive sequences, into stimuli toward which there can be only instantaneous response, yes or no... It is in this sense that the modern media call for, according to McLuhan, a greater degree of immediate participation, an incessant response, a total plasticity (Benjamin compares the work of the cameraman to that of the surgeon: tactility and manipulation).[85]

Baudrillard circles back to McLuhan's notion that "the medium is the message," and transforms it again to conclude that the medium controls the process of meaning through its styles and techniques.[86] Baudrillard further comments on—extending, perhaps to the point of distortion—McLuhan's notion of tactile, or acoustic media. Baudrillard argues that this sensory analysis underlies electronic culture, but he widens the argument so that it is the audience that is being touched and tested or palpated, by the media.

> And you understand why McLuhan saw in the era of the great electronic media an era of tactile communication. We are closer here in effect to the tactile than to the visual universe, where the distancing is greater and reflection [or contemplation] is always possible. At the same time as touch loses its sensorial, sensual value for us ... it is possible that it returns as the strategy of a universe of communication—but as the field of tactile and tactical simulation, where the message becomes the "massage," tentacular solicitation, test. Everywhere you're tested, palpated, the method is "tactical," the sphere of communication is "tactile."[87]

This may compare to McLuhan's notion that the media "massage" the audience, but for Baudrillard the media are not extensions of humans as they are for McLuhan. For Baudrillard, humans are terminals for the imploded media as the media reach in to touch humans. Kellner notes how Baudrillard "inverts" McLuhan's theory of extension to argue that people "internalize" the medium and "become terminals within media systems."[88]

Another idea appropriated from McLuhan, according to Kellner, is the typology of "hot" and "cool" media. Baudrillard adapts this concept to show how media take "hot" events like sports or wars and turn them into "cool" media events. For Baudrillard all media become "cool," thereby eliminating the troublesome distinction in which some media are "hot" and others are "cool." Furthermore, he believes that all "cool" media "neutralize meaning" and create a "flat, one-dimensional experience" that is passively absorbed by the audience.[89]

Kellner's analysis of Baudrillard lead him to call Baudrillard a "dangerous writer" who should be "entirely rejected."[90] He is also hostile to McLuhan, which is apparent in his acceptance of Fekete's critique of McLuhan's work as well as in his contention that Baudrillard one-ups McLuhan in terms of his technological determinism.

> Baudrillard out-McLuhan's McLuhan in interpreting television and all other media simply as technological forms, as machines which produce primarily technological effects in which content and messages or social uses are deemed irrelevant and unimportant... Like McLuhan, he anthropomorphizes the media, ...a form of technological mysticism ... as extreme as that of McLuhan. Like McLuhan, Baudrillard also globalizes media effects, thereby making the media demiurges of a new type of society and new type of experience.[91]

Kellner also finds Baudrillard has adopted McLuhan's methodology of "mosaic constellations of images and concepts" and his writing style, which involved juxtaposing ideas instead of following a logical, linear theoretical position.[92] This is the approach that Stamps identifies as dialectical theory. Calling Baudrillard a "new McLuhan ... who has repackaged McLuhan into new postmodern cultural capital," Kellner extends his critique of Baudrillard's theory to McLuhan and suggests that earlier critiques of McLuhan should be applied to Baudrillard.[93]

In an earlier essay, Kellner named Fekete as the author of that critique and he borrows Fekete's term, "McLuhanacy," to advise that Fekete's and other critiques of McLuhan "may need to be recycled a second time for the new McLuhan(cy)" [sic].[94] Kellner, in this critique, even blames McLuhan's media theory and its "formalism, technological determinism and essentialism" for the paucity of postmodern media theory.

In his final analysis, Kellner defined three major criticisms that link

Baudrillard and McLuhan as theorists. First, both reduce media to formal properties, although McLuhan gives more of a historical analysis. Second, both are essentialists, attributing essential natures to the media. Third, both eschew cultural and political analysis, focusing on abstractions.[95]

Ironically, Kellner's alternative to these theoretical approaches is a dialectical approach, which is much the same as McLuhan's. Baudrillard, however, has clearly rejected dialectical theory, as illustrated in his "requiem for the dialectic" and the monistic collapse of media and reality. So, although Kellner's analysis of Baudrillard may well deserved, McLuhan meets some of the criteria for media studies urged by Kellner.

Kellner accuses Baudrillard of dissolving a "dialectics of the media"—an accusation he does not level at McLuhan as forcefully— and argues for examining media under both capitalism and socialism. Kellner also urges the application of "a dialectic of form and content, media and society" that allows multiple roles for television and other media. This analytic approach far exceeds a simple model of media-induced effects. Inasmuch as McLuhan also is seen as an essentialist and technological determinist, Kellner finds that he subordinates a dialectical position, which would view media as "complex, many-sided institutions and technologies."[96]

Kellner more clearly described the "dialectics of the media" elsewhere, and expands on the dialectic of form and content in terms of ideology. He allows that the media do have formal effects that are dominant:

> I would propose grasping the dialectic of form and content in media communication, seeing how media forms constitute content and how content is always formed or structured, while recognizing that forms themselves can be ideological... For a dialectical theory of the media, television would have multiple functions (and potential decodings) where sometimes the ideological effects may be predominant while, at other times, a medium like television functions as mere noise or through the merely formal effects which Baudrillard puts at the centre of his analysis."[97]

Kellner's belief that "neo-Marxian theories of dialectics and mediations are preferable"[98] is one of the themes of this book, which offers the argument that McLuhan employed a Marxian theory of dialectics and mediations, in contrast to the critique of McLuhan offered by

Kellner and Fekete, as well as by Baudrillard himself. Baudrillard, as well as Kellner, has distorted McLuhan's hybrid media theory and his laws of the media. Kellner largely has done this by reducing McLuhan to the critical neglect that had befallen him in cultural studies as the heir of critical theory.

Baudrillard's Disservice to McLuhan

Baudrillard has done McLuhan's theories a disservice, even as he has embraced them, in the way that he has reduced them to a few uncritical theorems, and then altered and extended them to unrecognizable form as he outdistances McLuhan. For example, in reciting "the medium is the message" as an incantation, Baudrillard ignores the process that underlies this idea. This implies that media forms have psychological, social, political and economic effects—not just television or electronic media, or even books and newspapers, but every medium of communication, from clothes and cars to numbers and money—as they collide with former media in a complex process in which human autonomy is the key. McLuhan was trying to distance communication theory from its emphasis on content and its blindness—or deafness—to media forms. As Berland has noted, the content of a new medium is an old medium. As some cultural studies scholars have also written, this connects to McLuhan's notion of "rearview mirrorism," or the fact that new media look backward for content and meaning. McLuhan's theorem then, still clearly posits a difference between medium and message, and does not erase the message as does Baudrillard.

By declaring the death of the medium and the message, Baudrillard also ignores the important historical context provided by McLuhan. The mediated and the real, which Baudrillard asserts have collapsed in a hyperreality of mediated communication, have never been stable or separate in human experience, as all media, to use McLuhan's inclusive notion of media as a wide range of cultural products and social practices, have always altered, determined and negotiated the real. Much like television, the spoken word is itself a technology. By positing the end of history and the end of media as well as reality in hyperreality, Baudrillard has ignored that McLuhan's dialectical historical process is on-going. Television, about which McLuhan wrote very little, is perhaps the newest dominant medium but not the end of media, or history, or ideology.

The collapsing of "hot" and "cool" media, as a corollary, also distorts McLuhan's distinction between high-information, low-participation media, like print, and low-information, high-participation media, like television. The loss, again, is of becoming in a dialectical process. As Baudrillard collapses each of McLuhan's theorems that he encounters, Baudrillard moves further from McLuhan's approach because he abandons dialectical theory. It is this stance, which most cultural studies and postmodern critics have ignored, and that most violates McLuhan's legacy to communication theory. As this book has tried to demonstrate, McLuhan shared a dialectical approach that has much in common with the understanding of dialectics held by some cultural historians and other political theorists.

And it is dialectics that Kellner as well as other contemporary communication scholars call for in searching for methodologies that constitute multi-perspectival research approaches within and beyond the fields of cultural studies and postmodernism. It is to this field-wide call for new methodologies of, for example, critical rather than administrative theories, that the next chapter will turn, in order to argue for benefits to be found in reclaiming McLuhan for communication theory today. The next chapter will look at the current reappraisal of McLuhan and suggest that his dialectical theory should be reclaimed by critical theorists who have relied more on mainstream media rejection of McLuhan, as well as rejection by critical and cultural theorists, rather than on an examination of McLuhan's texts themselves.

NOTES

1. Jean Baudrillard, "Requiem for the Media," in *For a Critique of the Political Economy of the Sign* (St. Louis, MO: Telos Press, 1981), 164-184; Jean Baudrillard, *Simulations* (New York: Semiotext(e), 1983); Charles Jencks, *What is Post-Modernism?* (New York: St. Martin's Press, 1986), 47, 55; Mark Poster, *The Mode of Information: Post-Structuralism and Social Context* (Chicago: University of Chicago Press, 1990), 2, 15, 45, 76.

2. Donald M. Lowe, *History of Bourgeois Perception* (Chicago: University of Chicago Press, 1982); Mark Poster, *Foucault, Marxism and History: Mode of Production vs. Mode of Information* (Cambridge, MA: Polity Press, 1984); Mark Poster, "The Mode of Information and Postmodernity," in *Communication Theory Today*, eds. David Crowley and David Mitchell (Stanford, CA: Stanford University Press, 1994), 173-192; Janet Wolff, *The Social Production of Art*, 2nd ed. (New York: New York University Press, 1993), 35-40.

3. Douglas Kellner, "Resurrecting McLuhan? Jean Baudrillard and the Academy of Postmodernism," in *Communication: For or Against Democracy*, eds. Marc Raboy and Peter A. Bruck (Montréal: Black Rose Books, 1989), 131-146; Douglas Kellner, *Jean Baudrillard: From Marxism to Postmodernism and Beyond* (Stanford, CA: Stanford University Press, 1989), 60-76; Steven Best and Douglas Kellner, *Postmodern Theory:*

Critical Interrogations (New York: Guilford Press, 1991), 267-268; Stanley Aronowitz and Henry A. Giroux, Postmodern Education: Politics, Culture, and Social Criticism (Minneapolis: University of Minnesota Press, 1991), 192-193.

4. Marshall McLuhan, with Harley Parker, Through the Vanishing Point: Space in Poetry and Painting (New York: Harper and Row, 1968), 29.

5. Fredric Jameson, The Ideologies of Theory: Essays 1971-1986, vol. 1 (Minneapolis: University of Minnesota Press, 1988), 17.

6. Ibid., 67.

7. James M. Curtis, Culture as Polyphony: An Essay on the Nature of Paradigms (Columbia, MO: University of Missouri Press, 1978), 92.

8. Ibid., vii.

9. Aronowitz and Giroux, Postmodern Education.

10. Ibid., 192.

11. Best and Kellner, Postmodern Theory, 119, 267-268, 275.

12. Poster, Mode of Information.

13. Poster, Foucault, Marxism; Poster, "Mode of Information."

14. Poster, "Mode of Information," 2.

15. Ibid., 15.

16. Ibid., 45.

17. Jencks, What is Post-Modernism?, 50.

18. Walker, Art in the Age, 84.

19. Timothy J. Clark, The Painting of Modern Life: Paris in the Art of Manet and his Followers (Princeton, NJ: Princeton University Press, 1984); Janet Wolff, Aesthetics and the Sociology of Art (London: George Allen and Unwin, 1983).

20. Walker, Art in the Age, 80.

21. Ibid., 82.

22. Ibid.

23. Jencks, What is Post-Modernism? 10, 14, 16, 22.

24. Ibid., 8, 28.

25. Ibid., 29.

26. Ibid., 33, 34.

27. Ibid., 49-50.

28. Ibid., 54-55.

29. Ibid., 43-44.

30. Ibid., 46-48.

31. Wolff, Aesthetics, 11.

32. Ibid., 22-23.

33. Wolff, Social Production, 35-40.

34. Nick Stevenson, Understanding Media Cultures: Social Theory and Mass Communication (London: Sage, 1995), 162.

35. Ibid., 163.

36. Ibid., 164, citing Fredric Jameson, "Postmodernism and Consumer Society," in Postmodernism and its Discontents: Theories, Practices, ed. E. A. Kaplan (London: Verso).

37. John Fiske, Television Culture (London: Methuen, 1987); Patrick Brantlinger, Crusoe's Footprints: Cultural Studies in Britain and America (New York: Routledge, 1990); Ien Ang, "In the Realm of Uncertainty: The Global Village and Capitalist Postmodernity," in Communication Theory Today, eds. David Crowley and David Mitchell (Stanford, CA: Stanford University Press, 1994), 193-213; Roger

Silverstone, *Television and Everyday Life* (London: Routledge, 1994); John Hartley, *The Politics of Pictures: The Creation of the Public in the Age of Popular Media* (London: Routledge, 1992); James M. Collins, "By Whose Authority? Accounting for Taste in Contemporary Popular Culture," in *Communication Theory Today*, eds. David Crowley and David Mitchell (Stanford, CA: Stanford University Press, 1994), 214-231.

38. Brantlinger, *Crusoe's Footprints*, 171.
39. Ibid., 16.
40. Ang, "Realm of Uncertainty," 207.
41. Ibid.,
42. Collins, "By Whose Authority?" 228.
43. Nicholas Garnham, *Capitalism and Communication: Global Culture and the Economics of Information* (London: Sage, 1990), 1-2.
44. Hartley, *Politics of Pictures*, 147.
45. Ibid., 121.
46. Brantlinger, *Crusoe's Footprints*, 172, 175.
47. Ibid., 72.
48. Hartley, *Politics of Pictures*, 15.
49. Ibid., 87-88.
50. Fiske, *Television Culture*, 105.
51. Ibid., 254.
52. Ibid.
53. Donald Lowe, *History of Bourgeois Perception* (Chicago: University of Chicago Press, 1982), 9.
54. Silverstone, *Everyday Life*, 88.
55. Ibid., 180, citing Mike Featherstone, "Global Culture: An Introduction," *Theory, Culture and Society* 7 (2/3): 1-14.
56. Brantlinger, *Crusoe's Footprints*, 25.
57 Ibid., 130.
58. Ibid., 163.
59. Baudrillard, *For a Critique*.
60. Kellner, *Jean Baudrillard*, 70, 73.
61. Ibid., 66.
62. Ibid., citing Jean Baudrillard, review of Marshall McLuhan, *Understanding Media*, in *L'Homme et la Société*, 5 (1967): 277.
63. Ibid., 67.
64. Baudrillard, *For a Critique*, 164.
65. Ibid., 165.
66. Ibid., 166.
67. Ibid., 169.
68. Ibid., 168-170.
69. Ibid., 170.
70. Ibid., 172.
71. Ibid.
72. Ibid., 177.
73. Ibid., 175.
74. Ibid., 175-176
75. Ibid., 176-177.
76. Kellner, *Jean Baudrillard*, 68.

77. Ibid.
78. Ibid.
79. Baudrillard, *Simulations*, 54.
80. Kellner, *Jean Baudrillard*, 68.
81. Kellner, *Jean Baudrillard*, 68-69, citing Jean Baudrillard, *In the Shadow of the Silent Majorities* (New York: Semiotext(e), 1983), 102-103.
82. Baudrillard, *Simulations*, 76-77.
83. Ibid., 98-99.
84. Ibid., 102.
85. Ibid., 119.
86. Ibid., 123.
87. Ibid., 123-124.
88. Kellner, *Jean Baudrillard*, 71.
89. Ibid., 69-70.
90. Mike Gane, introduction to Jean Baudrillard, *Symbolic Exchange and Death* (London: Sage, 1993), ix.
91. Kellner, *Jean Baudrillard*, 70.
92. Ibid.
93. Ibid., 73.
94. Kellner, "Resurrecting McLuhan?" 144, citing John Fekete, "McLuhanacy: Counterrevolution in Cultural Theory," *Telos* 15 (spring 1973): 75-123.
95. Kellner, *Jean Baudrillard*, 73-74.
96. Ibid., 74.
97. Kellner, "Resurrecting McLuhan?" 140.
98 Ibid., 144.

Reclaiming McLuhan for Critical Theory

Communication Theory Reacts to McLuhan

Faced with McLuhan's sweeping conclusions, mainstream mass communication researchers, especially those in the United States, rejected both the substance of his arguments and the style in which they were presented. Only one communication journal dealt substantively with McLuhan: the *Journal of Communication* began planning a symposium a year before McLuhan died in 1980 and published nine articles in an issue in 1981.[1] Expressing reservations about McLuhan's substance, a recurrent criticism among social scientists in mainstream communication research was his disregard of scientific method and his disdain of logic. His concepts could be neither accepted nor rejected on the basis of empirical testing because they were not structured to be submitted to scientific scrutiny. In contrast, the publication of a special double issue on McLuhan in the *Canadian Journal of Communication* in 1989 and the publication of political theorist Judith Stamps' work in 1995 are examples of the greater degree of receptivity to McLuhan's work in Canadian scholarship.[2] Critical theories of cultural studies and postmodernism are also retrieving McLuhan. This chapter will reassess criticisms of McLuhan and urge that his dialectical theory be recognized and given a prominent place within the pluralistic communication theory community.

In the 1960s and 1970s, McLuhan's writing did not take the usual form of communications studies. Many of his books barely resembled books. His premises and labels seemed to shift with each discovery and his processes were usually not phrased in ways that facilitated testing.[3] His methodology seemed to put him in the realm of poets and prophets rather than academic scholars. His evidence was derived from the arts rather than traditional historical and empirical facts, and his writing violated all the rules of scholarly exposition.[4] In empirical research, one measure of the usefulness of a theory is the extent that it contributes to the development of a specific body of knowledge. This can be done only if the theory is explicit and specifies a methodology for testing the theory. McLuhan did not state his hypotheses clearly and did not establish his thinking within the framework of a social science research tradition.[5]

Reacting against his style, scholars also dismissed McLuhan because he refused to be made accountable for his theory and because he became a popular culture figure in the mass media, which was considered to be an unorthodox way to promote scholarly activity. In his thesis that media-induced sensory environments supersede logic, he alienated social scientists by attacking logic itself. According to McLuhan, sensory balance determines the intellectual mode in use, whether it is logic or analogy.[6] He also rejected public documents and other evidence normally used in historical research because he claimed that evidence only expresses conscious thought patterns. For evidence, he turned to art and artists, as the "antennae of the race."[7]

McLuhan's work was anathema to empirical social scientists, who have built most of today's mass communication theory using scientific method instead of literary rhetoric. McLuhan also was rejected by other literary scholars such as Donald Theall, for his loose interpretations of James Joyce and other literary figures.[8] Educators criticized him for abandoning the values of the literate tradition of book culture and uncritically embracing television culture.[9] As if this double-barreled rejection were not enough, critical communication theorists in the Marxist camp, despite the fact that they too were wary of quantitative positivist methodologies, rejected McLuhan's work for being apolitical or totalitarian.

Reflecting on the divergent history of administrative and critical research in North America, media theorist Hanno Hardt cites a 1970s list of "elder statesmen" that included McLuhan.[10] Discussing US cultural studies, Hardt names "the technological determinism of Harold Innis and Marshall McLuhan" as one of its influences.[11] Hardt also points to McLuhan's metaphor of communication as environments as one of the ideas of communication systems that is included in the cultural studies approach, where culture is considered the social context for creating meaning.[12]

In a longer reflection on McLuhan, Hardt retraces the typical US mass communication approach, both within and outside critical theory and cultural studies. Hardt cautions cultural studies scholars against succumbing to the "cheerful negative classicism" of McLuhan, who, quoting literary scholar Patrick Brantlinger, prescribes that "all will be well because all will be well."[13] After using McLuhan as an example of how the humanities approaches social research—combining an aesthetic appreciation combined with self-promotion and an "irresistible

pop philosophy"[14]—Hardt recalls that McLuhan "almost single-hand-
edly took on the media and defined their function in modern society."[15]
His slogans led to discussion, and often rejection, of his theories,

> but also exposed the isolation of a communication research
> establishment that was locked into its own social-scientific
> culture, unable or unwilling to deal with McLuhan's assertions
> about the potential effect of the medium itself and the struc-
> ture of communication found in the realm of everyday experi-
> ence in which information moved the mind.[16]

Paradigm Conflict in Media Research

McLuhan's weaknesses might have been interpreted as strengths had
he developed his media theories in a time more receptive to his critical
dialectical approach. Communication research, which had rejected
McLuhan, changed dramatically after the 1960s with the emergence of
critical theory approaches. So much so that in 1983, the *Journal of
Communication* devoted a special issue to debating the cleavage
between the emergent critical theory and its opposite, administrative or
mainstream theory. McLuhan received some attention, although not a
new reading, as a critical theorist. The journal revisited these issues in
1993 but at this point the authors had abandoned McLuhan as a relevant theorist.

In 1983, eminent US media scholar Steven H. Chaffee identified
McLuhan and Innis as the source of the idea that media change "modes
of thought and social organization," an idea Chaffee suggests researchers
are familiar with.[17] Another eminent researcher, Elihu Katz, credited
Innis and McLuhan with inspiring interest in the social history of the
media.[18] Commenting on McLuhan's "tremendous impact" on the
return of theoretical analysis and new theoretical approaches to media
research, especially French research, media researcher Francis Balle
called the 1960s the "decade of McLuhan's theories," arguing that "the
same message could have very different effects, depending on the media
used to transmit it."[19] But in his discussion of British cultural studies,
US cultural studies scholar James Carey reiterates his rejection of
McLuhan as "the oddest creature of the lot," and critiques the combination of New Criticism and Innisian influence in his work.[20]

The only sustained discussion of McLuhan is conducted by communications and culture Robert White, who credited him with broadening

the idea of media effects and introducing a "new form of cultural interpretation."[21] According to White, McLuhan interpreted what he saw as a problematic idea that technology is neutral as "one of the major contemporary threats to freedom of the human spirit." His "central quest" was to discover a method to create awareness of the impact of new technology on consciousness in order to be "better able to direct the technological construction of reality." Moving from a causal analysis of media effects to an analogical method of cultural analysis, White contended that McLuhan is drawn close to the methods of cultural studies, and that his "laws" are more metaphors than scientific terms.[22] This reading of McLuhan as focused on intervening in the "potentially humanizing or dehumanizing effects of technology" is a far cry from Carey's "oddest creature" characterization. Despite his more positive analysis, White moved on from this position to cite Carey's and British cultural studies founder Raymond Williams' critique of McLuhan's abstraction from historical context, as well as his failure to explain the "sources of alienation" in political and economic terms. White concluded that overall, McLuhan is lacking a structural link from media change to more general social change.[23]

McLuhan is absent from much of the rest of the 1983 discussion on the conflict between critical and administrative research. In that discussion, communications researcher Jennifer Daryl Slack and Martin Allor provided the historical ground of the debate, defining administrative research as American empiricism and critical theory as European theory. However, the two strains attempted a cross-fertilization in 1938 when social scientist Paul Lazarsfeld brought critical theorist Theodor Adorno to Princeton's radio project. Lazarsfeld defined administrative research as an activity carried out in the service of an administrative agency. He posed critical research as the study of the general role of media in the social system. Slack and Allor argued that Lazarsfeld's early attempt at convergence of these two approaches failed because he did not appreciate the political and epistemological differences between the two.[24]

Slack and Allor contend that Adorno felt that administrative research precluded the analysis of the system itself and its cultural, social and economic premises. He said the rift was more than a difference of theory and methods. Adorno wanted to study the process of communication critically. Slack and Allor go on to suggest that administrative research was unable to confront the political and epistemological bases of the social order and its role in that order.[25]

Furthermore, Slack and Allor contend that recent attempts to

accommodate the critical and administrative approaches have dupli-
cated the same pitfalls as befell Lazarsfeld. They argue against casting
administrative versus critical research in simple dichotomies.
Administrative research is not simply empirical, quantitative, func-
tional, positivist and effects-oriented. And critical theory is more than
qualitative, Marxist, structuralist, and owner/control-oriented. They
also argue against mainstream research adopting aspects of critical theory such as communication context, ethical aspects and multimethod
approaches. Critics say this convergence amounts to co-optation of
critical theory.[26]

Searching for the deeper boundaries separating administrative and
critical approaches, Slack and Allor found that many models of communication developed in the administrative camp since the 1950s
adhere to the basic linear causality reflected in the earliest sender-mes-
sage-receiver model. Administrative research still treats communication
as a process without context in which each element can be isolated.
Adding bits of social context only adds a layer of sophistication to the
simple linear terms.[27]

The two authors defined critical theory as a range of alternative
approaches to research in such areas as international communication,
new technologies, political economy, sociology and cultural studies.
The common thread is the role of communication in the exercise of
social power, a premise that leaves critical theory in opposition to liberal social theory. Critical approaches share a rejection of the linear
causal model, adopting positions ranging from Marxist sociology to
dependency theory and the Frankfurt School.

Slack and Allor argue that all critical approaches consider media
institutions and mass communication to be intertwined with other
social institutions such as the family, the State and the economy.
Individuals are viewed as members of social groups defined by class,
gender, race and subculture. For example, Marxist studies look at the
complex and often contradictory interrelationships between politics,
economics and culture. This approach looks at the struggle over social
meaning between dominant and oppressed groups. Political economy
studies look at the structures of the institutions involved in the production and distribution of communication.[28] Cultural studies measures
power in terms of hegemony, or the idea of rule by consent. Hegemony
describes the process by which oppressed classes come to experience
the world in terms created by the ruling class.[29]

The authors see all these approaches to critical theory as offering an
opportunity for communication research by redefining old research

questions and opening new areas of inquiry. The challenge to the field is confronting the role of power and epistemology in communication institutions and research itself.[30]

However, Slack did not count McLuhan among those practicing critical research, and called his position "an unusually explicit example of a simple causal position."[31] Despite her support of critical theory, Slack excludes McLuhan and, by doing so, cites among her sources the work of Carey,[32] who Canadian scholar media Liss Jeffrey argued is the most cited critic of McLuhan. It was Carey, Jeffrey contends, whose misleading and often incorrect criticism of McLuhan set the tone for academic rejection of McLuhan.[33] As a result, Carey's position discourages direct reading of McLuhan's work.[34]

In addition, Slack did not use the term dialectics in proffering a model of understanding the relationship between technology and society, yet her descriptions of "expressive causality" and its systemic version, "structural causality" rest on Hegelian dialectic and build on Marxist analysis as it has been extended through cultural studies.[35] These two forms of causality are opposed to Western rational variations of causality, including mechanistic and simple conceptions.[36] It is in this discussion of simple causal conceptions that she places McLuhan.[37]

However, the language she uses to describe "expressive causality" clearly describes dialectics, and her entire discussion of both expressive and structural causality mirrors the media galaxies of McLuhan. While tracing expressive causality from Marxism to its variations in British cultural studies and the Frankfurt School, Slack based the concept on Hegelian dialectic.

> Georg Lukacs is a seminal figure in this Marxist variant of expressive totality... Lukacs's conception of totality is based on the appropriation and adaptation of the Hegelian articulation of totality. Hegel posits a universal, infinite totality characterized by three stages. In the first stage there is unity between subject and object... In the second stage, individuals become knowing subjects, which causes them to perceive and live in oppositions... Individuals thus become alienated from nature... The higher unity is realized when we come to an awareness ... that ... we must be self-conscious and therefore separated from nature and such at the same time that we are integral to it.[38]

This "expressive causality" is based on Hegel's dialectic, which is turned by Marxists into a materialist dialectic and further varied by members of the Frankfurt School such as including Horkheimer and Marcuse, and also by Williams in British cultural studies.[39] Although McLuhan was excluded from this dialectical perspective, the foregoing description of his method and his media and culture galaxies should rescue him from the unfair designation as a technological determinist and single-causation theorist, reclaiming him for the critical theory camp.

Adding to the 1983 debate, Canadian communications research pioneer Dallas Smythe and co-author Tran Van Dinh asserted that the ideological orientation of the researcher is inescapably linked to the choice of problems and methods. They argued that all researchers are predisposed to either try to change the existing political-economic order or to preserve it: value-free scientific inquiry is a myth. Smythe and Van Dinh set the two camps in sharp, unreconcilable contrast as they define each approach in terms of problems, methods and ideological perspective.[40]

The authors argued that administrative research focuses on how to make organizations more efficient, for example, how to innovate word processors within a corporation. Administrative methods comprise neopositivist behavioral theory applied to individuals. Administrative ideology means linking these problems and tools with results that either support or do not disturb the status quo. Conversely, critical theory researches problems of how to reshape or create institutions to meet the needs of the community. The critical method is an historical materialist analysis of the contradictory dialectical processes of the real world. And critical ideology links these problems and methods with results that involve radical changes in the established order.[41]

Smythe and Van Dinh stressed the transdisciplinary scope of critical theory, which extends to the humanities, the arts and social sciences. They state that critical theory must include criticism of the contradictory aspects of phenomena in systemic context, regardless of whether it is Marxist or not. The authors note that Marxist work was repressed in the United States until the 1960s, when research, teaching and publishing spread rapidly. They cite a study that concluded Marxism is viewed as a serious alternative approach, although they find no contact between Marxist work in social sciences and Marxist work in communication.[42]

Smythe and Van Dinh stated that the objectives of critical research are the demystification of science and technology; the decentralization and democratization of media institutions; the formulation of praxis, where theory and practice intersect; and mass mobilization for action. Sketching needs for future critical research, they suggested that researchers should study the communication theories and practices of independence, liberation and revolutionary movements, the action of multinational corporations and Third World alternatives for horizontal media. Community research could involve projects to help people resist imposed communications systems. Researchers should work with labour, feminist, religious and environmental groups as well as political parties.[43]

Sociologist Gaye Tuchman took more of a middle position in the critical versus administrative theory debate. Tuchman argued that theoretically and empirically sound studies of the "production of culture" can be done without adhering to a linear causality model.[44] In other words, Tuchman's approach tries to accommodate the empirical demands of administrative research with the dialectics of critical research.

Tuchman writes that the social movements of the 1960s made American media researchers expose themselves to ideas familiar to Europeans who looked at media as the study of the formation of consciousness. Tuchman's concern with consciousness forces consideration of dominant ideologies, the maintenance of power, the control and integration of social change, and the praxis for resistance to media hegemony. The model implicit in this perspective is that production influences content, which in turn influences social behavior and structure, which then influences production processes.[45] Neither Smythe and Van Dinh nor Tuchman mentioned McLuhan.

Reassessing the paradigm conflict at the end of the 1980s, media researcher Clifford Kobland wrote that the call for diverse methodologies embracing quantitative and qualitative research approaches had been intermittent throughout the decade, but there appeared to be renewed interest in linking methods.[46] Kobland suggested that the ideal of a multiperspectival methodology would aim at combining the promised explanatory power of positivism with the interpretation of text and the critical inquiry of institutional structures. He further stated that despite resistance from narrowly focused positivists and critical theorists, both camps are grudgingly accepting the "unavoidable final solution" of methodological pluralism.[47] At the same time, he questioned whether "considering these widely divergent positions ... if we can ever hope to find some common ground between critical and empirical schools."[48]

Suggesting that it is Marxist ideology that is the focus of the schism,

Kobland contended that critical theory need not be Marxist. Critical theory can also be interpretive, humanist, or structuralist, among other approaches. Hoping for a more broad-based methodology that does not reject critical theory on ideological grounds, Kobland reasoned that the merger could be justified in that empiricism is often void of direction due to a lack of communication theories.[49] He offers three approaches, including cultural studies, that exhibit some elements in his proposed solution of "multiperspective methodology" and "methodological synthesis."

Kobland borrowed from Hardt in proposing what he called, "an Americanized version of Hegelianism," or, "a dialectical synthesis of extant methodology."[50] The dialectical synthesis would accept technical considerations, as well as the idea that knowledge is ideological. The synthesis would combine "the insightfulness, detail, and analytical thought of the rational approaches with the generality, technique and economy of empiricism."[51] Kobland envisioned a "dialectical methodology" involving a research team as a "dialectical synthesizer" in which the members studying a phenomenon "critique and inform each other" as they apply multiple methods.[52]

If Hegelian dialectics, as the forerunner of Marxist dialectics, is recognized as the basis of the solution to the paradigm conflict between the dialectical theorists of critical theory and the linear theorists of administrative theory, the synthesis may be construed as a victory for dialectics and critical theory.

The likelihood of such a synthesis, however, which would require a seismic shift in the dominant empirical paradigm, is not promising, Kobland laments

> But the time is running out... Save for a few notable exceptions, positivism does not appear to be loosening its stranglehold on communication studies... Without such an experience [of exposure to diverse methodologies], I fear that the field will continue to become more fragmented and schismatic with scholars from various, compartmentalized perspectives, working on the margin, churning out research that only serves to reinforce their own pre-existing view of knowledge rather than providing a force for a promethean heuristic of what is actually happening in the world.[53]

Reassessing Conflict in the 1990s

The methodological schism between critical and administrative research has receded in the minds of US communications scholars whose essays appear in two 1993 special issues of the *Journal of Communication*. The editors offered the "provocative proposition" that past controversies of the theoretical order have been resolved by "a comfortable acceptance of theoretical pluralism."[54] For communication scholars responding to this proposition, however, methodological issues continued to be a question, as did other issues closely related to the critical theory approach of McLuhan.

The discussion revolved around several themes. First, there seemed to be a backing away from Marxist communication studies and an overall decline in critical theory. Dialectically, there were renewed calls for methodological pluralism, multi-perspective theories and dialectical perspectives in communication research. However, much of this discussion, even when it centred on contributions made at least in part by McLuhan's dialectical and pluralistic analysis, ignores McLuhan. It is symptomatic of the continued negative assessment of McLuhan in the United States that his name is absent, even in instances where authors mention his mentor, political economist Harold Innis, and his derivatives, humanities scholar Walter Ong and communications scholar Joshua Meyrowitz.

In his comparison of the contemporary conflict in research paradigms with the conflict as it existed ten years earlier, media researcher Karl Rosengren dismisses critical theory. He finds that what he called the "sociology of radical change," including critical theory and Western Marxism, is on the wane.[55] According to Rosengren, because Marxism has proved politically "unviable" and Marx has been relegated to a "niche ... in the mausoleum of the classics," communication scholars have abandoned labels like "Marxist" or "socialist" in favour of more vague terms such as "critical," "radical" and "left." In ascendance, instead, he points to humanistically-oriented research in sociology, noting a stronger focus on the human individual and on the historical perspective.[56] Both emphases, despite the dropping of the "critical" label, would indicate areas in which McLuhan was working: at the level of individual perception, and at the historical level of media systems.

Another author, journalism researcher Douglas Gomery, proposes that media economics should move into the centre of communication studies; an indirect focus of McLuhan's. But Gomery rejects both Marxist critical studies and free-market studies because they presuppose the answers. The former assumes a conspiracy of media monopolies, while the latter assumes efficient operation is the only goal for any economic institution. He proposes an emphasis on the changing conditions of quality, or performance.[57] This openness is also similar to McLuhan.

In their essay, communications researcher Monahan and Lori Collins-Jarvis apply a historical approach to the field's most salient academic value: theoretical and methodological diversity in communication research. They document a shift from the dominance of a positivist, behavioral science perspective in the 1950s and 1960s to the rise by the 1980s of an "eclectic mix of scholars" with a diversity of theoretical and methodological approaches including critical and cultural perspectives. The authors propose a value hierarchy for the field's future, including a return of creativity and social relevance as guiding values.[58]

Downplaying the methodological divide, communications scholar Dervin describes such theoretical polarities as critical versus administrative research symptoms rather than the disease itself.[59] The disease, she argues, is the issue of difference, which, as Stamps noted throughout her work, was a key issue in the critical theories of McLuhan, Innis and the Frankfurt School.

Also downplaying the theoretical schism, communications researcher Joli Jensen argues that epistemological differences become oversimplified between, for example, scientists and humanists, messages and meaning. For her, divisions such as the one between critical and administrative research "get flattened" and differences lose meaning. The solution is one that would appeal to the dialectical tradition that, according to Stamps, McLuhan embraced as a dialectical communication strategy: conversation. As Jensen writes: "My purpose here is simply to suggest that a conversation ... is necessary and fruitful."[60]

To meet the challenge of unifying and diversifying communication research, researcher Austin Babrow assumes that a dialectic of theoretical pluralism and broad perspectives is desirable.[61] As communication becomes thought of as a multiple process, dialectical perspectives have particular significance in communication research, along with several other perspectives. The dialectical themes of opposition, totality and change, applied to communication, could reveal many distinct relational processes and lead to multiple-process theorizing.[62]

The work of social science scholars Kurt Lang and Gladys Engel Lang mention Innis in an analysis centered on the impact of a new medium on the existing balance between power groups, for example, between culture and military force, or alphabet-based knowledge monopolies and those based on the oral tradition. They suggest that "none has written more suggestively" about the issues Innis raised, but they "crop up time and again in different terms and in modern contexts. This is where the real challenge lies."[63] The work of Innis is also mentioned, along with that of Ong and Meyrowitz, as essential elements of any telecommunications curriculum to study the exponents of the diverse work on the rise and characteristics of electronic culture.[64] No mention is made of McLuhan.

Media research scholar Klaus Krippendorff articulates a theme of McLuhan's without acknowledging McLuhan's influence as a forerunner. Krippendorff argues that dominant message-driven scholarship is slowly being challenged by "reflexive" explanations.[65] Thus the choice for communication scholars sounds like one faced by McLuhan forty years ago: narrow the domain of inquiry to message-driven studies or embark "on an exciting path of reconstructing our field." The end of theories listed by Krippendorff includes the linear, message-driven theories of Harold Lasswell, Claude Shannon, Warren Weaver, and others. These are the ones McLuhan heralded the end of many decades ago.

Meyrowitz, who has written much on McLuhan, posed a basic question of communication research that was McLuhan's first question: "This essay argues that a fair amount of confusion in media studies has resulted from the lack of explicit treatment of the most basic of questions: 'What are media?'"[66] He then meditates on the metaphors for media as conduits, languages and environments.

Clearly, treating media as languages with their own grammars—to be understood dialectically—is a McLuhan project. Similarly, treating media as environments is classic McLuhan. According to Meyrowitz, who cites anthropologist Edmund Carpenter and, in an endnote, McLuhan, these three metaphors yield three functionally different types of media studies that foster hidden ferment because they obscure the different assumptions underlying each.[67]

Other recent scholarship on McLuhan has continued to probe his continued relevance to communication research. Media scholar Marjorie Ferguson, for example, meditates ambivalently on McLuhan's relationship with and importance for postmodernism.[68] On the one hand, McLuhan's critique of popular culture predates Roland Barthes and semiotics by a decade, making him a "founding father ... for later practitioners of the texts, rhetorics or discourses of popular cultural artifacts and media technologies."[69] However, "the weight of the evidence is that McLuhan arose from and remained embedded within the scholarly traditions of modernity."[70] Still, Ferguson finds his reappearance likely, if not wholly welcome:

More significantly, McLuhan may be in line for intellectual recycling within the fashionable realm of communication theory... The 1990s may be ripe for "neo-McLuhanisms." If this should prove to be the case, the man and his "isms" will join an already crowded room filled with "neo" or "post:" Marxisms, structuralisms, Freudianisms, positivisms... In this intellectual space, McLuhan might be castigated as a "neotechnological determinist" but celebrated as the harbinger of postmodernist, non-sequitur, bricolage methods tuned to a global system of information and culture.[71]

Two recent studies finding McLuhan's theories applicable come from the diverse realms of psychology and critical studies.[72] Psychologist Michael Bross set out to test McLuhan's sensory theory against the findings of contemporary psychophysical research. Bross integrates McLuhan's theory with the theory of cybernetics, making McLuhan's theory "a more useful tool for analyzing and understanding how changes in media technologies affect individuals and societies."[73] Bross finds that despite the cascades of criticism against McLuhan:

All this does not detract, however, from the overall contributions of McLuhan's general theory of the relationship between media and the individual's experience of life; it must be remembered that for McLuhan the entire world as it reveals itself to us through our senses is one immense media event. To this end he was absolutely correct in insisting on the primary role of sensory functions as the cornerstone of any understanding of how individuals apprehend and interact with their environments.[74]

Communications and physiology researchers Barry Brummett and Margaret Carlisle Duncan follow another of McLuhan's central theses—that media are extensions of the self—and argue that the perspective is more consistent with the everyday experience of communication and so should be applied in critical studies:[75]

We have argued that one good way to study the bricolage of actual communication is through the metaphor of media as extensions of the self. That metaphor would enroll the different fields of communication into one perspective that asks how people create subject positions as well as the experience itself by seeking extensions of the self... We have also made the media, understood as extensions of the self, the key metaphor underlying the study of communication in its everyday manifestations.[76]

In more current research, McLuhan's tetrad is the theoretical basis for an analysis of a CD-ROM multimedia novel, *Myst*, which the author suggests may be understood by applying McLuhan's fourth law of the media—retrieval of long obsolete art forms.[77] Researcher David Miles casts doubt on McLuhan's claim to have completed Hegel's dialectic by adding the law of retrieval and suggests that the tetrad is derived from Innis, James Joyce and Giambattista Vico's four cyclical stages of history.[78] Still, Miles found the law of retrieval, as well as the reading of the phrase "the medium is the message" to mean that the content of a new medium is an old medium, thus providing the basis of his analysis of an extremely new medium, the CD-ROM multimedia novel.

Canadian Voices on McLuhan

In Canada, McLuhan has never suffered the eclipse and negative readings that he suffered in the United States; for example, Canadian political and social theorist Arthur Kroker approvingly calls him a "technological humanist."[79] Nevertheless, his work has gone through a renaissance even in Canada. McLuhan's pervasive influence in media studies can be seen in his subtle dominance in the Canadian textbook *Communication in History*.[80] The text itself is not McLuhan-centered, and it includes just one excerpt of McLuhan's writing. Still, its many contributors cite McLuhan more than any other individual. McLuhan is mentioned in a variety of contexts and evaluations, although most acknowledge his contribution to various aspects of communication and history. When one simply counts the number of references, however, his ideas can be seen as touching on the work and thought of many writers and researchers in communication, at least in the Canadian context.

In the mid-1980s, Kroker depicted McLuhan as representing "technological humanism" in the Canadian discourse on technology. According to Kroker, McLuhan's technological humanism approach represents one of two conflicting sides in that discourse—the other being that of "technological dependency," which he defines as a "poetic, always tragic reflection" on the cost of technology.[81] He further notes that McLuhan is an "emblematic" thinker who elevates the "utopian" potential of technology in opposition to the technological dependency perspective of Canadian philosopher George Grant, who offers a "tragic lament." For Kroker, Innis completes the perspectives of the "Canadian mind," offering a critical perspective called "technological realism."[82]

Had Kroker's essay replaced those of Carey, Williams or semiotician Umberto Eco, or even literary scholar John Fekete's or Marxist analyst Hans Enzensberger's interpretation of McLuhan as a humanist rather than a determinist—important though flawed—it would have substantially changed the history of readings of McLuhan in critical theory, cultural studies and postmodernism. Situating McLuhan further within an historic perspective, another Canadian scholar, Paul Tiessen, imbeds McLuhan's theoretical landscape within the context of four activists and intellectuals in Canada who anticipate elements of McLuhan's work. These four antecedents of McLuhan do not include those usually identified as his progenitors, including Innis.[83]

The reassessment of McLuhan in Canada is evident in the double issue of *Canadian Journal of Communication* (*CJC*) devoted to McLuhan in 1989. Theall, the editor, credited McLuhan with opening up substantial areas of then-neglected concerns that have since grown in significance for communication studies. From the importance of rhetoric and dialectics, to the centrality of orality and literacy, the arts and literature, and the need for a multidisciplinary approach to cultural studies, McLuhan's contributions outweigh his academic shortcomings. These articles returned McLuhan's work to serious discussions of social science or argued for its continued relevance.[84]

Countering the widespread dismissal of McLuhan, McLuhan scholar Liss Jeffrey argues for a reassessment and notes his reemergence in communications research via the works of Ong, media theorist Neil Postman, Meyrowitz, and communication historian Paul Heyer.[85] She compares McLuhan's work to that of science historian Thomas Kuhn, saying that both focus on the understanding that, as Kuhn is quoted, "when paradigms change, the world itself changes with them."[86] A grand theorist, McLuhan sought to explain how cultures change course. Both he and Kuhn attempt to account for radical shifts in world views.[87] The key to McLuhan's approach, which should place him in the dialectical camp, is his contention that his was the "only communication theory of transformation" rather than of transportation.[88] The very idea of transformation is the key to totalizing in dialectical thinking.

In assessment, McLuhan is accorded the role of catalyst in the emergent "interdiscipline" of communications. This claim is based first on McLuhan's writings and his own words about how his approach differed from the orthodoxy of the fifties and early sixties, namely that he had a theory of transformation while the US communications establishment offered linear theories of transportation.[89]

Jeffrey, however, calls McLuhan's process simply "pattern watching," suggesting that he uses the technique of Symbolist poets as well as Edgar Allen Poe's metaphor of the man in the maelstrom who studies its action as a way of surviving.[90]

Jeffrey compares McLuhan to Williams, another literary critic who turned to communication studies. Although Williams took an openly neo-Marxist approach, McLuhan "was a North American pioneer in a similar (if non-Marxist) vein."[91] But Jeffrey also defends McLuhan against charges levelled primarily by Carey that McLuhan was a technological determinist. Jeffrey contends that this charge seems untenable when considering all of McLuhan's work.[92] McLuhan may be regarded as a precursor to a time when mainstream social science research dominated, and before imported ideas from Europe in cultural studies and poststructuralism filled the void.[93]

Heyer argues that McLuhan's decline and subsequent rise occurred in the 1980s because, for the first time, attention was given to the historical side of his work—beginning with the oral tradition and then looking at the print revolution. Heyer finds that what has survived of McLuhan is his continuation of the tradition, following Innis, of communication history.[94]

Theall mines McLuhan's theory of communication for its sources in the works of James Joyce, who was also an interest of semiotician Umberto Eco. Theall argues that Joyce should be given an important place in communication theory. Among his contributions, Joyce explored the shift from orality to literacy before McLuhan or any of his other references, offering many insights about the interplay of these two forms.[95]

> A genuinely enriched theory of the relation between communication and the knowledge revolution can be attained by going back to McLuhan's source to question anew the poets, artists, especially Joyce, about how they conceived the socio-historical drama of changing concepts of time and space, the nature of human communication, and the emergence of powerful technologies which transform knowledge and communication.[96]

Another reassessment of McLuhan from a Canadian perspective, by communications researchers James Winter and Irving Goldman, is organized around the dialectics of four disciplines that represent four levels of thought in the work of Innis.[97] The political dialectic's "contraries" are power and knowledge; the historical dialectic's are space and time; the economic dialectic's are margin and metropolis. Fitting McLuhan into Innis' political dialectic, Winter and Goldman contend that McLuhan shared Innis' interest in the effects of discourse on democracy. However, they note that the early interest—expressed in *The Mechanical Bride: Folklore of Industrial Man* through a fear of monopolies of knowledge—had been transformed to technological determinism by *The Gutenberg Galaxy*.[98] The authors contend that the early critical perspective of McLuhan, as reflected in his dialectical approach, only remained in remnants in his later work.

The inclusion of an explication of the just-published *Laws of Media* by Eric McLuhan in the special McLuhan issue of the *CJC* rounded out a Canadian reassessment of McLuhan[99] that included an open hearing on his later ideas such as the tetradic laws; a historical approach; a theoretic-biographical interpretive approach; a literary approach and a dialectic analysis—all reflecting a diversity of perspectives and a receptiveness to McLuhan.

Dialectics, Cultural Studies, and Postmodernism Today

The contemporary re-emergence of McLuhan's theories among a diverse group of theorists in cultural studies and postmodernism illustrates McLuhan's continued relevance to critical communication theories. From Canadian communication historians David Crowley and David Mitchell to sociologist John B. Thompson and Meyrowitz, McLuhan maintains a central position.[100] McLuhan also has been revisited by neo-Marxists like Armand Mattelart and included in the social semiotics of Klaus Jensen and the ethnographic studies of James Lull.[101] Cultural studies, with its methodological openness and defiant position, itself embodies McLuhan's spirit. Furthermore, even as postmodernists label McLuhan a technological determinist and attempt to move beyond him, much of his dialectical analysis seems ever more applicable and relevant to them.[102]

Crowley and Mitchell, who have compiled an overview of contemporary communication theory that includes one Canadian contributor, focus on four themes in theory today, including one theme that was central to McLuhan: mediation, or the role of the media in shaping the social world.[103] The focus on media messages and social effects in media research, however, marginalized other media and social theorists such as Innis, McLuhan, and Ong. Innis is identified as seeing a "dialectic in history, where one media asserted a primacy in a society, followed by effort to bypass the social power that gathered around the control of that medium, with the predictable championing of alternatives and the rise of new social actors around those alternatives."[104]

Among contemporary theorists, Thompson and Meyrowitz incorporate the theories of the "Toronto circle of medium theorists." Thompson integrates their model of media-induced social change with Habermas's theory of the public sphere and hermeneutics. Meyrowitz connects the work of McLuhan and Ong with the sociological model of Erving Goffman.[105]

Thompson refers to the work of Innis and McLuhan as having lasting significance but he focuses more on Innis' exploration of communication media and social power in terms of time and space.[106] Meyrowitz builds McLuhan into the fabric of his research.[107] In his reprise for Crowley and Mitchell, Meyrowitz elevates Innis and McLuhan to among the unique medium theorists whom he recognizes based on the sweep of history and culture that they undertake to analyze.[108]

Returning to dialectics and McLuhan in recent years, Mattelart takes media theory beyond dialectics and has been more accepting of McLuhan.[109] He notes that the Frankfurt School employed dialectics in analyzing personal and social perceptions of self and society, and goes on to suggest that these theorists saw individuals adjusting dialectically to development and change marked by conflict. Beyond individual socialization, dialectical thought promoted the idea of historical contradiction and development toward a specific end. He argues, however, that dialectical theory is in crisis because the "philosophies of negativity are blurred," as is the "distinction between the positive and the negative, power and counterpower."[110] The dialectical theory that helped analyze the formation of the State and social classes is unable to help analyze societies, such as Western countries, that have "metabolized" State and class and that have new "topologies of individuality."[111]

In his critical history of mass communication theory, Mattelart invokes McLuhan's work as the "paradigm" of a media theory that replaces the "ideology of progress" with the "ideology of communication" and proposes communication as the foundation of society.[112] Mattelart continued to read McLuhan as a technological determinist of the "planetary village" who contended that technological change propels social change and renders political revolution obsolete in the name of the "communications revolution."[113] But Mattelart recognizes an early McLuhan, who began as a "critical spirit" analyzing the cultural context of new media. Not a technological determinist, this McLuhan has been left behind.[114] Despite his change into a "prophet in a new age of grace," McLuhan counts among those important thinkers who freed communication from its Enlightenment fetters and influenced Mattelart:

> Above and beyond these thinkers' different evolutions, one must remember that their major impact is to have exploded the postulate of the priority of content over form, that is, to have insisted on the fact that the medium itself determines the character of what is communicated and leads to a new type of civilization. This postulate, nurtured by pedagogues of Enlightenment philosophy, and the "typographic men" of the Gutenberg galaxy, had for too long inhibited understanding of the nature of changes brought about by electronic networks.[115]

McLuhan's ideas survive him in succeeding theorists. For example, Zbigniew Brzezinski adapted the idea of the "global village" and transforms it into the "global city"; altered because the "global nervous system" is more like a "city," which is "nervous, agitated, tense, and fragmented," than a "village," which is stable and intimate, and based on shared values and traditions.[116]

Jensen touches on McLuhan when introducing a discussion of postmodernism and "rearview mirrorism," which is McLuhan's concept for the problem posed by the analysis of new media. New media tend to be analyzed in terms of former media—the present in terms of the past. Jensen also points out that "rearview mirrorism" is a correlate of "the medium is the message," asserting that the content of a new medium is an older medium. Taking McLuhan's idea further, he asserts that "the implication is that new media seldom realize their full potential because they are made in the image of older media. For example, television news formats traditionally have been constrained within the formats of print journalism."[117] Applying "rearview mirrorism" to communication theories in general and postmodernism in particular, Jensen takes a position of qualified support for McLuhan:

> On the one hand, despite McLuhan's eclecticism and rampant metaphors, his diagnosis of the literate bias of communication scholarship and his emphasis on the material specificity of

other media than writing and print remain underestimated contributions to mass communication theory ... which offer insight into the long waves of social and cultural history.[118]

Jensen calls postmodernism "a grand narrative, announcing the end of another grand narrative in its rearview mirror."[119] McLuhan, as a guide for scholars, "helped teach our field to look beyond the rearview mirror of print and Logos to contemporary popular culture."[120] Jensen argues that although McLuhan overstated the effects of moving from a print culture to an electronic culture, the fast-changing media technologies of recent decades have created a "qualitatively new form of media environment."[121]

Working within the rubric of cultural studies ethnographic audience research, Lull invokes McLuhan's notion of media as "extensions," adapting it so that "television viewing is an 'extension'—not only of the human senses, as McLuhan had argued, but of individual viewers, households, and cultures."[122] Lull points out that when McLuhan published *Understanding Media* in 1964, television was only a decade old as a part of daily life. Lull finds in McLuhan's work an "insight that still has theoretical currency": the notion that the media are extensions of perceptual senses, both physical and psychological.[123] Television, Lull asserts, is an extension of viewers' senses and bodies, but it is also "extensions of audience members' most basic and common mental and behavioral orientations, nested and constructed within culturally diverse circumstances."[124] His analysis stems from the categorization of viewing as an extension of the person, the household, and the culture.[125] More recently, Lull characterized McLuhan as "never coherent" and "not critical," and finds that he is not concerned with economic or cultural content issues in media. He also compares Thompson's work to Innis, McLuhan, and Meyrowitz, although he states that Thompson is more like Innis in that he looks at social structure as a critical factor in organizing time and space.[126]

Concerned with the theme of postmodernity, historian Mark Poster's work analyzes the impact of electronic media, especially the computer, on individual and political discourses. He defines this relationship between shifting forms of media and social relations as the "mode of information."[127] Although McLuhan and other medium theorists are not mentioned in this work, Poster's historical analysis approximates theirs. He argues that as print culture fostered a contradictory "critical distance" for readers along with an intensified exposure to persuasion, so do electronic media and computers simultaneously create a playful "electronic cafe" as well as an increased surveillance "technology of power."[128]

Poster defines the "mode of information" as "electronically mediated communication," that "challenges and reinforces systems of domination that are emerging in a postmodern society and culture." Poster summarizes his thesis using a postmodern sensibility in a way that resembles McLuhan's electronic media culture. Poster argues that the electronic mode of information radically changes language so that the rational, autonomous individual disappears. The new human, instead, is "multiplied, disseminated, and decentered," as well as "unstable."[129]

In a postmodern critique of Marx, Poster sounds remarkably like McLuhan in faulting Marx, along with other social theorists of his time, for neglecting language and communication. Poster calls Marx an "heir" of the Enlightenment, which was "profoundly rooted in print culture," as its notion of the rational individual was largely the product of that print-based culture.[130] In Poster's view, because of the linearity, stability, and order of the printed page, print culture separates readers from authors and promotes the idea of individualism critically responding in isolation from political and religious power. He argues that it also promotes the authority of the author, in contrast to the fleeting nature of oral communication. It was print culture, then, that gave Marx and other intellectuals the idea of the individual as subject. Poster suggests that although Marx realized that individuals change with the changing social relations created by the mode of production, he ignored the mode of communication.[131]

The mode of information, which Poster defines as forms of electronic media, changes the constitution of the individual and society, replacing the characteristics of print culture with instability and multiplicity, while eroding the reader/author relationship. In Poster's thesis, minorities such as women, children and people of colour, whom McLuhan envisioned as emerging into visibility in the global village, can no longer be ignored but are also alienated as the "other."[132]

As well as basing his theory on the contrast between the print mode of information and the electronic, Poster also employs a dialectic of contradictory tendencies in each of the cultures. These tendencies resemble the tensions in McLuhan's hybrid media model and the tetradic laws of the media. For Poster, electronic communication separates senders and receivers while bringing them together.[133]

> These opposing tendencies—opposite from the point of
> view of print culture—reconfigure the position of the

individual so drastically that the figure of the self, fixed in time and space, capable of exercising cognitive control over surrounding objects, may no longer be sustained... Electronic communication systematically removes the fixed points, the grounds, the foundations that were essential to modern theory.[134]

Poster explores the work of Jean Baudrillard, as well as postmodernist Michel Foucault and deconstructionist Jacques Derrida, in commenting on the changes being wrought by electronic media. All three offer post-Marxist critiques that also reflected on McLuhan's Marxist critique. Poster attempts to extract Baudrillard's "critical impulse" without his "monolithic vision," which helps extend a critique of Marxism.[135] Marxists believe, for example, that computer databases are a new type of commodity controlled by corporations, thus reinforcing and extending class divisions.[136] The problem with this analysis, Poster argues, is that it ignores the change in the notion of the individual from a stable, rational being who is struggling against institutions in a dialectic of social forces.[137] Sounding like McLuhan in his view of the idea of privacy and the class struggle, Poster asserts that the privacy of Marxism and liberalism is cancelled by computer databases that blur the distinctions between individuals and institutions: "Information flows today double the action of individuals and subvert models which presuppose either privacy or the class struggle. Society is now a double movement: one of individuals and institutions; another, of information flows."[138]

Like critical historian Donald Lowe, Poster draws on Foucault's discourse theory to help analyze the impact of electronic media. A Marxist critique would focus on State and corporate use of computer databases to maintain a system of oppression, and thereby positing the antagonistic distinction between the individual and the State. Foucault, however, saw connections instead of opposition, rejecting the dualism between mind and body, and ideology and institution. Applying Foucault's thinking to databases, Poster argues that electronic technologies negate the dualism of private and public. In the case of electronic writing, such as electronic mail. the tendency of print to remove author from text and reader is heightened. But electronic writing also subverts print culture by being volatile rather than fixed and blurs the distance between author and reader.[139]

Poster draws on Derrida's counter-position on writing as fixed and authorial in the effort by scholars of deconstruction to show the multiplicity of meanings, the subversive opportunities of the reader to create meaning and undermine the author's intention, and potential to "destabilize the march of univocal meaning in written texts."[140] Poster applies Derrida's approach in contrasting print and electronic forms of writing. Thus, deconstruction becomes a tool of the electronic mode of information used to analyze the previous mode of print culture.

In writing about the mode of information theory in broader terms, Poster credits the Frankfurt School with recognizing the "stalled dialectic" as the experience of the century led to the dwindling of the labour movement and "suspending the dialectic of the class struggle." According to Poster, Western Marxism in general attributed this situation to the effect of mass culture on the working class; however, Western Marxism developed a theory that did not account for the construction of the individual "through the language patterns of the mode of information."[141]

Poster argues that communication theory must be placed at the centre of social theory because media change social life itself. Media theory must also become relational and relative rather than universal and absolute, tied to changing historical conditions; what he called "self-reflexivity"—or the dependence of truth on context—which is the core of dialectical theory, as well as the core approach to history espoused by McLuhan, Marx, and Western Marxism in general.[142]

Believing that communication theory produces a "new kind of truth" not tied to "universality," Poster writes that "the first principle of communication theory in the age of electronic technology, then, is that there is no first principle, only a recognition of an outside of theory, an Other to theory, a world that motivate theory."[143]

Poster argues that Marxist writing on communication takes the mode of production as a fixed element and focuses questions on it, neglecting issues not related to class structure. Sounding much like Marxist dialectical theorists, Poster then calls for an end to these Marxist ideas: "For communication theory, the turn to history must sustain a sense of an open field, not a closed totality, a sensitivity to the new, not a confirmation of the already given."[144]

Postmodern critics Steven Best and Douglas Kellner also call for a multiperspectival and multidimensional critical theory of the media and society; one that is dialectical and relates all dimensions of society—from the cultural to the social, political and economic—to each other and to the dominant mode of social organization. Advertising, for example, would not only be studied in terms of how it affects capitalist economics, but also how it adapts cultural forms and affects cultural life, as well as how it has changed politics.[145]

More generally, Best and Kellner define dialectics as relating specific social conditions to overall productive relations. Dialectical analysis would preserve the specific, even as it attempts to connect it to broader social forces. They note that dialectical theory is open to historical events and adapts its analysis to historical change. In alliance with critical theory, dialectics also focuses on social problems, conflicts and struggle, looking toward positive resolution. Dialectical critical theory then, is political. Stressing multiple perspectives, Best and Kellner advocate using many approaches, theories and disciplines such as Marxism and feminism, critical theory and postmodernism, or economics, sociology and philosophy. By multiple dimensions, Best and Kellner mean that each dimension of society is treated as relatively autonomous, thus inviting analysis from diverse disciplines or perspectives.[146]

Best and Kellner cite McLuhan, as well as Baudrillard and some unnamed Marxists, as bad examples of multiperspectival critical theory. McLuhan and Baudrillard are faulted for theorizing strictly as technological determinists, and the Marxists are accused of analyzing modern culture strictly in economic terms. McLuhan and Baudrillard also are denigrated for studying television solely as a medium, without including its political role, its readings by audiences, or its content and ideologies.[147] According to Best and Kellner, in general, postmodern theory is thought to have rejected dialectical theory.[148]

Today cultural studies attempts to remain an open field by defying method and tradition. An example of this approach can be found in an introduction to a prominent cultural studies anthology. In it Cary Nelson, Paula Treichler, and Lawrence Grossberg discuss the cultural studies research domain, methodologies, and an intellectual legacy of its tradition and language, and suggest that cultural studies averts being a traditional discipline, and is even anti-disciplinary. Cultural studies crosses domains, or disciplines—from Marxism and feminism to psychoanalysis and postmodernism. Cultural studies also has no identifiable methodology and can best be described as a "bricolage" of textual analysis, semiotics, deconstruction, ethnography, content analysis, survey research, and other methods. However, any or all theories and methodologies employed are ideally used self-reflexively and in context.[149]

Despite the difficulties of reigning in such a diverse discipline, the authors attempt a general definition of cultural studies that would include domain, methodology, and traditions—some of which are shared with McLuhan. Cultural studies is inter-, trans-, and counter-disciplinary. It maintains a tension between broad anthropological concepts and narrow humanistic concepts of culture. It studies primarily modern industrial societies, insists on treating high and popular culture as equals in cultural production, and compares these cultural products to other social and historical forms. It is "committed to the study of the entire range of a society's beliefs, institutions, and communicative practices."[150] Culture itself is conceptualized both as a way of life and a set of cultural practices, the former including "ideas, attitudes, languages, practices, institutions and structures of power," and the latter including "artistic forms, texts, canons, architecture, mass-produced commodities" and so forth. In terms of its traditions, cultural studies has political aims, studying cultural change with the intent of intervening in it, although these aims differ in the British and US versions.[151]

McLuhan's work can also be understood as interdisciplinary and anti-disciplinary, oscillating between narrow and broad cultural and historical sweeps. He mixed high and popular culture and compared media products to other social and historical forms. He also looked at culture as a way of life, as ideology, and as a set of practices. And, contrary to older readings of McLuhan, he was very much interested in intervening in the cultural-technological process.

In a less forgiving analysis of cultural studies, John Hartley searches for its definition and identifies two levels of response: institutional and genealogical. First, he finds cultural studies to be an "intellectual enterprise of the left" from the 1960s transformed, for the worse, into an "academic subject increasingly of the centre" in the 1980s and 1990s.[152] Second and more ironically, cultural studies becomes a list of names (including McLuhan's) of "prodigal parents" who begat a field that detests orthodoxy, avoids authority, and is committed to interdisciplinarity, yet "has no unified theory, textual canon, disciplinary truths, agreed methodology, common syllabus, examinable content or professional body."[153]

Reclaiming McLuhan

Within this pluralistic group of critical communication scholars, McLuhan's work offers relevance, both theoretically and methodologically, to research in cultural studies and postmodernism. McLuhan's dialectical methodology, allied with other critical theory paradigms and their dialectic methods, offers a bond that would bridge diverse researchers. Stripped of mythology and reinforced in his dialectic and historical methodology, McLuhan's work offers a theory of media evolution and human intervention that Marxism has missed. McLuhan's methodology forms a bond with Hegelian and Marxist dialectics and its descendants in the critical theory of Benjamin, Adorno, and Horkheimer as well as in the new generation of cultural studies scholars, postmodernists and more generally, in Canadian media theory.

The theoretical and methodological similarities between McLuhan, critical theory, and dialectics can serve as a theoretical base for studying the dialectical relationship of media production and consumption, evolving media systems, and of social systems. McLuhan's analysis could be applied to hegemony and ideology, as well as praxis. All are formulated under other concepts by McLuhan.

Researchers could devise studies that reflect hegemonic ideology—the beliefs, values, and way of living that are promoted as common-sense explanations for the relationship between social and economic classes—and its relationship to media forms. Both McLuhan and critical theory have suggested that the mass media create false consciousness when the dominated media consumers believe the interests of other groups are their own. In the larger context, McLuhan's theory and method would also provide a theoretical framework for interpreting empirical research data if were reformulated in critical, historical and empirical terms. McLuhan's dialectics could help form a bridge that would move communications research in the direction of methodological synthesis. Using McLuhan's analysis, critical theory research would be given an expanded opportunity to question the ends of media and political systems, and ask systemic questions about what the media should be.

McLuhan, like Marx, may have overemphasized aspects of his dialectical theory in making his ideas popular, and in doing so made a rich dialectical process oversimplified. In an article written between *The Mechanical Bride* and *The Gutenberg Galaxy* , when his critics argue he lost his critical approach, McLuhan wrote about shifting his emphasis. In his own words, he made a mistake by criticizing the new acoustic culture of the electronic age, a postmodern media and social galaxy, using arguments based on enlightenment values. Here he attempts a critique of these clashing cultures with a critique of all values. This position, in which he admittedly dropped the approach he put forward in *The Mechanical Bride*, is shown as the chosen path that McLuhan stayed with in all of his later works. It is in the spirit of this stance that McLuhan's legacy is most notable:

When I wrote *The Mechanical Bride* some years ago I did not realize that I was attempting a defense of book culture against the new media. I can now see that I was trying to bring some of the critical awareness fostered by literary training to bear on the new media of sight and sound. My strategy was wrong, because my obsession with literary values blinded me to much that was actually happening for good or ill. What we have to defend today is not the values developed by any particular culture or by any one mode of communication. Modern technology presumes to attempt a total transformation of man and his environment. This calls in turn for an inspection and defense of all human values. And so far as merely human aid goes, the citadel of this defense must be located in analytical awareness of the nature of the creative process involved in human cognition. For it is in this citadel that science and technology have already established themselves in their manipulation of the new media.[154]

The technological transformation is well under way. Defending an old regime may be laudable, but the battle looms in the future, facing the new media, not in celebration, but in defence. As McLuhan wrote in *Understanding Media: The Extensions of Man*, the actions of corporate owned media that are stripping individual privacy and rights should raise a call to the ramparts. If the response is anything less with regard to the new media, the result will be a "banana-skin pirouette and collapse."

Once we have surrendered our senses and nervous systems to the private manipulation of those who would try to benefit from taking a lease on our eyes and ears and nerves, we don't really have any rights left. Leasing our eyes and ears and nerves to commercial interests is like handing over the common speech to a private corporation, or like giving the earth's atmosphere to a company as a monopoly... As long as we adopt the Narcissus attitude of regarding the extensions of our own bodies as really *out there* and really independent of us, we will meet all technological challenges with the same sort of banana-skin pirouette and collapse.[155]

McLuhan's increasing concern about the formal effects of media, and their negotiation through praxis, is made clear in his distillation of the concept of the new acoustic media's "discarnate man." Biographer

Philip Marchand located several letters and interviews from the 1970s in which McLuhan expresses an increasingly "gloomy view of present reality" spurred by the development of discarnate man—someone who is on the telephone or watching television and who "could be present, minus his body, in many different places simultaneously, through electronics." According to McLuhan, living "between fantasy and reality," "discarnate man" is losing his or her personal identity and privacy, and discarnate children are "aimless, undisciplined, and illiterate."[156] Discarnate existence is marked by violence as a last-ditch effort to achieve meaning and identity, as the primary human activity becomes surveillance and espionage.[157]

McLuhan continued to search for a method of overcoming this state of alienation. He wrote:

> Politically, discarnate man may have an image, but not a physical body. There is a corresponding loss of personal identity and responsibility which creates separatism in private life and family life and in all institutional existence. When one becomes aware of this hidden *ground* and its effects, one should be better prepared to cope with, and to counteract, these effects. Ours is surely the first human generation that has ever encountered such an undermining disease which afflicts us at all levels of church and state.[158]

McLuhan addressed the issue of learning disabilities to then-US President Jimmy Carter, including a document that he had sent to California Governor Edmund G. Brown Jr. In it he offered a "brief diagnosis and outline of positive therapy." He describes discarnate man as needing to make little motor response to electronic media, whereas reading requires extensive motor activity. "My own interest in the electronic media has often been taken as evidence of my indifference to the visual and literate values of our society. The enclosure will, I hope, dispel that fallacy."[159] It is hoped that this book also has worked to dispel the fallacy that McLuhan was either celebrative or indifferent to the media, and that his dialectical theory will be reclaimed for critical communication research, in order that, as McLuhan said, society "may think things out before we put them out."

The Method is the Message

NOTES

1. "The Living McLuhan," *Journal of Communication* 31, no. 3 (summer 1981): 116-199.

2. "The Medium's Messenger: Understanding McLuhan," *Canadian Journal of Communication* 14, nos. 4 and 5 (winter 1989): 1-160.

3. Bruce E. Gronbeck, "McLuhan as Rhetorical Theorist," *Journal of Communication* 31, no. 3 (summer 1981): 118-119.

4. David R. Olson, "McLuhan: Preface to Literacy," *Journal of Communication* 31, no. 3 (summer 1981): 136-137.

5. Ibid., 140.

6. Paul Levinson, "McLuhan and Rationality," *Journal of Communication* 31, no. 3 (summer 1981), 185.

7. James M. Curtis, "McLuhan: The Aesthete as Historian," *Journal of Communication* 31, no. 3 (summer 1981): 149.

8. Donald F. Theall, *Understanding McLuhan: The Medium is the Rear View Mirror* (Montréal: McGill-Queen's University Press, 1971), 144-145.

9. Richard Gambino, "McLuhan: A Message that Muddles," *The Midwest Quarterly* 21 (autumn 1979): 71-80.

10. Hanno Hardt, *Critical Communication Studies: Communication, History and Theory in America* (London: Routledge, 1992), 168.

11. Ibid., 196.

12. Ibid., 218.

13. Ibid., 203, citing Patrick Brantlinger, *Bread and Circuses: Theories of Mass Culture as Social Decay* (Ithaca, NY: Cornell University Press, 1983), 270.

14. Ibid., 203-204.

15. Ibid., 204.

16. Ibid.

17. Everett M. Rogers and Steven H. Chaffee, "Communication as an Academic Discipline: A Dialogue," *Journal of Communication* 33, no. 3 (summer 1983): 25.

18. Elihu Katz, "The Return of the Humanities to Sociology," *Journal of Communication* 33, no. 3 (summer 1983): 52.

19. Francis Balle, with Idalina Cappe de Baillon, "Mass Media Research In France: An Emerging Discipline," *Journal of Communication* 33, no. 3 (summer 1983): 150.

20. James Carey, "The Origins of Radical Discourse on Cultural Studies in the United States," *Journal of Communication* 33, no. 3 (summer 1983): 312.

21. Robert White, "Mass Communication and Culture: Transition to a New Paradigm," *Journal of Communication* 33, no. 3 (summer 1983): 284.

22. Ibid., 285.

23. Ibid., 286.

24. Jennifer Daryl Slack and Martin Allor, "The Political and Epistemological Constituents of Critical Communication Research," *Journal of Communication* 33, no. 3 (summer 1983): 209-210.

25. Ibid., 211.

26. Ibid., 212.

27. Ibid., 213.

28. Ibid., 214.

29. Ibid., 215-216.

30. Ibid., 217.

31. Jennifer Daryl Slack, *Communication Technologies and Society: Conceptions of Causality and the Politics of Technological Intervention* (Norwood, NJ: Ablex, 1984), 56-57.

32. James Carey and John Quirk, "The Mythos of the Electronic Revolution," Part II: *The American Scholar* 39 (summer 1970): 398-399.

33. Liss Jeffrey, "The Heat and the Light: Towards a Reassessment of the Contribution of H. Marshall McLuhan," *Canadian Journal of Communication* 14, nos. 4 and 5 (winter 1989): 19.

34. Ibid., 21.

35. Slack, *Communication Technologies*, 64-92.

36. Ibid., 53-63.

37. Ibid., 56.

38. Ibid., 70-71.

39. Ibid., 71-72, 73-76.

40. Dallas Smythe and Tran van Dinh, "On Critical and Administrative Analysis: A New Critical Analysis," *Journal of Communication* 33, no. 3 (summer 1983): 117-118.

41. Ibid., 118.

42. Ibid., 123.

43. Ibid., 126-127.

44. Gaye Tuchman, "Consciousness Industries and the Production of Culture," *Journal of Communication* 33, no. 3 (summer 1983): 330.

45. Ibid., 330-332.

46. Clifford Kobland, "Toward a Synthesis of Multiple Methodologies," (paper presented at the annual meeting of the Association for Education in Journalism and Mass Communication, Washington, DC., August 1989), 1, 4.

47. Ibid., 3, 4.

48. Ibid., 14.

49. Ibid., 14-15.

50. Ibid., 21, citing Hanno Hardt, "The Return of the 'Critical' and the Challenge of Radical Dissent," *Communication Yearbook 12* (Newbury Park, CA: Sage, 1989, 558-600.

51. Ibid.

52. Ibid., 23.

53. Ibid., 25.

54. Mark Levy and Michael Gurevitch, "Editor's Note," *Journal of Communication* 43, no. 3 (summer 1993), 4.

55. Karl Erik Rosengren, "From Field to Frog Pond," *Journal of Communication* 43, no. 3 (summer 1993): 7.

56. Ibid., 7-8.

57. Douglas Gomery, "The Centrality of Media Economics," *Journal of Communication* 43, no. 3 (summer 1993): 190-191.

58. Jennifer Monahan and Lori Collins-Jarvis, "The Hierarchy of Institutional Values in the Communication Discipline," *Journal of Communication* 43, no. 3 (summer 1993): 151-152, 155-156.

59. Brenda Dervin, "Verbing Communication: Mandate for Disciplinary Intervention, *Journal of Communication* 43, no. 3 (summer 1993): 45.

60. Joli Jensen, "The Consequences of Vocabularies," *Journal of Communication* 43, no. 3 (summer 1993): 69, 73.

61. Austin Babrow, "The Advent of Multiple-Process Theories of Communication," *Journal of Communication* 43, no. 3 (summer 1993): 110.

62. Ibid., 115-116.

63. Kurt Lang and Gladys Engel Lang, "Perspectives on Communicuson," *Journal of Communication* 43, no. 3 (summer 1993): 95.

64. Willard D. Rowland, "The Traditions of Communication Research and Their Implications for Telecommunications Study," *Journal of Communication* 43, no. 3 (summer 1993): 214.

65. Klaus Krippendorf, "The Past of Communication's Hoped For Future," *Journal of Communication* 43, no. 3 (summer 1993): 34.

66. Joshua Meyrowitz, "Image of Media: Hidden Ferment—and Harmony—in the Field," *Journal of Communication* 43, no. 3 (summer 1993): 55.

67. Ibid., 64.

68. Marjorie Ferguson, "Marshall McLuhan Revisited: 1960s Zeitgeist Victim or Pioneer Postmodernist?" *Media, Culture and Society* 13, no. 1 (1991), 71-90.

69. Ibid., 83.

70. Ibid., 86.

71. Ibid. 81.

72. Michael Bross, "McLuhan's Theory of Sensory Functions: A Critique and Analysis," *Journal of Communication Inquiry* , 16, no. 1 (1992): 91-107; Barry Brummett and Margaret Carlisle Duncan, "Toward a Discursive Ontology of the Media," *Critical Studies in Mass Communication* 9, no. 3 (1992): 229-249.

73. Bross, "McLuhan's Theory," 91.

74. Ibid., 105.

75. Brummett and Duncan, "Discursive Ontology," 229.

76. Ibid., 247.

77. David Miles, "The CD-ROM Novel *Myst* and McLuhan's Fourth Law of Media: *Myst* and Its 'Retrievals,'" *Journal of Communication* 46, no. 2 (spring 1996): 4-18.

78. Ibid., 7.

79. Arthur Kroker, *Technology and the Canadian Mind: Innis/ McLuhan/ Grant* (Montréal: New World Perspectives, 1984).

80. David Crowley and Paul Heyer, *Communication in History*, 2nd. ed. (White Plains, NY: Longman, 1995).

81. Kroker, *Technology and Canadian Mind*, 13-14.

82. Ibid., 15.

83. Paul Tiessen, "From Literary Modernism to the Tantramar Marshes: Anticipating McLuhan in British and Canadian Media Theory and Practice," *Canadian Journal of Communication* 18 (1993): 451-467.

84. Donald F. Theall, guest editor's introductory remarks, *Canadian Journal of Communication* 14, nos. 4 and 5 (winter 1989): vii-viii.

85. Jeffrey, "Heat and Light," 3.

86. Ibid., 5, citing Thomas Kuhn, *The Structure of Scientific Revolutions*, 2nd. ed. (Chicago: University of Chicago Press, 1970), 111.

87. Ibid., 6.

88. Ibid., 13.

89. Ibid., 23.

90. Ibid., 15.

91. Ibid., 18.

92. Ibid., 20.

93 Ibid., 24.

94. Paul Heyer, "Probing a Legacy: McLuhan's Communications/History 25 Years

After," *Canadian Journal of Communication* 14, nos. 4 and 5 (winter 1989): 31-32.

95. Donald Theall and Joan Theall, "Marshall McLuhan and James Joyce: Beyond Media," *Canadian Journal of Communication* 14, nos. 4 and 5 (winter 1989): 54.

96. Ibid., 63.

97. James P. Winter and Irving Goldman, "Comparing the Early and Late McLuhan to Innis's Political Discourse," *Canadian Journal of Communication* 14, nos. 4 and 5 (winter 1989): 92-93.

98. Ibid., 96-97.

99. Eric McLuhan, "The New Science and the Old," *Canadian Journal of Communication* 14, nos. 4 and 5 (winter 1989): 80-91.

100. David Crowley and David Mitchell, eds., *Communication Theory Today* (Stanford, Calif.: Stanford University Press, 1994); John B. Thompson, "Social Theory and the Media," in *Communication Theory Today*, 27-49; Joshua Meyrowitz, "Medium Theory," in *Communication Theory Today*, 50-77.

101. Armand Mattelart, *Mapping World Communication: War, Progress, Culture*, trans. Susan Emanuel and James A. Cohen (Minneapolis: University of Minnesota Press, 1994), 125-128; Klaus Bruhn Jensen, *The Social Semiotics of Mass Communication* (London: Sage, 1995), 4-5, 11, 98-99; James Lull, *Inside Family Viewing: Ethnographic Research on Television Audiences* (London: Routledge, 1990), 23, 149, 171.

102. Mark Poster, "The Mode of Information and Postmodernity," in *Communication Theory Today*, ed. David Crowley and David Mitchell (Stanford, CA: Stanford University Press, 1994), 173-192; Steven Best and Douglas Kellner, *Postmodern Theory: Critical Interrogations* (New York: Guilford Press, 1991), 267-268.

103. Crowley and Mitchell, *Theory Today*, 6.

104. Ibid., 8.

105. Ibid., 9.

106. Thompson, "Social Theory," 29.

107. Joshua Meyrowitz, *No Sense of Place: The Impact of Electronic Media on Social Behavior* (New York: Oxford University Press, 1985).

108. Meyrowitz, "Medium Theory," 52.

109. Armand Mattelart and Michele Mattelart, *Rethinking Media Theory*, trans. James A. Cohen and Marina Urquidi (Minneapolis: University of Minnesota Press, 1992); Mattelart, *Mapping*.

110. Mattelart, *Rethinking*, 115.

111. Ibid., 167.

112. Mattelart, *Mapping*, 125.

113. Ibid., 126.

114. Ibid., 127-128.

115. Ibid., 128.

116. Ibid., 134, 135.

117. Jensen, *Social Semiotics*, 4.

118. Ibid., 4-5.

119. Ibid., 11.

120. Ibid.

121. Ibid., 99.

122. Lull, *Family Viewing*, 23-24.

123. Ibid., 149.

124. Ibid.

125. Ibid., 151.

126. Ibid., 25, 27.
127. Poster, "Mode of Information," 15.
128. Ibid.
129. Ibid., 173.
130. Ibid.
131. Ibid., 174.
132. Ibid., 174-175.
133. Ibid., 176.
134. Ibid.
135. Ibid., 179.
136. Ibid.
137. Ibid., 180.
138. Ibid., 181.
139. Ibid., 183-185.
140. Ibid., 186.
141. Ibid., 187.
142. Ibid., 188.
143. Ibid., 189.
144. Ibid.
145. Best and Kellner, *Postmodern Theory*, 263-264.
146. Ibid., 264-265.
147. Ibid., 267, 268.
148. Ibid., 223.
149. Cary Nelson, Paula A. Treichler, and Lawrence Grossberg, "Cultural Studies: A User's Guide to This Book," in *Cultural Studies*, eds. Lawrence Grossberg, Cary Nelson, and Paula Treichler (New York: Routledge, 1992), 1, 2.
150. Ibid., 4.
151. Ibid., 5.
152. John Hartley, *The Politics of Pictures: The Creation of the Public in the Age of Popular Media* (London: Routledge, 1992), 16.
153. Ibid., 17
154. Marshall McLuhan, "Sight, Sound, and the Fury," in *Mass Culture: The Popular Arts in America*, eds. Bernard Rosenberg and David Manning White (New York: Free Press, 1957), 489-495, reprinted from *Commonweal* 60 (1954): 168-197.
155. Marshall McLuhan, *Understanding Media: The Extensions of Man* (New York: Mentor, 1964), 73.
156. Philip Marchand, *Marshall McLuhan: The Medium and the Messenger* (New York: Ticknor and Fields, 1989), 238.
157. Ibid., 239.
158. Marshall McLuhan, *Letters of Marshall McLuhan*, eds. Matie Molinaro, Corinne McLuhan, and William Toye (Toronto: University of Toronto Press, 1987), 528.
159. Ibid., 531-532.

Afterword

Considering McLuhan and Multimedia Culture

The emergence of the Internet and the World Wide Web could give McLuhan's legacy a boost, even on the WWW itself. However, new readings of McLuhan's legacy as a critical voice may be thwarted as these new twists of the electronic media forces, which greatly concerned McLuhan, come into being. The old readings of McLuhan as the happy harbinger of technologies beyond human control or intervention could continue to dominate interpretations of McLuhan's work.

On a WWW site promoting a new video of old discussions with and lectures by McLuhan, called "The Living McLuhan," US cultural studies scholar James Carey's review has been distributed to help explain the McLuhan revival. The theorist who described McLuhan as a technological determinist for thirty years makes no mention of that label now. Giving McLuhan some of his due, Carey writes that "communication technology has developed along lines he anticipated with great prescience." McLuhan "grasped the consequences of the globalization of communications, the extension of the body as image and the world as simulation for the human imagination," Carey writes, inserting a humanistic element into McLuhan's analysis.[1]

The University of Toronto McLuhan Program in Culture and Technology also has launched a Web site that describes the program as a teaching and research unit whose associates "study, explore, and comment on the impacts of technology on culture."[2] The site leads to biographical information on McLuhan, as well as details on the program and its academic and continual learning units. At least one media critic, though, has recently quoted McLuhan program director Derrick de Kerckhove as emphasizing the independent and mechanically grinding advance of technologies beyond human control.[3]

In addition to dozens of other McLuhan Web sites, the Internet can lead to citations of books published about McLuhan in 1996 and 1997. At least one of these books explores McLuhan's connection to critical theory and postmodernism, based on a dissertation directed by literary theorist Fredric Jameson.[4] Among the other books is *McLuhan for Beginners,* which has a comic-text format similar to that of *Marx for Beginners.*[5]

Afterword

The crucial question in this resurgence of McLuhan's communication theory is whether it continues to reify McLuhan as the uncritical usher of media-induced change, or whether it recognizes his critical humanist approach, as do Canadian political theorist Judith Stamps, cultural studies scholar Jody Berland, and literary scholar Glenn Willmott, as well as British sociologist Nick Stevenson.[6] Now appears to be one of those "break boundary"[7] times that create a "moment of freedom and release"[8] during which social and media activists—McLuhan's artists — can work to achieve "an increase of human autonomy."[9] The opportunity is here to wrest control of the media from dehumanizing economic and political forces that try to naturalize these media trends toward corporate control and alter the media's technical effects on society. Unless challenged, the media and their handlers will have their way with us.

The Internet and McLuhan's Method

If McLuhan speaks more to the media activist than to the media executive, what can we conclude about an analysis and recommendation for social action and change based on McLuhan's dialectical method? Having argued that McLuhan's method, like Marx's dialectic, is open-ended and process-oriented, it would be rash to predict predetermined media effects of any new media. But some thoughts on the emergence of the Internet and the World Wide Web—filtered through McLuhan's and Marx's shared method of being, non-being or alienation, becoming and reversal—might indicate the usefulness of McLuhan's perspective to social action and media activism.

In McLuhan's terms, what qualities of the Internet enhance what qualities of existing media? What qualities obsolesce existing media qualities? What qualities retrieve aspects of previous media? And what qualities suggests a reversal of the Internet from existing media into a new media culture?

One of the central dialectical contradictions of the World Wide Web may be the struggle between private/corporate control or public/state control of this new medium. Growing out of an elite, but public, educational communication system used by scientists, the Internet has engendered a struggle for its control by both public and private forces. The struggle between corporate and public control of public space has involved critics seemingly as diverse as McLuhan and critical media scholar Herbert Schiller.[10] There is the threat that the Internet will be taken over by globalized corporate media; at the same time, there is the promise that it will be preserved by the public and the government.

This is not a new story: in the past, research and development in electronic media technologies funded by the US government led way to a privatized, commercial telegraph system, radio system, and television system. The US government was a reluctant partner in regulating the telegraph. But State involvement was part and parcel of the introduction of radio and of television as a "public service" that required government regulation in the "public interest." However, it took sixty years for broadcasters to effectively eliminate public government controls, and to do that took the deregulatory fervor of the Reagan administration. Outside of the United States, Canada and Western European countries have a history of public-service broadcasting only recently eroded by the emergence of US-style corporate and commercial private media.

In this struggle, what does the Internet enhance or extend? The Internet could enhance contradictory qualities. Certainly, it threatens to extend corporate commercial media control, and it could extend globalization of the private media, if corporate control prevails. The Internet also could extend the existing media's technology gap between information haves and have-nots, as enclaves of technologically advanced and connected communities, such as academics and affluent economic groups, communicate in social isolation.

On the other hand, the Internet enhances global communication. Discussion groups traverse time and space, making it possible to leap over national boundaries in a way that television, in McLuhan's analysis of its properties, only hinted at. Although it has taken much abuse from cultural studies and critical theory and postmodernism, the notion of the "global village" need not carry with it the globalization of a dominant, hegemonic culture that destroys traditional and indigenous cultures, as well as opposition cultures, in its wake. McLuhan envisioned the global village not as a place of totalized, primitive conformity, but as a place where minority issues and views cannot be ignored, where difference and diversity are celebrated. With the Internet, minority views are given ultimate exposure; as a medium the Internet thrives on difference, as it offers the potential to extend the global village in this humanist sense.

Which potentially enhanced qualities will prevail depends on human intervention and on the qualities of the existing media that could be made obsolete by the Internet media culture. As corporate mass media threaten to extend their control over the Internet, the Internet threatens to obsolesce the *mass* quality of the existing electronic mass media of television, radio, magazines, and newspapers. The "massness" of these media has been slowly eroding for decades, as their audiences have fragmented. This occurred first with radio, then magazines, then television, and now newspapers. But throughout this process the media owners have still controlled the means to produce and deliver messages to media consumers. The Internet threatens these traditional forms because, along with matching their "mass" capabilities, it is individualized and interactive—consumers can truly become media producers. We can make meaning not only in the process of decoding mass-mediated messages, the part of the process on which cultural studies has largely focused for twenty years, but we can make meaning by encoding mass-distributed messages that are individually created.

By potentially obsolescing the massness of the media and interfering with the media's control of production of messages, the Internet offers an opportunity to retrieve some of the elements of print culture. At the same time, it integrates print culture with the still and moving images, as well as the sound, of the acoustic media of radio, film, and television. The Internet is a text-based medium, with storage and retrieval of all messages possible for all individuals—a retrieval with a vengeance of the individualism and democratization of print culture. Individuals and groups have their own "home" pages, with intricate systems of links to other home pages. The language is one of print culture. Each home page has an address, which is personal, specific, and one of a kind.

This building of an electronic community of individuals may lead to the re-emergence of another aspect of print culture: the public. If a sense of community can be retrieved from the mass of mass culture and mass media, there stands a better chance of combating corporate, global, commercial media control. This public community of print culture could be further strengthened and changed by the return of an element of oral culture lost in both print and electronic media cultures. That element is dialogue, conversation, interaction. The public that emerged in print culture—which also gave rise to Marxist thinking—could interact only sporadically and through few media. The Internet offers a historic opportunity for mediated interaction and conversation at the public level. Moreover, an opening exists for public and government involvement in the Internet that could disrupt the status quo of privately owned media. Through this opening, enough public will could be exerted to prevent the corporatization of a globalized, totalized Internet that would be nothing more than television under conglomerate and advertiser control writ large.

Addressing the last phase of McLuhan's and Marx's dialectic: into what media culture could these potential enhancements, obsolescences and retrievals of the Internet reverse or flip into in the "reversal of the overheated medium"? Last fall I was exploring the relevance of McLuhan's ideas with a group of students in a multimedia class. I brought up McLuhan's distinction between "hot" media's high-definition and low-participation and "cool" media's low-definition and high-participation. One student, unfettered by the limits of the hot and cool media debate, may have innocently answered the question of potential reversal: What would the World Wide Web flip into?

The student offered the alternative of high-definition and high-participation interactive multimedia. The Internet could break through the binary opposition and dialectic of hot and cool, visual and acoustic media, to create a new media more like direct experience than any previous media. New multimedia could provide the high-participation of everyday interaction with the high-definition of our experience of the world through all five senses. If multimedia could capture the high participation of cool media and the high definition of hot media combined, then the high stakes that so concerned McLuhan as we leased our eyes and ears to the electronic media's economic and political handlers would become the even higher stakes of this new multimedia culture.

Reorienting Cultural Studies and Postmodernism

For McLuhan, if the electronic media could reverse into a high-definition, high-participation multimedia culture, the call to resistance, as well as to adjustment, would lead invariably to the artist. Broadly defined, artists are the humanists and scientists in all fields who can mediate the unmitigated effects of these new technologies and can help us think things out before we put them out. In media studies, McLuhan's avant garde today no doubt would include cultural studies and postmodernist critical scholars and activists who would both accede to and resist the social and media forms they study.

McLuhan's contribution to cultural studies would, I think, be his insistence on studying media forms and message production as well as their effect on individuals and cultures. Cultural studies scholar James Lull describes quite well, although unintentionally, I think, the quandary that cultural studies has created in largely abandoning its Marxist roots and focusing on the decoding of messages by audiences. A gulf exists between the hegemonic media production of messages and the individual and social act of making meaning out of these hegemonic texts in ways that can resist, if not reject, dominant meanings.[11]

Studies of Madonna's fans reading her as a subversive text, for example, which John Fiske carried out, fail to answer the question of how to change the media that produce Madonna in the first place.[12] Studying ideological codings in television crime dramas for opportunities to decode oppositional readings begs the question of whether television culture itself should go unchallenged. McLuhan's focus on form and encoding, as well as the formal effects on reading texts, could help reorient cultural studies to include production as well as consumption. McLuhan's method would argue that the tension between media production and media consumption cannot be resolved. With the rise of something akin to virtual media, the need to continue to make cultural meaning in the face of diminishing odds and opportunities also becomes more important.

The Internet could offer that opportunity to both produce and make meaning as an act of autonomy and resistance, unless we sell our rights to corporate media. The outcome, applying McLuhan's open-ended dialectic, also is open-ended. It is not an end run for technological determinism. Apologists of the existing information order will need to find another standard bearer. Technological determinism also has been attractive to some postmodernist scholars. Exemplified by Jean Baudrillard, postmodernism could seem resigned in the face of the collapse of media and reality into this high-definition, high-participation "hyperreality" of multimedia. With the dissolution of the individual as an effective social actor, postmodernism can call upon post-Marxism and post-colonialism to help neutralize media and social activism.

McLuhan's sense of postmodernism, however, has much greater historicity than this. McLuhan's method would argue that we live in a world of post's, as well as pre's, as part of an ongoing process that does not reverse modernism but transcends it in becoming and reversal. The danger of the postmodern critique is that it abandons the possibility of even the need for social action. Much of this political philosophy has also abandoned Marxist principles as these principles become part of the modernism that has succumbed to its successor. Although McLuhan appears not to have used the term postmodernism often, his take on it is more along the lines of the humanist, positive stance reflected in the works of critic Charles Jencks and art historian John Walker.[13] This involves the retrieval of past cultures, of the simultaneous existence of many cultures and pasts, and an acceptance of that abundance and diversity. Willmott regards McLuhan as a double-coded figure himself, living postmodernism. He paints McLuhan as a modernist who helped bring about the ideas of postmodernism and embodied postmodernism.[14] McLuhan abolished the distinction between high culture and popular culture, including the media.[15] Although Willmott contends that McLuhan's dialectics were not Marxist because it did not stem from economics and materialism,[16] he argues that McLuhan was part of a "radical culture" articulated by the New Left and its rejection of technocratic authority in favour of cultural utopianism.[17]

Broadening this stultified idea of Marxist dialectics to include the many forms of cultural and radical Marxist dialectical method would help channel McLuhan's media dialectic for a rich and diverse reading of the postmodern world. Intensifying the postmodern trends in media and culture would serve greater human self-expression and creativity, which are, in the end, at the heart of McLuhan's media and culture universe. The human is the measure of McLuhan's method, where Canadian scholar Arthur Kroker's label of him as a "technological humanist" most properly applies.[18] In addition to enriching cultural studies and postmodernism, McLuhan's media theories and dialectical method can help retrain their critical focus, retrieving the human being from technological structures. Ultimately, his ideas forecast the potential reversal of a highly technological media culture into a human one.

NOTES

1. Carey, James, "Review by James Carey," http://www.videomcluhan.com/carey.htm, in *The Video McLuhan* (Toronto: Video McLuhan Inc., 1996).
2. "McLuhan Program in Culture and Technology," http://www.fis.utoronto.ca/mcluhan/ (Toronto: University of Toronto, 1997).
3. James P. Winter, *Democracy's Oxygen* (Montréal: Black Rose Books, 1997), 156.
4. Glenn Willmott, *McLuhan, or Modernism in Reverse* (Toronto: University of Toronto Press, 1996).
5. W. Terrence Gordon, *McLuhan for Beginners* (London: Writers and Readers, 1997).
6. Judith Stamps, *Unthinking Modernity: Innis, McLuhan and the Frankfurt School* (Montréal: McGill-Queen's University Press, 1995); Nick Stevenson, *Understanding Media Cultures* (London: Sage, 1995); Jody Berland, "Angels Dancing: Cultural Technologies and the Production of Space," in *Cultural Studies*, ed. Lawrence Grossberg, Cary Nelson, and Paula Treichler (New York: Routledge, 1992), 38-51; Willmott, *Modernism in Reverse*.
7. Marshall McLuhan, *Understanding Media* (New York: Mentor, 1964), 49.
8. Ibid., 63.
9. Ibid., 59.
10. Ibid., 73; Herbert I. Schiller, *Culture Inc.: The Corporate Takeover of Public Expression* (New York: Oxford University Press, 1989).

11. James Lull, *Media, Communication, Culture: A Global Approach* (New York: Columbia University Press, 1995).

12. John Fiske, "British Cultural Studies and Television," in *Channels of Discourse*, ed. Robert C. Allen (Chapel Hill, N.C.: University of North Carolina Press, 1987), 254-289.

13. Charles Jencks, *What is Post-Modernism?* (New York: St. Martin's Press, 1986); John A. Walker, *Art in the Age of Mass Media* (London: Pluto Press, 1983).

14. Willmott, *Modernism in Reverse*. 156.

15. Ibid., 158-160.

16. Ibid., 33.

17. Ibid., 200.

18. Arthur Kroker, *Technology and the Canadian Mind: Innis.McLuhan/Grant* (Montréal: New World Perspectives, 1984).

Bibliography

Althusser, Louis. *For Marx*. Translated by Ben Brewster. New York: Pantheon, 1969.

Ang, Ien. "In the Realm of Uncertainty: The Global Village and Capitalist Postmodernity." In *Communication Theory Today*. Edited by David Crowley and David Mitchell, 193-213. Stanford, CA: Stanford University Press, 1994.

———. *Living Room Wars: Rethinking Media Audiences for a Postmodern World*. London: Routledge, 1996.

Aristotle. *The Basic Works of Aristotle*. Edited by Richard McKeon. New York: Random House, 1941. Quoted in Marshall McLuhan, "Laws of the Media," *Et Cetera* 34, no. 2 (June 1977): 175-178.

Aronowitz, Stanley, and Henry A. Giroux. *Postmodern Education: Politics, Culture, and Social Criticism*. Minneapolis: University of Minnesota Press, 1991.

Babrow, Austin. "The Advent of Multiple-Process Theories of Communication." *Journal of Communication* 43, no. 3 (summer 1993): 110-118.

Balle, Francis, with Idalina Cappe de Baillon. "Mass Media Research In France: An Emerging Discipline." *Journal of Communication* 33, no. 3 (summer 1983): 146-156.

Baudrillard, Jean. Review of *Understanding Media: The Extensions of Man*, by Marshall McLuhan. *L'Homme et la Societe*, 5 (1967): 277. Quoted in Douglas Kellner, *Jean Baudrillard: From Marxism to Postmodernism and Beyond* (Stanford, CA: Stanford University Press, 1989).

———. *For a Critique of the Political Economy of the Sign*. St. Louis: Telos Press, 1981.

———. "Requiem for the Media" In *For a Critique of the Political Economy of the Sign*. St. Louis: Telos Press, 1981.

———. *Simulations* . New York: Semiotext(e), 1983.

———. *In the Shadow of the Silent Majorities*. New York: Semiotext(e), 1983. Quoted in Douglas Kellner, *Jean Baudrillard: From Marxism to Postmodernism and Beyond* (Stanford, CA: Stanford University Press, 1989).

Bibliography

Benjamin, Walter. "The Work of Art in the Age of Mechanical Reproduction." In *Illuminations*. Edited by Hannah Arendt. Translated by Harry Zohn. New York: Schocken Books, 1969.

Berger, John. *Ways of Seeing*. London: British Broadcasting Corp. and Penguin Books, 1972.

Bergman, P.G. "Relativity," In *Encyclopaedia Brittanica*. 15th ed. 1974: *Macropaedia*. vol. 15. Quoted in Donald Lowe, *History of Bourgeois Perception* Chicago: University of Chicago Press, 1982.

Berland, Jody. "Angels Dancing: Cultural Technologies and the Production of Space." In *Cultural Studies*. Edited by Lawrence Grossberg, Cary Nelson, and Paula Treichler, 38-51. New York: Routledge, 1992.

Best, Steven, and Douglas Kellner. *Postmodern Theory: Critical Interrogations* . New York: Guilford Press, 1991.

Brantlinger, Patrick. *Bread and Circuses: Theories of Mass Culture as Social Decay*. Ithaca, NY: Cornell University Press, 1983.

———. *Crusoe's Footprints: Cultural Studies in Britain and America*. New York: Routledge, 1990.

Bross, Michael. "McLuhan's Theory of Sensory Functions: A Critique and Analysis." *Journal of Communication Inquiry* 16, no. 1 (1992): 91-107.

Brummett, Barry, and Margaret Carlisle Duncan. "Toward a Discursive Ontology of the Media." *Critical Studies in Mass Communication* 9, no. 3 (1992): 229-249.

Carey, James. "Harold Adams Innis and Marshall McLuhan." In *McLuhan: Pro and Con*. Edited by Raymond Rosenthal, 270-308. Baltimore, MD: Penguin, 1968.

———. "McLuhan and Mumford: The Roots of Modern Media Analysis." *Journal of Communication* 31 (summer 1981): 162-178.

———. "The Origins of Radical Discourse on Cultural Studies in the United States." *Journal of Communication* 33, no. 3 (summer 1983): 311-313.

Carey, James, with John Quirk. "The Mythos of the Electronic Revolution," Part II. *The American Scholar* 39 (summer 1970): 395-424. Quoted in Jennifer Daryl Slack, *Communication Technologies and Society: Conceptions of Causality and the Politics of Technological Intervention* (Norwood, N.J.: Ablex, 1984).

———. "Walter Benjamin, Marshall McLuhan, and the Emergence of Visual Society." *Prospects: An Annual of American Cultural Studies* 12 (1987): 29-38.

———. "Mass Communication and Cultural Studies." *Communication* as Culture: Essays on Media and Society, 37-68. Boston: Unwin Hyman, 1989.

———. "Review by James Carey," http://www.videomcluhan.com/carey.htm. In The Video McLuhan. Toronto: Video McLuhan Inc., 1996.

———. "Space, Time, and Communication: A Tribute to Harold Innis." In Communication as Culture: Essays on Media and Society, 142-172. Boston: Unwin Hyman, 1989.

Carey, James, with John J. Quirk, "The Mythos of the Electronic Revolution." In Communication as Culture: Essays on Media and Society, 113-141. Boston: Unwin Hyman, 1989.

Clark, Timothy J. The Painting of Modern Life: Paris in the Art of Manet and his Followers. Princeton, NJ: Princeton University Press, 1984.

Collins, James M. "By Whose Authority? Accounting for Taste in Contemporary Popular Culture." In Communication Theory Today. Edited by David Crowley and David Mitchell, 214-231. Stanford, CA: Stanford University Press, 1994.

Crowley, David, and David Mitchell, eds. Communication Theory Today. Stanford, CA: Stanford University Press, 1994.

Crowley, David, and Paul Heyer, eds. Communication in History. 2nd. ed. White Plains, NY: Longman, 1995.

Curtis, James M. Culture as Polyphony: An Essay on the Nature of Paradigms. Columbia, MO: University of Missouri Press, 1978.

———. "McLuhan: The Aesthete as Historian." Journal of Communication 31 (summer 1981): 144-152.

Czitrom, Daniel J. Media and the American Mind: From Morse to McLuhan . Chapel Hill, NC: University of North Carolina Press, 1982.

Dervin, Brenda. "Verbing Communication: Mandate for Disciplinary Intervention." Journal of Communication 43, no. 3 (summer 1993): 15 51.

Eco, Umberto. Travels in Hyper Reality. Translated by William Weaver. San Diego: Harvest/Harcourt, Brace, Jovanovich, 1990.

Eliot, T.S. The Use of Poetry and the Use of Criticism . London: Faber and Faber, 1933. Quoted in Marshall McLuhan, Culture is Our Business. New York: McGraw-Hill, 1967.

Enzensberger, Hans M. The Consciousness Industry. New York: Seabury Press, 1974.

Featherstone, Mike. "Global Culture: An Introduction." Theory, Culture and Society 7 (2/3): 1-14. Quoted in Roger Silverstone, Television and Everyday Life. London: Routledge, 1994.

Bibliography

Fekete, John. "McLuhanacy: Counterrevolution in Cultural Theory." *Telos* 15 (spring 1973): 75-123.

———. *The Critical Twilight: Explorations in the Ideology of Anglo-American Literary Theory from Eliot to McLuhan*. London: Routledge and Kegan Paul, 1977.

———, ed. *The Structural Allegory: Reconstructive Encounters with the New French Thought*. Minneapolis: University of Minnesota Press, 1984.

———. *Moral Panic: Biopolitics Rising*. Montréal-Toronto: Robert Davies Publishing, 1994.

Ferguson, Marjorie. "Marshall McLuhan Revisited: 1960s Zeitgeist Victim or Pioneer Postmodernist?" *Media, Culture and Society* 13, no. 1 (1991): 71-90.

Finkelstein, Sidney. *Sense and Nonsense of McLuhan*. New York: International Publishers, 1968.

Fiske, John. *Television Culture* . London: Methuen, 1987.

———. "British Cultural Studies." In *Channels of Discourse*. Edited by Robert C. Allen, 254-289. Chapel Hill, NC: University of North Carolina Press, 1987.

Fromm, Erich. *Marx's Concept of Man*. New York: Ungar, 1961.

Gadamer, Hans. *Hegel's Dialectic: Five Hermeneutical Studies*. Translated by P. Christopher Smith. New Haven, CN: Yale University Press, 1976.

Gambino, Richard. "McLuhan: A Message that Muddles." *The Midwest Quarterly* 21 (autumn 1979): 71-80.

Gane, Mike, introduction to *Symbolic Exchange and Death* by Jean Baudrillard. London: Sage, 1993.

Garnham, Nicholas. *Capitalism and Communication: Global Culture and the Economics of Information*. London: Sage, 1990.

Gitlin, Todd. *The Whole World Is Watching: Mass Media in the Unmaking of the New Left*. Berkeley, CA: University of California Press, 1980.

Gomery, Douglas. "The Centrality of Media Economics." *Journal of Communication* 43, no. 3 (summer 1993): 190-198.

Gordon, W. Terrence. *McLuhan for Beginners*. London: Writers and Readers, 1997.

Gronbeck, Bruce E. "McLuhan as Rhetorical Theorist." *Journal of Communication* 31 (summer 1981): 117-128.

Grosswiler, Paul. "The Shifting Sensorium: A Q-Methodology and Critical Theory Exploration of Marshall McLuhan's Visual and Acoustic Typologies in Media, Aesthetics and Ideology." Ph.D. diss., School of Journalism, University of Missouri, Columbia, MO., 1990.

————. "A Dialectical Synthesis of Marshall McLuhan and Critical Theory." Paper presented at the annual meeting of the International Communication Association, Chicago, Ill., May 1991.

————. "The Dialectical Methods of Marshall McLuhan, Marxism, and Critical Theory." *Canadian Journal of Communication* 21 (winter 1996): 95-124.

Hall, Stuart. "On Postmodernism and Articulation: An Interview with Stuart Hall." Edited by Lawrence Grossberg. In *Stuart Hall: Critical Dialogues in Cultural Studies.* Edited by David Morley and Kuan-Hsing Chen, 131-150. London: Routledge, 1996.

Hardt, Hanno. "The Return of the 'Critical' and the Challenge of Radical Dissent." *Communication Yearbook 12.* Newbury Park, CA: Sage, 1989. Quoted in Clifford Kobland, "Toward a Synthesis of Multiple Methodologies," (paper presented at the annual meeting of the Association for Education in Journalism and Mass Communication, Washington, D.C., August 1989).

————. *Critical Communication Studies: Communication, History and Theory in America* . London: Routledge, 1992.

Hartley, John. *The Politics of Pictures: The Creation of the Public in the Age of Popular Media.* London: Routledge, 1992.

Hauser, Arnold. *The Sociology of Art.* Translated by Kenneth J. Northcott. Chicago: University of Chicago Press, 1982.

Hayes, Carleton. *Historical Evolution in Modern Nationalism.* New York: Smith Publishing, 1931. Quoted in Marshall McLuhan, *The Gutenberg Galaxy: The Making of Typographic Man.* Toronto: University of Toronto Press, 1962.

Heyer, Paul. "Probing a Legacy: McLuhan's Communications/ History Twenty-Five Years After." *Canadian Journal of Communication* 14 (winter 1989): 30-45.

Horkheimer, Max, and Theodor Adorno. *Dialectic of Enlightenment.* Translated by John Cumming. New York: Continuum, 1987.

Jameson, Fredric. *The Ideologies of Theory: Essays 1971-1986.* Vol. 1. Minneapolis: University of Minnesota Press, 1988.

————. "Postmodernism and Consumer Society." In *Postmodernism and its Discontents: Theories, Practices.* Edited by E. A. Kaplan. London: Verso, 1988. Quoted in Nick Stevenson, *Understanding Media Cultures: Social Theory and Mass Communication.* London: Sage, 1995.

Jeffrey, Liss. "The Heat and the Light: Towards a Reassessment of the Contribution of H. Marshall McLuhan." *Canadian Journal of Communication* 14 (winter 1989): 1-29.

Bibliography

Jencks, Charles. *What is Post-Modernism?* New York: St. Martin's Press, 1986.

Jensen, Joli. "The Consequences of Vocabularies." *Journal of Communication* 43, no. 3 (summer 1993): 67-74.

Jensen, Klaus Bruhn. *The Social Semiotics of Mass Communication.* London: Sage, 1995.

Katz, Elihu. "The Return of the Humanities to Sociology." *Journal of Communication* 33, no. 3 (summer 1983): 51-52.

Kellner, Douglas. "Resurrecting McLuhan? Jean Baudrillard and the Academy of Postmodernism." In *Communication: For or Against Democracy.* Edited by Marc Raboy and Peter A. Bruck, 131-146. Montréal: Black Rose Books, 1989.

Kellner, Douglas. *Jean Baudrillard: From Marxism to Postmodernism and Beyond.* Stanford, CA: Stanford University Press, 1989.

Kobland, Clifford. "Toward a Synthesis of Multiple Methodologies." (Paper presented at the annual meeting of the Association for Education in Journalism and Mass Communication, Washington, D.C., August 1989).

Krippendorf, Klaus. "The Past of Communication's Hoped For Future." *Journal of Communication* 43, no. 3 (summer 1993): 6-17.

Kroker, Arthur. *Technology and the Canadian Mind: Innis/McLuhan/Grant.* Montréal: New World Perspectives, 1984.

Kuhn, Thomas. *The Structure of Scientific Revolutions.* 2nd. ed. Chicago: University of Chicago Press, 1970. Quoted in Liss Jeffrey, "The Heat and the Light: Towards a Reassessment of the Contribution of H. Marshall McLuhan," *Canadian Journal of Communication* 14 (winter 1989): 1-29.

Lang, Kurt, and Gladys Engel Lang. "Perspectives on Communication." *Journal of Communication* 43, no. 3 (summer 1993): 92-99.

Levinson, Paul. Introduction to "Laws of the Media," by Marshall McLuhan, *Et Cetera* 34, no. 2 (June 1977): 173-174.

―――. "McLuhan and Rationality." *Journal of Communication* 31 (summer 1981): 179-188.

Levy, Mark, and Michael Gurevitch. "Editor's Note." *Journal of Communication* 43, no. 3 (summer 1993): 4-5.

"The Living McLuhan." *Journal of Communication* 31, no. 3 (summer 1981): 116-199.

Lowe, Donald M. *History of Bourgeois Perception.* Chicago: University of Chicago Press, 1982.

Lull, James. *Inside Family Viewing: Ethnographic Research on Television Audiences.* London: Routledge, 1990.

Marchand, Philip. *Marshall McLuhan: The Medium and the Messenger.* New York: Ticknor and Fields, 1989.

Marvin, Carolyn. "Innis, McLuhan and Marx." *Visible Language* 23 (summer 1986): 355-359.

Marx, Karl. "Theses on Feuerbach." *The Marx-Engels Reader.* Edited by Robert C. Tucker. 2nd ed. New York: Norton, 1978.

Mattelart, Armand. *Mass Media, Ideologies and the Revolutionary Movement.* Atlantic Heights, NJ: Sussex, 1980.

Mattelart, Armand, and Michele Mattelart. *Rethinking Media Theory.* Translated by James A. Cohen and Marina Urquidi. Minneapolis: University of Minnesota Press, 1992.

Mattelart, Armand. *Mapping World Communication: War, Progress, Culture.* Translated by Susan Emanuel and James A. Cohen. Minneapolis: University of Minnesota Press, 1994.

McCallum, Pamela. "Walter Benjamin and Marshall McLuhan: Theories of History." *Signature: A Journal of Theory and Canadian Literature* 1, no. 1 (1989): 71-89.

McLuhan, Eric. "The New Science and the Old." *Canadian Journal of Communication* 14 (winter 1989): 80-91.

McLuhan, Marshall. *The Mechanical Bride: Folklore of Industrial Man.* New York: Vanguard Press, 1951.

———. "Sight, Sound and the Fury." In *Mass Culture: The Popular Arts in America.* Edited by Bernard Rosenberg and David Manning White, 489-495. New York: Free Press, 1957.

———. *The Gutenberg Galaxy: The Making of Typographic Man.* Toronto: University of Toronto Press, 1962.

———. *Understanding Media: The Extensions of Man.* New York: Mentor, 1964.

———. Introduction to *The Bias of Communication*, by Harold A. Innis. Toronto: University of Toronto Press, 1964.

———. *Culture is Our Business.* New York: McGraw-Hill, 1967.

———. With Quentin Fiore and Jerome Angel. *The Medium is the Massage: An Inventory of Effects.* New York: Bantam, 1967.

———. With Quentin Fiore and Jerome Angel. *War and Peace in the Global Village.* New York: Bantam Books, 1968.

McLuhan, Marshall. With Harley Parker. *Through the Vanishing Point: Space in Poetry and Painting.* New York: Harper and Row, 1968.

———. *Counterblast.* New York: Harcourt, Brace and World, 1969.

McLuhan, Marshall. With Wilfred Watson. *From Cliche to Archetype.* New York: Pocket Books, 1971.

Bibliography

McLuhan, Marshall. With Barrington Nevitt. *Take Today: The Executive as Dropout*. New York: Harcourt, Brace Jovanovich, 1972.

McLuhan, Marshall. "McLuhan's Laws of the Media." *Technology and Culture* 16, no. 1 (January 1975): 74-78.

———. "Laws of the Media." *Et Cetera* 34, no. 2 (June 1977): 173-179.

———. *Letters of Marshall McLuhan*. Edited by Matie Molinaro, Corinne McLuhan, and William Toye. Toronto: Oxford University Press, 1987.

———. With Eric McLuhan. *Laws of Media: The New Science*. Toronto: University of Toronto Press, 1988.

———. With Bruce Powers. *The Global Village: Transformations in World Life and Media in the Twenty-first Century*. New York: Oxford University Press, 1989.

"McLuhan Program in Culture and Technology." Http://www.fis. utoronto.ca/mcluhan/. Toronto: University of Toronto, 1997.

"The Medium's Messenger: Understanding McLuhan." *Canadian Journal of Communication* 14, nos. 4 and 5 (winter 1989): 1-160.

Meyrowitz, Joshua. *No Sense of Place: The Impact of Electronic Media on Social Behavior*. New York: Oxford University Press. 1985.

———. "Image of Media: Hidden Ferment—and Harmony—in the Field." *Journal of Communication* 43, no. 3 (summer 1993): 55-66

———. "Medium Theory." In *Communication Theory Today*. Edited by David Crowley and David Mitchell, 50-77. Stanford, CA: Stanford University Press, 1994.

Miles, David. "The CD-ROM Novel *Myst* and McLuhan's Fourth Law of Media: *Myst* and Its 'Retrievals.'" *Journal of Communication* 46, no. 2 (spring 1996): 4-18.

Mills, C. Wright. *The Power Elite*. New York: Oxford University Press, 1959. Quoted in James Carey, "Mass Communication and Cultural Studies," *Communication as Culture: Essays on Media and Society* (Boston: Unwin Hyman, 1989), 37-68.

Monahan, Jennifer, and Lori Collins-Jarvis. "The Hierarchy of Institutional Values in the Communication Discipline." *Journal of Communication* 43, no. 3 (summer 1993): 150-157.

Mumford, Lewis. *Technics and Civilization*. New York: Harcourt, Brace and World, 1934. Quoted in Philip Marchand, *Marshall McLuhan: The Medium and the Messenger* (New York: Ticknor and Fields, 1989).

Nairn, Tom. "McLuhanism: The Myth of Our Time." In *McLuhan: Pro and Con*. Edited by Raymond Rosenthal, 140-152. Baltimore: Penguin, 1968.

Nelson, Cary, Paula A. Treichler, and Lawrence Grossberg. "Cultural Studies: An Introduction." In *Cultural Studies*. Edited by Lawrence

Grossberg, Cary Nelson, and Paula Treichler, 1-22. New York: Routledge, 1992.

Olson, David R. "McLuhan: Preface to Literacy." *Journal of Communication* 31 (summer 1981): 136-143.

Ong, Walter. *Orality and Literacy: The Technologizing of the Word*. New York: Methuen, 1982.

Peritore, N. Patrick. "Radical Dialectics." Unpublished paper, Department of Political Science, University of Missouri, 1985.

Poster, Mark. *Foucault, Marxism and History: Mode of Production vs. Mode of Information*. Cambridge, MA: Polity Press, 1984.

————. *The Mode of Information: Post-Structuralism and Social Context*. Chicago: University of Chicago Press, 1990.

————. "The Mode of Information and Postmodernity." In *Communication Theory Today*. Edited by David Crowley and David Mitchell, 173-192. Stanford, CA: Stanford University Press, 1994.

Postman, Neil. *Amusing Ourselves to Death: Public Discourse in the Age of Show Business*. New York: Penguin, 1985.

Rius. *Marx for Beginners*. New York: Pantheon, 1976.

Rogers, Everett M., and Steven H. Chaffee. "Communication as an Academic Discipline: A Dialogue." *Journal of Communication* 33, no. 3 (summer 1983): 18-30.

Rosengren, Karl Erik. "From Field to Frog Ponds." *Journal of Communication* 43, no. 3 (summer 1993): 6-17.

Rowland, Willard D. "The Traditions of Communication Research and Their Implications for Telecommunications Study." *Journal of Communication* 43, no. 3 (summer 1993): 207-217.

Schiller, Herbert I. *Culture, Inc.: The Corporate Takeover of Public Expression*. New York: Oxford University Press, 1989.

Schwartz, Tony. *The Responsive Chord*. New York: Anchor Books, 1974. Quoted in Marshall McLuhan, with Eric McLuhan, *Laws of the Media: The New Science* (Toronto: University of Toronto Press, 1988); and Marshall McLuhan, with Bruce Powers, *The Global Village: Transformations in World Life and Media in the Twenty-first Century*. New York: Oxford University Press, 1989.

Silverstone, Roger. *Television and Everyday Life*. London: Routledge, 1994.

Slack, Jennifer Daryl, and Martin Allor. "The Political and Epistemological Constituents of Critical Communication Research." *Journal of Communication* 33, no. 3 (summer 1983): 208-218.

Slack, Jennifer Daryl. *Communication Technologies and Society: Conceptions of Causality and the Politics of Technological Intervention*. Norwood, NJ: Ablex, 1984.

Bibliography

Smythe, Dallas, and Tran van Dinh. "On Critical and Administrative Analysis: A New Critical Analysis." *Journal of Communication* 33, no. 3 (summer 1983): 117-127.

Spigel, Lynn. Introduction to *Television: Technology and Cultural Form*, by Raymond Williams. Hanover, NH, and London: Wesleyan University Press, 1992.

Stamps, Judith. "The Bias of Theory: A Critique of Pamela McCallum's 'Walter Benjamin and Marshall McLuhan: Theories of History.'" *Signature: A Journal of Theory and Canadian Literature* 1, no. 3 (1990): 44-62.

———. *Unthinking Modernity: Innis, McLuhan and the Frankfurt School.* Montréal: McGill-Queen's University Press, 1995.

Stevenson, Nick. *Understanding Media Cultures: Social Theory and Mass Communication.* London: Sage, 1995.

Theall, Donald F. *Understanding McLuhan: The Medium is the Rear View Mirror.* Montréal: McGill-Queen's University Press, 1971.

———. Guest editor's introductory remarks. *Canadian Journal of Communication* 14, (winter 1989): vii-ix.

Theall, Donald F. and Joan Theall, "Marshall McLuhan and James Joyce: Beyond Media." *Canadian Journal of Communication* 14 (winter 1989): 46-63.

Thompson, John B. *Ideology and Modern Culture.* Stanford, CA: Stanford University Press, 1990.

———. "Social Theory and the Media." In *Communication Theory Today.* Edited by David Crowley and David Mitchell, 27-49. Stanford, CA: Stanford University Press, 1994.

Tiessen, Paul. "From Literary Modernism to the Tantramar Marshes: Anticipating McLuhan in British and Canadian Media Theory and Practice." *Canadian Journal of Communication* 18 (1993): 451-467.

Tuchman, Gaye. "Consciousness Industries and the Production of Culture." *Journal of Communication* 33, no. 3 (summer 1983): 330-341.

Tucker, Robert C., ed. Introduction to *The Marx-Engels Reader.* 2nd. ed. New York: W. W. Norton, 1978.

Turner, Graeme. *British Cultural Studies: An Introduction.* Boston: Unwin Hyman , 1990.

Walker, John A. *Art in the Age of Mass Media.* London: Pluto Press, 1983.

Warren, Scott. *The Emergence of Dialectical Theory: Philosophy and Political Inquiry.* Chicago: University of Chicago Press, 1984.

White, Robert. "Mass Communication and Culture: Transition to a New Paradigm." *Journal of Communication* 33, no. 3 (summer 1983): 279-301.

Williams, Raymond. "Paradoxically, If the Book Works It to Some Extent Annihilates Itself." In *McLuhan Hot and Cool.* Edited by Gerald E. Stearn, 188-191. New York: Dial Press, 1967.

———. *Marxism and Literature.* Oxford: Oxford University Press, 1977.

———. *The Year 2000.* New York: Pantheon, 1983.

———. *Television: Technology and Cultural Form.* Hanover, NH, and London: Wesleyan University Press, 1992.

Willmott, Glenn. *McLuhan, or Modernism in Reverse.* Toronto: University of Toronto Press, 1996.

Winter, James P. *Democracy's Oxygen.* Montreal: Black Rose Books, 1997.

Winter, James P., and Irving Goldman. "Comparing the Early and Late McLuhan to Innis's Political Discourse." *Canadian Journal of Communication* 14 (winter 1989): 92-99.

Wolff, Janet. *Aesthetics and the Sociology of Art.* London: George Allen and Unwin, 1983.

———. *The Social Production of Art.* 2nd ed. New York: New York University Press, 1993.

Wood, Michael. "The Four Gospels." *New Society* (December 18, 1969). Quoted in Marshall McLuhan, *Letters of Marshall McLuhan*, ed. Matie Molinaro, Corinne McLuhan, and William Toye. Toronto: Oxford University Press, 1987.

Index

Index

Index

Index

Index

DEMOCRACY'S OXYGEN

How the Corporations Control the News

James Winter

A book that presents the hard facts that illustrate the complicity between government and corporate media interests as it asks the questions 'who owns newspapers in Canada and what influence have they on content?'

Once the hinge of democracy, the media now specialize in 'junk food news'—Winter's analysis is strong. **—Globe and Mail**

James Winter has hit on a hot topic. Contains truths which only those in an advanced state of denial could ignore. **—Ottawa Citizen**

An important book because it enhances the political discourse on a critical subject. **—Literary Review of Canada**

Winter's book is an invaluable reference tool. Its research is particularly strong in the profiles of Black, his fellow baron Paul Desmarais, and the publishing giant Québecor. **—Quill & Quire**

In the increasingly stifling atmosphere of Canadian democracy, Winter's book is a breath of fresh air. **—Canadian Dimension**

A timely release. **—Briarpatch**

A valuable resource. Winter presents a well-documented case that Black has a definite political agenda, and his acquisition of newspapers the world over is a conscious grab for political power. **—Hour Magazine**

Democracy's Oxygen *is a fact-packed examination of the influence of ideology and ownership in the media.* **—Now Magazine**

In the wake of Conrad Black's grab of Southam, James Winter's book could not be more timely. I unreservingly recommend it. **—The Peak**

This book is a must for all of us concerned about the direction Canada is heading. **—Howard Pawley, Former Premier of Manitoba**

This book is about nothing less than the corporate takeover of public expression. Read it. **—Maude Barlow, Council for Canadians**

The combination of his [Winter's] deep desire for fundamental political and media reforms, and his relentless examples backed up by facts, figures and quotations makes his a distinct voice at a distinct intersection.
—Barrie Zwicker, publisher of Sources and media critic for Vision TV

294 pages, bibliography, index
Paperback 1-55164-060-0 $23.99
Hardcover 1-55164-061-9 $52.99

also by James Winter

COMMON CENTS *Media Portrayal of the Gulf War and Other Events*

PERSPECTIVES ON POWER
Reflections on Human Nature and the Social Order
Noam Chomsky

This is the first collection to bring together questions of philosophy, ethics, and foreign policy. It includes essays on linguistics; on responsibilities of writers; and on international affairs, drawing links between foreign policy decisions, the state of intellectual culture, the role of the media, and the potential for democratic societies. His views of the world and the nature of things are supported by a wealth of detail. In a rare article Chomsky reveals his own personal goals and visions for change.

276 pages, bibliography, index
Paperback   1-55164-048-1 $23.99
Hardcover   1-55164-049-X $52.99

YEAR 501
The Conquest Continues 2nd printing
Noam Chomsky

From the brutality of Columbus to the persecution in East Timor, a powerful and comprehensive discussion of the incredible injustices hidden in our history.

...Year 501 offers a savage critique of the new world order whose roots Chomsky traces to European colonization.   **—MacLean's Magazine**

Tough, didactic, [Chomsky] skins back the lies of those who make decisions, accumulate wealth, spread influence.   **—Globe and Mail**

Here, at last, a book that is a much-needed defense against the mind numbing free market rhetoric.   **—Latin America Connexions**

331 pages, index
Paperback ISBN: 1-895431-62-X $19.99
Hardcover ISBN: 1-895431-63-8 $48.99

RETHINKING CAMELOT
JFK, the Vietnam War, and U.S. Political Culture
Noam Chomsky

This book is a thorough analysis of the Kennedy years. For those who turn to Hollywood for history, and confuse creative license with fact, Chomsky proffers an arresting reminder that historical narrative rarely fits neatly into a feature film.

...a fascinating and disturbing portrait of the Kennedy dynasty and the structures of power that touch all world leaders.   **—Briarpatch**

...a particularly interesting and important instance of media and power elite manipulation...well-documented.   **—Humanist In Canada**

...by far the most important contribution to the ongoing public and private discussions about JFK.   **—Kitchener-Waterloo Record**

172 pages, index
Paperback   1-895431-72-7 $19.99
Hardcover   1-895431-73-5 $48.99

MANUFACTURING CONSENT

Noam Chomsky and the Media   2nd printing

Mark Achbar, editor

This companion volume to the acclaimed documentary charts the life of America's most famous dissident, from his boyhood days in Manhattan running his uncle's newsstand to his current role as outspoken social critic. Included are exchanges between Chomsky and his critics, historical and biographical material, filmmakers' notes, a resource guide, more than 270 stills from the film, and, 18 "Philosopher All-Stars" Trading Cards!

A juicily subversive biographical/philosophical documentary bristling and buzzing with ideas.   **—Washington Post**

You will see the whole sweep of the most challenging critic in modern political thought.   **—Boston Globe**

One of our real geniuses...an excellent introduction.   **—Village Voice**

An intellectually challenging crash course, laying out his [Chomsky's] thoughts in a package that is clever and accessible.   **—Los Angeles Times**

...challenging controversial.   **—Globe and Mail**

...a rich, rewarding experience, a thoughtful and lucid exploration of the danger that might exist in a controlled media.   **—Edmonton Journal**

...lucid and coherent statement of Chomsky's thesis.   **—Times of London**

...invaluable as a record of a thinker's progress towards basic truth and basic decency.   **—Guardian**

264 pages, 270 illustrations, bibliography, index
Paperback 1-55164-002-3
  $19.99 within Canada / $23.99 outside Canada
Hardcover 1-55164-003-1
  $48.99 within Canada / $52.99 outside Canada

BEYOND HYPOCRISY

Decoding the News in an Age of Propaganda, Including a Doublespeak Dictionary for the 1990s

Edward S. Herman

Illustrations by Matt Wuerker

This spirited book offers abundant examples of duplicitous terminology, ranging from the crimes of free enterprise to media coverage of political events. Also included is an extended essay on the Orwellian use of language.

Rich in irony and relentlessly forthright.   **—Montréal Mirror**

Makes us think and thinking is what protects our minds, otherwise we are going to join Orwell's characters.   **—Times-Colonist**

Edward Herman starts out with a good idea and offers a hard-hitting and often telling critique of American public life.   **—Ottawa Citizen**

239 pages, illustrations, index
Paperback ISBN: 1-895431-48-4 $19.99
Hardcover ISBN: 1-895431-49-2 $48.99

BLACK ROSE BOOKS

has also published the following books of related interest

Balance: Art and Nature, *by John Grande*

Beyond Boundaries, *by Barbara Noske*

Desert Capitalism: What are the Maquiladoras?, *by Kathryn Kopinak*

Former "State Socialist" World, *by David Mandel*

Free Trade: Neither Free Nor About Trade, *by Christopher D. Merret*

History of Canadian Business 1867-1914, *by R. T. Naylor*

Killing Hope: US Military and CIA Interventions Since World War II, *by William Blum*

Military in Greek Politics, *by Thanos Veremis*

Nationalism and Culture, *by Rudolf Rocker*

Oceans are Emptying: Fish Wars and Sustainability, *by Raymond A. Rogers*

Other Mexico: North American Triangle Completed, *by John W. Warnock*

Philosophy of Social Ecology, *by Murray Bookchin*

Politics of Social Ecology, *by Janet Biehl and Murray Bookchin*

Politics of Obedience, *by Etienne de la Boétie*

Politics of Sustainable Development, *by Laurie E. Adkin*

Triumph of the Market, *by Edward S. Herman*

Women Pirates and the Politics of the Jolly Roger, *by Ulrike Klausmann, Marion Meinzerin, Gabriel Kuhn*

Zapata of Mexico, *by Peter Newell*

send for a free catalogue of all our titles
BLACK ROSE BOOKS
C.P. 1258
Succ. Place du Parc
Montréal, Québec
H3W 2R3 Canada

To order books in North America: (phone) 1-800-565-9523
(fax) 1-800-221-9985
In Europe: (phone) 44-081-986-4854 (fax) 44-081-533-5821

Web site address: http://www.web.net/blackrosebooks

Printed by the workers of
VEILLEUX IMPRESSION À DEMANDE INC.
Boucherville, Quebec
for Black Rose Books Ltd.